A PILGRIM IN UNHOLY PLACES
Stories of a Mustang Colonel

Thomas D. Phillips

EAGLE EDITIONS
2004

EAGLE EDITIONS
AN IMPRINT OF HERITAGE BOOKS, INC.

Books, CDs, and more—Worldwide

For our listing of thousands of titles see our website
at
www.HeritageBooks.com

Published 2004 by
HERITAGE BOOKS, INC.
Publishing Division
65 East Main Street
Westminster, Maryland 21157-5026

COPYRIGHT © 2004 THOMAS D. PHILLIPS

All rights reserved. No part of this book may be reproduced or transmitted in any form or by any means, electronic or mechanical, including photocopying, recording or by any information storage and retrieval system without written permission from the author, except for the inclusion of brief quotations in a review.

International Standard Book Number: 0-7884-3200-1

TO NITA AND LAURA AND KAREN: YOU LIGHT UP MY LIFE.

TO ALL THOSE WHO HAVE WORN OUR NATION'S UNIFORM WITH HONOR AND PRIDE: THANK YOU FOR YOUR SERVICE TO OUR COUNTRY.

CONTENTS

Foreword	vii
Prologue	1
Chevrons	7
R & R A Moran Story: Setting an Example	33
Epaulets	35
R & R A Moran Story: The Five-Star Restaurant	67
Gold and Silver Leaves	69
R & R A Moran Story: The Painless Veterinarian	101
Eagles	105
R & R A Moran Story: The Sign	145
Incoming Rounds	147
R & R A Moran Story: A Growing Friendship	175
Comm Checks	177
R & R A Moran Story: The Ivory Fan	185
Situation Reports	187
R & R A Moran Story: The Discount	205
Bull Sessions	207
R & R A Moran Story: The Pet Monkeys	221
After Action Report	223

FOREWORD

There is a scene in the movie "She Wore a Yellow Ribbon" in which John Wayne, as Captain Nathan Brittles, a cavalry officer about to retire, is sharing "war stories" with another cavalryman. As the two of them reminisce, Brittles notices a young woman listening. Thinking (mistakenly, as it turns out) that she has little interest in their conversation, as both explanation and apology, he shrugs, "Old soldiers, Miss ..."

Captain Brittles' concern is a legitimate one: especially for those who have not been closely touched by the military, a few "war stories" can go a long way. During the course of a 36-year career, I listened to innumerable "war stories" and participated in the bull sessions that usually accompanied them. The residue from most of those encounters is best retired for safekeeping, eligible for recall – like veterans who have completed their active service – when a smile or mental companionship is needed on a cold winter night.

Some though, are worth remembering, and repeating, if only because they are funny, or poignant, or so intense that they evoke special memories that form *part* of a Soldier, Sailor, Airman, or Marine – so deeply ingrained in ways both visible and invisible that they help shape and define the person as a unique human being.

The most special tales can also serve another – higher – purpose: they put a human face on our nation's conflicts and policies. They teach, preserve an organization's heritage, and instill institutional memory. Collectively, they help glue a military service and its constituent parts together from squad to headquarters, from one-stripe airman to four-star general. And, although the route is more indirect, they attach the unit and the individual warrior to the country and its citizens.

I share Captain Brittles' apprehension about "war stories": they can easily be overdone. I hope the ones included in this book will strike the appropriate chord and that readers will appreciate them for their humor, or because they are touching, or searing, or too important not to be told. If any do not meet those standards, perhaps those who have worn the uniform will understand the explanation and accept the apology. Like the ones offered by Captain Brittles, they come with a shrug: "Old soldiers ..."

/////

I enlisted in the Air Force in 1960, never intending to make the military a career. I served in enlisted status for six years. It was a very proud moment in my life when I was called "Sarge" for the first time. In 1966, I received a commission through the Airmen Education and Commissioning Program perhaps confirming, as several friends insisted, that even the best organizations periodically make mistakes. Nonetheless, three decades later I retired as a "Mustang" colonel.

As a Chinese proverb says, some generations are "condemned to live in interesting times." Over those 36 years, events often conspired in ways that singled out Americans in uniform as star-crossed by especially "interesting times": the Cuban Crisis, Vietnam, Grenada, Panama, the Gulf War, Bosnia, and others. For much of that period, the Cold War formed a backdrop, like a gray tapestry on a Pollock painting that bound the edges of our environment and sometimes linked the dots together.

The stories in this book are told in a loose chronology of those "interesting times" as they unfolded. While many of the episodes describe people or units in peril, others do not. An equal or greater number recount anecdotes and reminiscences that trace a 36 year career in military service. Whether dramatic or mundane, humorous or tragic, official or unofficial, all taught lessons or instilled memories over a lifetime in uniform.

PROLOGUE

In the military, "Mustang" refers to an officer who "came up" through the ranks. The stories in this book chronicle nearly four decades as a "Mustang" in a career that began by messing up so badly that on my third day of boot camp I almost got kicked out of the Air Force. Thirty-six years later I retired as a colonel after leading some of the first American troops into Sarajevo.

It was never my intention to be a "lifer." When I enlisted as an 18 year-old farm boy, I wanted mainly to see if life existed outside of Lancaster County, Nebraska. The military was supposed to be just an interlude before getting on with the serious business of life. Complete my service obligation, maybe see some of the world, then come home and finish college: that was the plan.

For the next three decades, "the plan" was repeatedly disrupted. The Air Force caused the problem: I kept getting sent to interesting places, being given responsible jobs, and meeting fascinating people. Over the years, each time I reached a decision point I decided to "stay a little longer." Eventually, "staying a little longer" led to 36 years and retirement as a colonel.

At my farewell dinner I remarked that while on the way to the banquet I had finally just about decided to make the military a career. The line drew a nice laugh from a group of people who could not envision a gray-haired colonel as being – or wanting to be – anything other than an Air Force officer. But, while it may have stretched the point a bit, it was really like that in many ways – year by year, job by job, move by move being inexorably drawn along through life by the enjoyment and excitement of it all.

Somewhere along the journey I realized that it was more than just the travel, the jobs, the people, although those things were enormously important parts of the fabric. I stayed because something about it became part of me. It touched my soul. I loved it more as the years went by. It became the way I defined myself as a human being: an American Air Force officer. It was the importance of the "mission," of being one of the few chosen – honored – to wear that uniform. And it was so many other things.

The intermission had become the drama itself.

/////

Ironically, some of the scenes with the highest drama occurred on my very last job in the Air Force ... in Sarajevo.

Sarajevo: January, 1996

Sarajevo provoked biblical metaphors. To my closest friend, the ruins "looked like Hell with the fires out." At a hospital where Serbs had dragged Croatian and Muslim patients outside and shot them so they could use the beds for their own wounded, one of my young sergeants muttered partly to himself, partly to me, and partly, I think, to humanity, "We are pilgrims in an unholy place."

It was a haunting, yet exciting place – a place whose promise seemed strangely withheld. There was an awesome beauty about it: three quarters ringed by mountains, tucked inside a valley formed by those converging peaks just wide enough and flat enough to set a city amidst rugged hills that build into snowcaps visible in the distance. Bisecting it, right through the very heart of the city, ran a fast moving mountain stream. If not for the devastation, the landscape might have been mistaken for parts of the American West.

When the air was still, a distinct smell associated itself with the city. It was usually faint and not always unpleasant; it was the residue of dust, shattered masonry, broken water mains, ruptured gas lines, and the death that still lay covered and unclaimed under the rubble of the ravished streets.

Bosnia, and Sarajevo in microcosm, were places to which numbers attached themselves. Depending on whose numbers one believed, two and a half to seven and a half million land mines, two hundred thousand dead, two and a half million refugees. So much promise violated by smart, handsome people who seem almost genetically predisposed to do harm to one another. There was a number attached to me as well. This would be my last year in uniform, so I wanted this job to go well, to contribute even if in some small way, to be able to look back years from now and to believe the things we did might have helped make a difference. Perhaps most of all, I wanted to bring home safely the young men and women who accompanied me and who, as I've shared their lives with them, have become in ways that no outsider can understand, closer than family.

It was perhaps prophetic that the first sight visitors saw at the sandbagged and shattered airport was a sign that said "Welcome to Sarajevo." It had been mostly shot away; the final 'e' was gone from "Welcome" and the 'j' was mostly missing from "Sarajevo."

For many years afterward I kept on my desk a small snapshot. The picture was of another sign located just past the last guard post on the road from the airport. In enormous letters it cautioned convoys not to stop or slow down. Down the road a short distance was a hard right turn that aimed travelers straight down Sniper Alley into the core of the city. Visible in the background of the photo, half off the road in the right hand ditch, was a gutted tank. When the hulk was removed several days later, two corpses were found beneath it.

Months of bitter fighting had devastated the city: block after block torn apart by shelling and house to house fighting; burned out buildings — one almost looked as if it has been melted by the heat and the blast; piles of rubble, destroyed tanks and armored vehicles. Streetcars were a favorite target. Their shot-up remains lay scattered all over the city. There was an entire cemetery of murdered streetcars in an open field along Sniper Alley.

At exposed intersections, freight car containers or destroyed trolleys were used for protection from snipers. They were placed so that vehicles — there were not yet very many in the city — could move between the barriers; hugging close to them afforded pedestrians some protection from the sniper fire that had until so recently raked the major streets.

The city was mostly black at night, but there were hundreds of people of all ages out walking. Dozens of young people strolled arm in arm through the downtown area. They were anxious to be outside, above ground, free from the nightly terror visited on them from the nearby hills, away from the cellars that have bounded their existence for so many months. Many took their promenade in their very finest clothes, luxuriating in the delicious air of the unthreatened dark.

Away from the downtown area, firing continued around the edge of the city, thunderclap reminders that there was still far to go and much to be done. The shooting was usually not continuous but rather a series of shots followed seconds or minutes later by another volley in a lethal ping pong that lasted through the night.

As I began to learn the city and move around in it, I found my way to Zetra stadium. I thought immediately of my daughters, both enthusiastic, knowledgeable fans of figure skating. At the 1984 Olympics, the skating competition was held at this poignant place. Here was where Torvill and Dean skated to "Bolero," perhaps the most famous routine in all of skating history. Now, the roof of the stadium has been torn apart as if at this one place in the entire world a massive, angry presence had sought vengeance on this particular spot. The rink where Torvill and Dean skated was filled with trucks, half tracks and armored personnel carriers. Incongruously – and perhaps the ultimate obscenity – above those implements of war, still hanging from a shattered beam, was the Olympic scoreboard. It was punctured with bullet holes and the Olympic rings were partly missing.

The sights of the city began to weave themselves into my consciousness where they will always remain. I found myself wondering, who can possibly replace all this broken glass? I don't think there is enough in all of Europe.

On a narrow street near the stadium were houses that had been vacated by owners who knew the territory would soon be given to their adversaries. Everything had been stripped from the homes: electric wiring, wall sockets, window frames, doors, door knobs, faucets, plumbing. Nothing remained but the frames.

An entire mountain side near Zetra Stadium was now a graveyard. Small parks and lawns in residential areas became burial sites when the shelling was fierce or the "real" cemeteries were filled. Some families disinterred the corpses of relatives from graveyards in sectors their opponents will occupy.

One evening I walked across the bridge where a Serbian nationalist assassinated an Austrian Arch Duke and precipitated the start of World War I. The ethnic and religious strains that prompted that long ago assassination still remain. I was reminded once again that there is so far to go.

But there were also lighter moments that I will carry with me as well. The young American GIs in Sarajevo said that if we go to war we should go with the British: "The food in their dining halls is *really* good." They were, as usual, wise beyond their years. I discovered the truth of their comment when I dined with British colleagues a few nights later. Even in the half-destroyed hotel which was their headquarters, they served dinner on regimental china.

The kids of Sarajevo were eager to shake hands and try their few words of English. They had marvelous smiles and luminous eyes. They liked American chewing gum.

It was the very old and the very young, those most vulnerable, whose smiles seemed most genuine.

Days later, on my way to catch my return flight, I bought a banana split at a small café the owner had resurrected from the ruins. A vender was selling flowers on a corner of Sniper Alley. There was an occasional streetcar. Perhaps in my American optimism – or my farm boy naiveté – I regarded these as tiny beginnings. Small prayers offered up from a still-heathen landscape. Most of the rubble had been cleared from the airport, another sign of progress.

I left with these impressions: devastation amidst breathtaking beauty, life returning to a place that has too many cemeteries, crowds of strollers relishing the freedom to walk in the evening air not far from where tracers light the night sky, glimmerings of hope in an uncertain future.

The young people with me also returned unharmed, and I believe in some small way we have helped others plant tiny seeds that may – there is no assurance – take deeper root. At least that is what I told myself, and that made it okay to leave.

/////

I wound up making several trips to Sarajevo. But these first impressions, formed within days of the signing of the Dayton Peace Accords, were the most lasting. They remain with me, burned into me, always a part of me.

Sarajevo was my final substantive duty: it was the place where, for all intents and purposes, I left the Air Force at the end of a career that began 36 years, 5 months, and 2 days earlier when I stepped off a bus in San Antonio, Texas ... and almost immediately got in trouble.

CHEVRONS

Boot Camp

"What the hell happened?" The shout came from another recruit standing just outside the doorway. He had obviously heard the crash.

"I'm probably gonna get court-martialed," I replied. It was the only thing I could think of to say.

"Wow, that would be fast," he said.

I mentally agreed that it would set some sort of record: shortest time between enlistment and prison. Then I just listened as Staff Sergeant Huttenmier, my Training Instructor (TI), charged up the stairs carrying the window screen ... that I had just knocked out of a second story window ... that had fallen into a courtyard below ... that had narrowly missed him and a group of recruits circled around him.

Seventy-two hours after enlisting in the Air Force I saw my military career coming to a close. I would, I was sure, be sent home in disgrace with no "war stories" to tell. Well, maybe one ... about the nightmare trip that brought me to this place to begin with.

Great Plains thunderstorms tore at the aircraft all along the route from Omaha to Kansas City to St. Louis through central Texas. Wind shears jerked the wings almost vertical and baggage spilled from the overhead compartments. Food service was not even considered. Streaks of lightening lit the cabin and the plane was randomly swallowed in sudden down drafts like the bottom dropping out of a spastic elevator. A cluster of recruits had formed at the St. Louis airport, brought together at that place by connecting flights from around the country. Now, cloistered inside that vibrating aluminum canister, we hoped that the remaining 3 years, 364 and one half days of our 4-year enlistments would not be anything at all like the first 12 hours.

The thunderstorm was the worst, but not the last, misadventure nature perpetrated on us that night. One final torture remained: the San Antonio airport was fogged in. We flew on to Austin and waited in the middle of the night for a "blue goose" Air Force bus to crawl the 90 miles to collect and carry us to our ultimate destination, Lackland Air Force Base.

We finally arrived in the still pre-dawn hours, a caravan of exhausted, disheveled, uncertain teenagers, greeted as we stepped off the bus by a foul-mouthed two-striper who for sure was not a morning person. I had been forewarned, so the blow torch approach had little effect; and, by this time, operating on adrenalin only, I was probably too numb for it too register anyway.

Actually, even then everything seemed exciting. It was a reaction I often felt just before the first pitch of a ball game: excitement, anticipation, apprehension, ready and eager for the game to begin but somehow – until the first pitch – dreading it just the same. Now the first pitch had been thrown. The game had begun, and it was a relief to get started.

The Air Force trains all its recruits at Lackland, a sprawling complex adjacent to the *barrios* on the southwest outskirts of San Antonio. Our early morning arrival was in many ways a blessing. Even in the late spring, the daytime heat on the plains of south central Texas often climbed to frying pan levels. One of our first – shouted – lectures dealt with the need to take salt tablets several times each day.

In the blackness of the night bus ride those that had remained awake hadn't been able to see much of the landscape. Now with the rising sun on our first real day in the Air Force, the open areas near the base appeared to be a jumble of stunted mesquite sprouting from a sand and soil base, light brown or yellowish in color. Running through it, like veins of ore through a mountain side, was a unique strain of cement-hard clay called – we were told later – *kaleche*.

Tired as we were on the bus ride, as we approached San Antonio all of us squinted to see if we could find the Alamo somewhere in the disorder of the modern buildings visible from the road. We had no idea where it was. Several weeks later on our first Saturday afternoon pass, we found it: the Alamo was the first pilgrimage almost all of us made.

It is a place not to be trifled with. As we walked through the old mission – the chapel with the picture post card façade – one of the recruits gave a normal tone of voice, running commentary about the battle and the building's history. A matronly docent – there were several of them – quickly scolded him: "Lower your voice young man! This is a sanctuary; the Shrine of Texas Liberty!" Duly chastened, he complied. Years later when a local historian concluded that Mexican losses during the battle had been overstated, the public was greatly outraged. The poor gentleman no doubt feared for his life.

Even apart from the Alamo, San Antonio has been a garrison town since time immemorial. Major army installations – Camp Bullis, Fort Sam Houston, and Brooke Army Medical Center – are scattered across it, and at the time it was further ringed with four large air bases: Randolph, Kelly, Brooks, and Lackland.

It was to Barracks 1337 on Lackland that the bus delivered us. Built in the early 1940s for intended three-year occupancy, the clapboard and tar paper building and its hundreds of siblings were still in use. Baked by the unrelenting sun, the structures had dried to the point that they were the focus of our first safety briefing: "Sombitches burn totally to the ground in three minutes," a sergeant assured us.

In that building on the third day of training, I was given an assignment: clean the TI's office. It was my first official duty. I was scrubbing extra hard, clearing dust from the window sill in the World War II vintage barracks, when the caulking cracked around the screen and the whole thing broke loose with a crash.

On the way down, the screen bounced off a power line connected to the building and caused it to ricochet and miss – just barely – the crowd SSgt Huttenmier had gathered around him. Fortunately, the power line held; otherwise, most of Lackland AFB might have been blacked out. Just what I would have needed to cap off an otherwise ideal day. SSgt Huttenmier picked up the screen, glared at me standing by the window, and raced up the steps. He burst into the room, window screen in hand.

"What the (blank) happened?" I told him what I had done and showed him the caulking. "Well, Phillips," he said, "you screwed up." (Or words to that effect.)

I said, "Yes sir, I did."

Then, miracle of miracles, SSgt Huttenmier appeared to smile, sort of; he put the screen back in place, and walked out.

I had been in the Air Force three days and already saw myself flirting with jail time. On my first day at Lackland, SSgt Huttenmier lined up us "rainbows" (no uniforms yet); and after making some routine announcements shouted, "Where the (blank) is the guy from Lincoln Northeast?"

I signaled my presence.

"Well," he said, "I just love to (blank) with guys from Lincoln Northeast."

Jeez, this could only happen to me. Seventy kids from all over the country, all over the world counting two from Panama and one from Ireland, and I happened to be the one whose high school had routinely kicked his school's butt back in Nebraska. I mean, in an Air Force of several hundred thousand people, what were the odds of getting a TI from *Beatrice, Nebraska*?

Fortunately, I guess, SSgt Huttenmier was a basketball player. I was not, although Northeast regularly beat Beatrice like a drum. I played baseball. Beatrice did not have a baseball team or we would have kicked their butts in that sport as well. I was astute enough not to mention that to him when he called me into his office later that day.

I suppose it was the Nebraska connection that got me assigned to clean his office. That way he could give me grief about my high school and the loose women he supposed attended it or ask hard-nosed questions about what was going on "back home."

At that time, one of the first tasks for recruits was to memorize ten security instructions ("Sir, my first security instruction is to protect any and all government property in sight."), know the Air Force chain of command, and recite the names of the President's cabinet members. I didn't have any trouble doing that kind of thing and on our first barracks inspection, I spat them all back at the inspecting officer.

SSgt Huttenmier was duly impressed. He commented to SSgt Dubois, the other TI assigned to our flight, that despite my having knocked the screen out of his office window, my performance that day showed the superior capabilities of people from the Midwest. Further, it was possibly an indication that I "might make it after all."

Even setting considerations of SSgt Huttenmier aside, boot camp was a special event. Only two of us, Larry Vehrs from Iowa and I, were from the central region of the country. There were a few Texans, a handful from Oklahoma and Arkansas, and a scattering of ones and twos from elsewhere. The great majority, probably 40 of the 70 in our flight, were from New York City, Philadelphia, and Pittsburgh. Apparently, the pattern of aircraft delays and arrivals had created some unusual groupings as the flights were made up.

Our group was a kaleidoscope of colors, backgrounds, and lineages. In addition to us Heinz 57 varieties types, there were African-Americans, Hispanics, and a Native American who was immediately dubbed "Chief," as most were at the time. Several of the New York City cadre were of Italian and Spanish descent. The names were marvelous: Cusimano, Santa Maria, Espinosa. For a farm kid from Nebraska, it was a great experience.

There were some fascinating matchups: Ken Leonard, a devout Southern Baptist from Oklahoma, marched beside George Schoenemann, a monumentally fouled-mouthed kid from New York City. Schonemann was the Michelangelo of profanity. I've never before or since heard anyone curse with such frequency, variety, or imagination. Schoenemann was kicked out of boot camp about half way through, sent home, I think, for mouthing off to a TI or an officer.

I've often wondered what happened to Georgie. I fully expected he would wind up in prison or as governor of New York. Despite his mouth, there was a quality of unassuming leadership about him that almost compelled people to like and work with him. I came to think that if I or my unit were ever in a tight spot, Georgie would be the kind of person I would want on my side: smart, tough, fiercely loyal.

Once when we were paired together on a detail, I got him out of a jam by showing him how to disassemble his problem piece by piece and then solve it a step at a time. That was in contrast to the high volume, off color bitching that was most often his immediate reaction, and Georgie thought it was neat.

Others could have done the same. An NCO mentor or a sharp first sergeant might have salvaged this kid. Clearly, there *are* people who for any number of reasons have no place in the military. Their ties with the service are best severed totally and immediately. But in the case of George Schoenemann, it was unfortunate to see that much natural leadership ability walk out the door. I thought the Air Force gave up on him too soon.

Since my plan was to stay four years and then get out, there didn't appear to be much possibility that I would ever be in a position to influence decisions like that. Still, the thought occurred to me that if I ever were, I would walk a while longer with guys like Georgie.

Another of my barracks-mates was a gangly kid who was instantly given the label "Tweety." The name just seemed to fit: he was scrawny, bird-like, and seemed to restlessly flit from place to place. During the first several days, he was sometimes the butt of disparaging remarks from a group whose social sensitivity scale could usually be read in negative numbers.

About midway through training, our flight was called on to pull extra guard duty and other details while our sister units were off doing something else. "Tweety" was all over the place, working extended shifts, taking additional details, filling in, helping everyone get their jobs done. He ended up being one of the most well-liked and most respected members of the flight. "Tweety" taught all of us a lesson about people and teamwork.

Boot camp turned out okay, even though the surprises continued right up to the end. For one thing, SSgt Huttenmier and SSgt Dubois recommended me for TI duty. That never happened. Soon some wiser head higher up the chain decided my time would be more profitably used at Weather Observer School. I was not uncomfortable with that decision.

Then, on the day we left, someone placed a piece of paper in my hand designating me as "Airman in Charge" of the plane full of recruits headed for technical training at Chanute AFB, Illinois. Either my later performance had overcome the window screen faux pas or else the general screw-up level in my group was such that despite it I still looked good in comparison. I could understand either possibility.

Years later, when someone asked me how I'd lasted 36 years, I told them with great sincerity that was a tough question to answer because I was always a bit surprised to have survived the third day of boot camp.

Tech Training

Harold Henthorn was the world's scrawniest individual. He was six feet tall or more and weighed, or so it appeared, about 125 pounds. How he passed the enlistment physical will always be a mystery. Harold was a member of my class at weather school. In the old "open bay" barracks, he had one of the top bunks in the long double rows that extended from end to end on the building's second floor. The springs on Harold's bunk sagged and he was so skinny that when the bunk was viewed at eye level, Harold could sometimes not be seen tucked away in the fold of the mattress.

That was the other thing about Harold: he slept. Harold slept a lot and he slept soundly. For his squad mates, every morning was an ordeal as they struggled to wake Harold and get him on the road. Harold's sleeping habits soon made him legendary.

One Sunday, as Harold was snoozing on his bunk, several of us decided to test how soundly he really slept. We loosely tied bed sheets around him, his bed springs and mattress, so, hopefully, he would not fall out. Then we carried him and his entire bunk down two flights of stairs and put it in the shower room. That's where Harold, still sound asleep, had to be awakened the next morning.

I first met Harold and my other future weather school classmates when we were thrown into "PATS (Personnel Awaiting Tech School) status" immediately after we arrived at Chanute AFB. Located a few miles north of Champaign-Urbana, Illinois, and 100 miles south and a little west of Chicago, Chanute was home to several Air Force technical training courses including weather, engine mechanic, and many others. Now closed, the base was glued to the small town of Rantoul (dubbed "Rangoon" by the GIs) like half of a set of conjoined twins cohabitating on the table top-flat farm land of central Illinois. Octave Chanute, a contemporary of the Wright Brothers had experimented with gliders in the area, hence the name of the base.

I successfully completed my "Airman in Charge" duties by taking a final head count and handing over the records of the troops that had flown with me from San Antonio. At least this time I hadn't knocked out a window screen, and the head count revealed that no one had fallen off the plane. Pleased with that modest success, I saluted and reported to "PATS Barracks."

PATS status was a holding pattern, an interim arrangement that made us available for details until our tech training classes began. My group did not intersect the training cycle at an optimum time. For us, it was a two-week wait until the first day of weather school. We spent a day or two working at the commissary and then the remainder of the time pulling KP at Dining Hall #3.

Dining Hall #3 was monstrous; all of Chanute's tech school students marched to it three times a day. It was an old facility with open, high beamed rafters. Sparrows sometimes got into the building and roosted on those metal beams. I never heard of anyone receiving an extra drop of protein in their cereal, but it surely must have happened.

But, *two weeks* of KP! Keeping even one set of our newly issued three sets of fatigues washed and ironed became a continuous, and often losing, struggle. I saw more dirty dishes than I ever expected to see in a lifetime. There were mountains of them. There is perspective to be gained from most things, though, and I developed a healthy and abiding respect for those who do this and other similar chores by profession or necessity.

Once the agony of PATS was over, weather school itself was a treat; it was one of the best training experiences of my career. More than a decade later, I remembered enough to teach the meteorology block of an Air Force ROTC Flight Instruction Program. Closer to home, once in awhile the training still enables me to impress my daughters – an otherwise almost impossible task – by casually throwing out a term like *cumulonimbus mammatus* or *altocumulus standing lenticularus*.

Mammatus was easy to remember: the name refers to the pouches — mammaries — that sometimes form under the base of a thunderstorm cloud. They do, in fact, look like breasts; and that was how we were taught to identify them. For a group of red-blooded 18- and 19-year old American males, picking out a *mammatus* cloud posed no problem at all. Forty years later, I'll bet that is the one cloud type that everyone in the class can still identify.

The other salient memory of weather school at Chanute is the marching. We marched to and from school, meals, and details. Through some unique chemistry, our flight -- the 30 of us in my class -- were *really* good. It just happened; I can recall no particular practices before our first graded session. The protocol was that as the tech training squadrons marched to class, they were graded once a week. Within each squadron, the flight that won got to march at the head of the line through the next week when the process was repeated. It was a big deal because the base VIPs came out to watch the graded march-bys.

We were a very junior flight when we won for the first time and then every week after that. The usual drill was for the flights nearing graduation to be pulled out of competition, so the "front of the line" honor could be passed around and used as motivation for other flights that still had considerable time remaining.

That didn't happen with us. We looked so sharp the squadron commander kept us at the front. Perhaps we were helping his report card as well. Finally, bitching from other flights about never having the opportunity to march at the head of the line caused us to be moved. Or maybe we got cocky. In any event, we were either given the honorary title of lead flight or the title was retired until we graduated. More to the point, we were moved out of the first slot. For a week we marched at the back of the line. We were not amused.

Then something wonderful happened. On the graded march-by the following week, the flight that had been moved to the head of the squadron line in our place screwed up heroically. From our position in back we couldn't see, of course, but their mistakes must have been special to behold. Before we started to class the next morning, the entire squadron was formed up in front of the

Orderly Room. The cadet commander was from Scotland, a veteran of the British Army, who joined the American military to accelerate his citizenship. From way up at the head of the squadron, he called all the way down the line to Paul Rector, our flight leader. With a majestic Scottish burr, he shouted "Ta'e 'um up frront Rrectorr!"

Music to our ears. We marched past the entire squadron to resume our rightful spot at the front. I doubt we ever looked sharper. One of the guys broke wind as we marched by the flight that had taken our place. I was concerned for a moment that we would be relegated to the back once again. We stayed at the front though, all the way until graduation day.

How neat it was to be the very best.

Minot AFB

There was an important lesson to be learned from two years at Minot AFB: it is the *people* that make a good assignment, not the *place*.

There is a reason you don't read much about the scenic grandeur of North Dakota. That much was apparent to Gene Bieber and me as we drove north to our first assignment after tech school. We were classmates in the weather observer course. When that was finished, after a few days leave, Gene picked me up in his mid-50s Hudson and we traveled together to Minot.

It was not an auspicious start. Snow began falling almost exactly the moment we crossed the border into North Dakota although it was mid-fall by the standards of much of the rest of the world. We arrived in Minot in the late evening only to be told that the Air Force Base was several more miles north of town. We resolved to get a good meal, spend the night in the city, then drive to the base and report in the following morning. That decided, we found a nice looking restaurant called "Larry's Café" near the motel and settled in for a much-anticipated dinner on our last night of leave.

Bad decision: the worst case of food poisoning I have ever experienced. Gene and I were up several times that night as everything in our bodies – stomach lining, enamel from our teeth, *everything* – came loose. Repeatedly. Fortunately, the timing was such that there was never a conflict over access to the sink, commode, or shower, but the explosions were happening so often that availability became a concern.

Late the following morning the worst spasms subsided and we trucked wanly out to the base. The sergeant who cleared us in took note of our condition and wondered aloud why we looked so peaked. Gene explained the Larry's Café experience and concluded by saying that we had "crapped our brains out." That summed it up pretty well for me, so I didn't say anything. I was too weak to talk, anyway.

Those first hours notwithstanding, Minot turned out to be a good assignment. Physically attractive, the place was not. The surrounding landscape was mostly flat, treeless plains and enormous wheat fields. "There are," one of my roommates believed, "only two fences posts between here and the North Pole to stop the wind."

We were, indeed, quite a ways north – about 60 miles from the Canadian border. Sometimes after a hectic shift, two or three of us would drive up there just to have a cup of coffee at a truck stop in a small town on the Canadian side. In those more benign times, the customs crossings on the border were occasionally completely unattended late at night.

But, the weather and the scenery notwithstanding, Minot turned out just fine. That was because our small weather detachment contained a solid group of guys and the officer and NCO leadership was quite good. The detachment commander was a crusty, veteran "CO" who took no prisoners. He was fair, highly respected, and he demanded excellence.

At Minot, three young lieutenants influenced a major decision in my life. The saga began when I was working a midnight shift with one of them, Second Lieutenant Gene Cutler. During a coffee break between plotting maps and preparing forecasts, Lt. Cutler mentioned that he had recently read an article in the "Air Force Times" about a commissioning program for enlisted people. Each year the Air Force took a few selected enlisted troops with a minimum of college credits, sent them to civilian universities to complete their bachelor's degrees and then to Officer Training

School. Cutler said "You'd be good at that. Why don't you give it some thought?" During the weeks that followed, two other lieutenants, Philip West and Russell Shablow, encouraged me to consider the commissioning program.

Several things remain a mystery to this day. I don't know what qualities they saw or thought they saw, and I do not know if the contacts were independently made or part of an orchestrated effort. Whatever, it had an impact.

I began looking into the possibility. The baseline requirement for the program was 30 semester hours of college credit. I had 31, but as the Base Education Office soon discovered, the Air Force was prohibited from accepting two of the credit hours – from Air Force ROTC, of all things! That left me one hour short. I enrolled in a college trigonometry correspondence course that would get me over the hump and later took a Logic and Scientific Methods course that would, hopefully, further enhance my prospects.

At one time or another each of the three lieutenants served as test proctors for the hour exams and finals. Early in the process, Cutler rattled the cage of program officials who initially lost my Air Force Officer Qualifying Test and then misfiled the results. West got a foot-dragging bureaucrat to administer a college GED test on short notice. There were four parts to that test. I took it in two bleary-eyed segments after midnight to eight AM shifts. I was skeptical of the outcomes – especially on the science portion; taking it in a sleep-deprived state made it a long shot. West had hammered the Education Office pretty hard to get them to respond, so I did not ask for it to be rescheduled. Fortunately, I struggled through.

Soon after, the process was delayed by a pending overseas assignment; people "on orders" for overseas could not apply for the program. Happily, Sidi Slimane AB, Morocco, was a "short tour" location so when I returned to the States, I resubmitted the application. At Frances E. Warren AFB, Mr. Crerar, a truly superb Education Officer, pushed the paperwork; and I was fortunate enough to be selected.

I do not know what prompted those three lieutenants to take an interest in me. I am very grateful that they did, because what they asked me to consider ultimately became how I defined myself as a human being: an American Air Force officer.

When I eventually became an officer, I sought to continue the example set by Cutler, West, and Shablow. I made it a goal on every assignment to seek out and guide at least one exceptional airman or NCO to a commission as an officer. One of my proudest achievements is that for 30 years I succeeded in doing that: at least one on every assignment. In fact, I am pleased to say that a version of the process has continued post-retirement. While working as a university administrator, I assisted two young graduate students through the OTS recruiting and application process. Both have now received their commissions and are serving on active duty.

/////

I was a young airman at Minot AFB when the base was transferred from Air Defense Command (ADC) -- according to some the acronym meant "Already Dead Command" -- to Strategic Air Command (SAC). One of the world's premier military establishments, SAC was an organization that sought and achieved unwavering excellence. Years later when I was assigned to SAC headquarters, one long-time SAC officer told me – only half jokingly – that the command's motto was "To err is human; to forgive is not SAC policy."

At any rate, the difference was apparent almost overnight: the guards at the main gate were sharper, the salutes were crisper, the base was cleaner, the BX was better stocked, the barracks were better maintained; SAC even improved the taste of the food in the mess hall. And always, always the focus was on the mission. After a year in the Air Force I found myself thinking "so this is how it is supposed to be."

The Sound of Silence

It was the only time in my life when I have been conscious of hearing my own heartbeat. In the moments after the fourth klaxon sounded, it was if the entire world had stopped, waiting ...

Sidi Slimane Air Base, Morocco, was my first overseas tour. With a brand new third stripe stitched on my sleeve, I arrived there in early October 1962. The place was right out of a Humphrey

Bogart movie: camels, palm trees, veiled women. Narrow alleys formed the streets of the nearby town from which the base drew its name. Congested and noisy, venders shouted from the small shops – pots, pans, and brassware hanging from every wall – that lined each side.

The base was 33 miles inland from the Atlantic, built on a sandy coastal plateau that quickly gave way to rolling hills and then to the Atlas Mountains visible in the distance. Across those mountains the Sahara awaited, a scorching immutable presence that eliminated any hint of casualness from considerations of life, travel, and habitation.

My timing was impeccable: a few days later we were, as Secretary of State Dean Rusk later said, "eyeball to eyeball with the Soviet Union." Like military installations around the world, Sidi Slimane went on alert immediately after U-2 photos confirmed the presence of Soviet missiles in Cuba. We listened over Armed Forces Radio Service to Secretary of Defense McNamara's description of the Soviet weapons and were glued to the radio during President Kennedy's address to the nation. Sidi Slimane was a Strategic Air Command "reflex" base (B-47 bombers rotated -- "reflexed" -- in and out from bases in the United States), thus we took particular note of the President's comment that any missile fired from Cuba would be "regarded as an attack on the United States by the Soviet Union" and would require "a full retaliatory response."

That picture remains etched in memory: everyone in our small detachment huddled around a radio in our tar paper "hooch" on the edge of the Sahara, listening to those words. They caused a collective intake of breath and many unfocused, far away looks as each individual became instantly absorbed in thoughts entirely his own.

The crisis continued to build. On October 22, B-52s were placed on airborne alert as SAC went to DEFCON 3. The next day, for the first time in its history, SAC moved to DEFCON 2, an additionally heightened state of alert that awaited only a final order to launch. Because the detachment operated around the clock, we were essentially on duty all the time, grabbing a few hours sleep or taking a short break whenever the situation allowed.

The tension was extraordinary; deep in the crisis when work was momentarily caught up, three of us walked to the bowling alley for a cup of coffee to get away from it all for just a few minutes. At Sidi Slimane, B-47s were fueled and loaded and the crews poised in or near the aircraft. Rumors were rampant regarding Soviet troop movements in Europe. Clearly, their forces were also at the highest levels of alert. Meanwhile, the radio in the bowling alley said that Russian ships carrying additional missiles were about to be intercepted on the high seas. While their intentions were unknown, there was no indication that they would do anything other than attempt to proceed to Cuba.

The procedure at the base was that the klaxons sounded at established times once or twice a day to confirm the present DEFCON status, or more significantly, at any time there was a change in alert status. At that moment, the implications of the latter were almost too ominous to contemplate. The sirens shrieked as we took our first sips of coffee. There was no way of knowing whether they would signal a continuation of the present DEFCON – it was nearing the normal time for that – or whether the world's worst nightmare was about to happen.

When the first klaxon screamed, *everything* stopped. Even in the bowling alley, there was no sound. Whatever they were doing people stopped, totally. Pin boys halted their work. Coffee cups were poised at half-raised positions. No one spoke. It was so quiet that any noise from the outside could be heard. But there was no noise. It seemed as if even the birds were quiet. There were no traffic sounds, none of the normal "static" of a busy base. Everyone stood – completely still – waiting.

Four klaxons would reaffirm DEFCON 2. Anything after four meant that war -- *nuclear war* – was underway. The interval after the fourth siren, spent in absolute silence in a motionless world, was the longest few seconds of my life. It took a moment to realize there was not going to be a fifth klaxon. In a universe where no one had been breathing, there was an exquisite sigh of relief. For awhile at least, there was still a chance.

Contrasts, a Flood, and an Interesting Way of Saying Thanks

Morocco is a country with enormous promise. The climate near the coast is hospitable for both people and agriculture; the beaches along the Atlantic and the Mediterranean are marvelous, as are the ski resorts in the Atlas Mountains; and it is home to some of the world's most intriguing cities: Casablanca, Tangier, Marrakech. Unlike many of its neighbors the country is stable, reasonably open, and progressive.

The country's moderate politics enable it to serve as an intermediary between contending parties in the region. The United States benefited greatly from its good offices during the hostage crisis with Iran.

But, elements of the population remain desperately poor. Indeed, to a visitor in Morocco in 1962, poverty was a first impression.

We took our weather observations from the control tower. From that vantage point we occasionally found ourselves in the middle of the action, helping guide security police to interlopers attempting to get into the base. The intruders would try to hide in the tall grass near the base perimeter, but the tower perch gave us unobstructed vision and its height allowed us to look down on the entire open area around the flight line.

Mostly, the visitors wanted to grab whatever they could and run. Copper was apparently an especially valuable commodity; on one occasion, thieves tried to cut a large cable leading to the bomb dump. It seemed to us that incidents like that spiked at about the time of the missile crisis, but that could have been active imaginations at work precipitated by daily events that already had a surreal quality all their own. Most of the transgressors were caught, turned over to local authorities and then, at least as scuttlebutt would have it, quickly turned loose.

/////

In early 1963, massive flooding occurred across a wide area around the base. At one time or another, most of us in the weather detachment were out and about in the countryside assisting in the recovery efforts. *Almost* always the help was appreciated by people poor to begin with, whose lives had been further devastated by a cruel and overwhelming act of nature. A few weeks later, three of us drove through the area and were warmly welcomed. No ugly Americans there.

During the worst days of the flooding, one of the guys in the detachment rode along on a U.S. helicopter sent to assist in the relief mission. They came upon a family totally isolated, huddled on the roof of a small shack surrounded by rising flood waters. The group was in dire straits: no food, nothing to drink, flood waters encroaching on their quickly diminishing sanctuary. They waved frantically to the chopper, pleading for help.

It took two trips, but eventually the entire family was lifted to safety. When the last of the group was secure on dry ground, the head of the family, almost overcome with emotion, clasped and kissed the hands of each of the crew members and thanked them in fervent and heartfelt Arabic.

And then he stole the toolbox from the helicopter.

Eddie Moran

Every good outfit has, or should have, at least one NCO like Eddie Moran. I met Eddie on the flight from Charleston AFB that took us first to the Azores and then to Nouasseur AB near Casablanca. From there, we had nearby seats on the bus ride to Sidi Slimane AB.

Eddie and NCOs like him are adhesives that hold units together. In his case, the glue came in a small container. A self described "tough little mick from Chicago," Eddie may have stood 5' 5" and weighed at most 130 pounds. He had been a B-24 tail gunner during World War II. Discharged immediately after the war, he stayed out six years, finally stopped kidding himself about not missing the military, and rejoined. He spent a few years in supply, a career field "frozen" for promotions as a result of the austere budgets of the time, before transferring to weather.

Eddie was about 41 when we met, a full 20+ years older than me. The age difference turned out not to be of much consequence. We shared an affinity for history, the Chicago Cubs, and playing softball. When our small detachment combined with the cooks to build a softball team, Eddie played second base and I played shortstop. Lots of free evenings were spent playing catch in the cool desert air. We quickly formed a rather nifty double play combination. Since I led off and Eddie batted second, we also worked with some success on a "hit and run" play.

When the initial shift rotations frequently paired us together, our friendship was further solidified. It remained over a lifetime even though after Sidi Slimane I only saw him twice. We always corresponded at Christmas and exchanged a few phone calls, the last one nearly 30 years after our first encounter when, even though I was by then a colonel, he called to check up on me during *Desert Storm.*

Eddie and I shared several things in common, but loquaciousness was not one of them. I didn't talk much at all. Eddie talked all the time. He talked to everyone: Arabs riding camels on the road outside the base, stuffy French waiters in restaurants, generals, one-stripers, clerks at the base exchange, school kids, anyone. Eddie never met a stranger.

His conversations sometimes had surprising consequences. Once he was chattering with a little Moroccan who sold coffee at a small stand near the base exchange. Eddie was prattling on as usual, but not much communication was happening: the Moroccan spoke very little English, and Eddie's French and Arabic were sparse to say the least. Finally, as we were about to leave, Eddie, fresh from a recent tour in Germany, jokingly said "Danke schoen mein Herr." To which, the Moroccan gentleman, tattered fez, frayed robe and all, responded "Bitte. Auf Wiedersehen!" For once, even Moran was stunned into silence.

It turned out that the little coffee vendor had been with the Moroccan contingent that fought with the French army during World War II and had spent considerable time in Germany. He spoke the language fluently. From that day forward, every time Eddie and I had coffee at the tiny stand, he and the vendor engaged in animated conversations – all in German – talking about events in general and reminiscing about their times in the Fatherland.

When Eddie and I walked down the streets of Kenitra, the nearest town of any size, or Sidi Slimane, a nearby village, it was a rare occasion when someone didn't recognize and call out to him. Apparently at some point Eddie had chatted them up; and now they were anxious to offer him coffee, sweet tea, or good bargains on brass ware, toy camels, wood carvings, sheep skin rugs or small scimitar-shaped knives. Moran loved to haggle, so on any excursion into town he was truly in his element.

Eddie's jokes and patter disguised his considerable sophistication: his wife was an artist who had enjoyed some success in Hollywood (she designed the cat motif on the "Mr. Lucky" TV series) and then worked around Taos and Albuquerque. At times, the noise he made and the laughter he created caused people to mistake how much he loved that uniform, the Air Force, and his country. Since I spent lots of time working with him and sharing time off, I got to know that side of him during serious conversations in his quieter moments. Others got the message rather quickly when they showed up wearing a uniform that did not meet his standards or when their work was less than satisfactory. Unless the screw-up was egregious he never got in their face in the presence of others. He always found a way to get to them though, whether "getting to them" meant a chewing out, a quiet talk, a reminder, or simply teasing the offender into a lesson learned: "Sorry that your barber died," "Try standing closer to your razor." Not everyone liked it, but they seldom failed to get the message.

At the base theater, where the "Star Spangled Banner" was played before the movie began, everyone would rise, remove their hats, and stand at attention. Moran was one of the few NCOs who would quickly seek out and jack up any showoff who failed to "honor the colors." Once per offender was enough; after that no one ever did it again.

Eddie and I were stationed together from October through the next July. Those ten months were an important part of my growing up time in the Air Force. I have never forgotten the education I received.

I've also never forgotten the stories Moran told. They usually had a military flavor and were always acted out. Whether it was a cockney accent, the exaggerated open hand salute and the foot stomping halt of the British Army, or the slurred speech of an inebriated soul, Eddie played all the parts.

When his stories weren't about himself, they often involved our allies or sister services. At the time we got to Sidi Slimane, the Army was going through one of its periodic attempts to make the service more humane and treat its soldiers with more compassion. According to Moran's story, that direction had just come in when a company commander was watching his grizzled "Old Army" first sergeant handle a formation out on the drill pad.

"Jackson," the first sergeant shouted, "your old lady just croaked. Fall out and get your butt home on emergency leave!"

The company commander was shocked. "Sarge, Sarge," he exclaimed, "we can't treat people like that any more. We've got to handle our soldiers gently. This is the 'New Army'!"

The company commander could see that the first sergeant was stunned and more than a little confused.

The next day just before roll call the commander handed the first sergeant a note saying that Private Jones' mother had died. The CO was especially anxious to see how the first sergeant would handle the situation. In the 'New Army' it was important to speak kindly to people and make them feel comfortable.

When the formation assembled, the commander could see the first sergeant staring at the note, perplexed about how to proceed under the compassionate 'New Army' guidelines.

Finally, after thinking about if for a few minutes, the first sergeant shouted "Everyone with a living mother take one step forward! WHAT THE HELL IS THE MATTER WITH YOU JONES? GET BACK IN LINE!"

Softball at Sidi Slimane

Sidi Slimane was scheduled for closure in the early fall of 1963, so during the spring and summer of that year the population was steadily "drawn down" as preparations were made to turn the base over to the Moroccan government. Because of mission requirements, units were not reduced at an even rate across the board. After the flying units left, the last major organization scheduled to shut down operations was the Global Communications Center. Even in "normal" times easily the largest outfit on the base, the first effect of the shut down schedule was that "Global Comm" soon came to "own" most of the remaining people on the base – something like 450-500 of the last 800 military people at Sidi Slimane were assigned to that unit.

Global Comm had a truly obnoxious commander, who had an even more obnoxious wife. At times, she accompanied her husband when he inspected Global Comm barracks. Her "Don't you think that locker could be a little neater?" sniffed with proper Brahmin accent was widely mimicked around the base. The second unfortunate effect of the draw down was that as Global Comm's proportion of the shrinking pie got larger and larger, so did the commander's and his lady's pretensions of royalty.

The third effect was that Global Comm dominated the sports competitions. Base officials had wisely laid on an ambitious softball season to help keep everyone occupied and entertained during the closure regimen – always a hectic time and one prone to producing anxieties, particularly among families preparing to depart. So, teams in the base fast pitch softball league played two, three, or more times each week. The games were well attended; on a week night at Sidi Slimane there wasn't much else going on.

Global Communications just ate the league up. They were 25-0 going into the last week of the season and most of the games weren't really very close. Our little weather detachment had 16 people total – just enough forecasters and weather observers to keep the station operating around the clock. As the softball season progressed there was some very creative swapping of shifts between softball players and non-softball players to make sure we could put a team on the field. Fortunately, we had a commander who understood the importance of all this and indulged the process as long as the station was always covered – which it was – and as long as everyone pulled the same number of shifts – which they did. Because we were so small, for softball purposes we combined with the cooks, another bunch of shift workers in a small unit who lived in the "hooches" next to us. The cooks usually provided two or three players – just enough to prevent us from having to forfeit any games.

During the season our patched together team did okay -- not great, but okay. We were 16-9 after a slow start. Fairly early in the year, we found a cook who said he thought he could pitch. He also turned out to be okay – not great, but okay. He was not typically a strikeout pitcher. What he could do well most nights was throw the ball over the plate. When the right shift workers were able to play, we had a fine defense that usually kept us in the game. The pitcher and the team both got better during the season, and we were riding the crest of a small winning streak when the last week of the season, and our game with Global Comm, rolled around.

They had killed us when we played them early in the year. The "mercy rule" was invoked in the fifth inning because they were so far ahead. Still, for several reasons an especially large crowd had showed up: (1) there wasn't much else to do; (2) we had been playing well and if Global Comm was going to get a serious challenge, most people realized it would likely come from us; (3) it would be one of the last games played at Sidi Slimane.

The crowd got larger each inning as the game progressed. The sizeable bleachers behind home plate and along the first and third base lines were entirely filled and became absolutely stuffed as more and more people came and crammed themselves in. By the late innings, people were standing along each baseline and lining the fences around the field. The reason was, miracle of miracles, we were ahead. Early in the game, someone had stuck his head in our dugout and said that the game highlights and inning by inning score were being announced over our small Armed Forces Radio station that broadcast news, music, and information. Eventually, at the end of the game, it seemed like the entire population of the base was at the ballpark.

We took an early lead and somehow, some way, managed to scrap and scrape and hold on as the innings went by. There were tons of fine defensive plays, timely hitting, and great base running. Our six weather guys and three cooks – that's all we had available to suit up – had our finest hours; in some way, at some point, during those incredible seven innings, everyone of us saved or won the game in one fashion or another.

Although each inning played like the "Perils of Pauline," rife with potential disaster, there was only one defensive breakdown. It was a big one though, a misplay in the outfield in the last inning that let Global Comm close within one run and left the tying and winning runs at third and second with one out. We managed to get the second out on an infield popup, and then our non-strikeout pitcher broke off a beautiful curve over the outside corner for a called strike three.

What happened next was absolute pandemonium. There was a diving, yelling, hugging, backslapping pile of players at the pitchers mound; people from the stands poured onto the field; car horns totted; the radio station dedicated its programming to us for the rest of the night, and someone risked courts-martial by sounding the base siren.

When the phone rang in our hooch for the first of countless times that night, our left fielder, "Okie" Davis, caught up in the excitement of the moment, picked up the receiver and shouted "Yeah, baby, we did it!" Then Okie got pale and quiet and turned the phone over to Eddie Moran. Our commander was on the other end of the line. The "CO" admonished Sergeant Moran to instruct Airman Davis on how to answer an official call in a proper military manner -- and then broke up laughing, congratulated Eddie, and said that there was champagne waiting at the club if anyone wanted to come pick it up.

What made all this even better was that our opponents took their defeat with their usual lack of grace. Their commander called our commander and accused us of having brought in "ringers" to play his boys in the big game. Our shortstop – me – was accused of being a ringer. I had played every game of the season: evidence of the kind of notice my playing normally attracted. Our centerfielder – Tony Smith – was accused of being a ringer. He had in fact been with us for several weeks on temporary duty from another base to help us keep our station running while we packed equipment and got the place ready to close. We really didn't know Tony was a ballplayer when he came to us; but with all due respect to Global Comm, he did look a lot like Mantle on that particular day.

Global Comm cried so much that a couple of days later Eddie Moran bought a sympathy card mourning their grievous loss and tacked it on the bulletin board in their orderly room. That immediately brought renewed howls from their first sergeant – another individual that most of us thought was destined to be disappointed on the first Easter after his death – and another call from their commander to our commander. Our quiet, devoutly religious boss was in on the prank; and, in fact, his was one of many signatures on the sympathy card. He surprised us all by telling the other guy to quit whining and get on with the mission.

That evening, outside under a desert sky with stars so close we could almost reach up and touch them, Eddie and I toasted that game with one last sip of the commander's champagne and thought that maybe, at that moment, life was about as good as it could get.

Francis E. Warren AFB

Cheyenne, Wyoming, is a western cow town. On its outskirts, Francis E. Warren AFB shares and extends that frontier heritage. Long past its days as a cavalry post, some of the original red brick buildings are now registered as national historic sites.

It is an unusual air force base: it has no flight line. The weather detachment was tucked away at the edge of the municipal airport to assist the occasional military transit traffic. The base eventually became the hub for outlying Minuteman and, later, Peacekeeper missile sites that radiate out from Warren like spokes on a gigantic wheel that leaves tracks across the corners of several states.

In 1963, the missiles had just begun to arrive. Much of the business of the detachment was to assist the unique C-133 aircraft – specially configured for the task – that carried the first Minutemen to the high plains of southeastern Wyoming. The missiles were a major topic of conversation as was the wind. Across the enormous open plateau, it blew incessantly.

Although I relished being within a day's drive of home, Francis E. Warren was the assignment I enjoyed least. Not that there weren't good people in the detachment; in fact, there were some first rate individuals. It was just that the cluster of individuals was a unit in name only. There was no special sense of pride, no *cohesion*, little sense of shared togetherness.

My feelings resulted in part from having just come from an overseas tour. Overseas units are often more "together" than stateside ones. There are usually fewer outside distractions, language barriers sometimes exist, and a greater portion of troops and families live on base. When the outside population is not culturally or emotionally supportive, people far from home often find reasons to band together. And then, of course, at Sidi Slimane there had been the high drama of the Cuban Missile Crisis.

I understood coming in that the esprit would likely not be as intense as I had experienced overseas. I did not expect it to be almost totally lacking. I missed it.

This was the only assignment I ever had where I felt that people were just showing up, putting in their time, then going home. Eight to four. Nothing special about it at all.

Some of that attitude came from the mission or lack of it at the time. There were no flying units at Warren and the Minuteman missiles were just being installed, so the place was not a hot bed of activity. But, I came to believe that most of the lethargy emanated from the commander. Just as sports teams often mirror the personalities of the coaches, military units frequently reflect the character of their commanders. The "CO" at Warren was a three-time divorcee, sloppy to the point of obesity, and more interested in flying with the base aero club than serving as commander of the detachment. The unit did in fact mirror his attitude: indifference.

One of my great bosses in later years often remarked "You can learn a lot from a bad example." That is true. Warren reinforced what I already knew: if I ever got to be a commander, I would lead in a totally different way.

Pool Tables and Other Things People Are Remembered By

At Colorado State University, where I was sent from Francis E. Warren AFB on an Air Force scholarship, I became part of a unique group of Air Force students. We studied together, played ball together – we had wickedly good softball and flag football teams – and became lifelong friends.

None of us had any money: in 1964, a staff sergeant's base pay was less than $300 per month. For young families especially, the

the program could be tough sledding financially.

At the time, the Air Force paid AECP students a stipend of $25 to buy text books each quarter. One young Air Force couple, Carl and Carol Marsalis, carefully hoarded those $25 checks. Their goal was to save enough to buy a vacuum cleaner because Carol had to borrow a carpet sweeper each time she cleaned her house. At long last they accumulated enough, and Carol sent Carl off with money in hand to buy a vacuum cleaner.

Intent on his mission, Carl walked into a department store ... where the first thing he saw was a pool table. Ironically, the pool table was priced almost the same as a vacuum cleaner. Carl immediately forgot the vacuum cleaner and bought the pool table.

Somehow, Carol got over her displeasure. That could not have been easy to do. *Buying* the pool table was bad enough, but that only presented another, bigger problem: *where to put it?* In their tiny rental, the only place large enough was the dining room – but only if all the furniture was removed from it.

The décor may not have suited *Good Housekeeping*, but good things and good times soon came from it. Complemented by Carl and Carol's hospitality, the Marsalis house and the pool table in its dining room became a magnet for Air Force students. The games of pool provided a welcome diversion from long hours at the books. Deep into many nights, that unprotesting cue ball took the heat for heavy course loads and the pressures of final exams.

Carol probably suffered the cruelest blow: in addition to being kept awake at all hours by the sound of ricocheting pool balls, she still needed to borrow a carpet sweeper to clean house; a chore which now included tidying up around the pool table in the middle of her dining room.

Carl recovered nicely: he grew up to become President of the Astrodome, one of the nation's premier attractions. That's a laudable achievement, of course; but to the guys in the Air Force program at Colorado State, buying a pool table with vacuum cleaner money will always rank as his finest accomplishment.

R & R

A MORAN STORY: SETTING AN EXAMPLE

A young British subaltern reported in to one of the most desolate outposts in the British Empire. It was his first duty station. He was eager to impress his men.

The only problem was the absence of female companionship. After several weeks he was unable to stand the pressure any longer. Finally, one evening he cleared his throat and called to the sergeant major. "Sergeant Major," said the young officer in an officious tone, "what do the men do when they, er, need relief?"

"Well sir," replied the sergeant major, "there's a camel tied to the side of the barracks ..."

"Say no more, say no more," responded the officer and proceeded on his way.

Soon afterward, the entire fort heard the camel snorting, braying, kicking at the corral fence, making a terrible racket. A few minutes later the officer appeared, uniform torn, hair disheveled, bleeding from various cuts and bruises.

"Well, Sergeant Major," he called proudly, "what will the men think of me now?"

"They'll be duly impressed, sir" replied the sergeant major, "normally they just ride the camel into town; it's right over that hill."

At boot camp as an enlisted recruit (left), I had no intention of being a "lifer."

Thirty-six years later, still on active duty, I went to Sarajevo as a colonel (bottom photo).

Lackland AFB, Texas
1960

Sarajevo, Bosnia-Herzegovina
1996

Talk about contrasts! From Minot AFB, North Dakota (left), where one of my roommates was sure that "there are only two fence posts between here and the North Pole," to the Sahara heat of Sidi Slimane Air Base, Morocco (right, in the bright sunshine, getting ready to pull a shift at the weather detachment). The low temperature at Minot during my tour was a minus 33 degrees, accompanied by a 30 knot wind. At Sidi Slimane the all-time high temperature was 124 degrees (but it only got to 114 while I was there).

A B-47 medium bomber arriving at Sidi Slimane during the Cuban Missile Crisis. A KC-97 tanker has just landed in the background.

"...like something out of a Humphrey Bogart movie."

(Right) Street scene. Fes, Morocco

(Left) We took weather observations from the control tower. The infamous "coffee bucket," just visible at the extreme right corner of the catwalk, was lowered by rope to a colleague working at the weather station at the base of the tower.

(Right) Near Tangier, Morocco. A photo famous in my family.

A self-styled "tough little mick from Chicago," Eddie Moran was a consummate story teller. He was my first real mentor in the Air Force. in the Air Force.

Eddie never met a stranger. With Moran (third from left) are Dris, a weather detachment employee (L), and two Moroccan trash collectors Eddie invited into the picture.

EPAULETS

Officer Training School

OTS Class 67-B (we graduated 13 September 1966 -- '67' referred to the fiscal year which at that time began on 1 July; 'B' meant that we were the second class commissioned in FY67), was one of the first on the bubble for the Vietnam War. Although the size was similar to the groups that had preceded us – we started with 600 and graduated 488 – our training was accelerated as the Air Force ramped up for the conflict. Eventually, two weeks were cut from our schedule. The trainees that came after us followed the same shortened training regime, but class sizes grew consistently larger: first 800, then 1000, finally 1200 or more graduated with each class.

The Air Force did a nice job of compressing so much instruction into so little time: leadership, officership, Air Force organization, Air Force history, customs and courtesies, drill and ceremonies, military justice, national power, international relations, weapons training, and so much more. The curriculum was a blend of material suited for the few prior service members as well as nuts and bolts information essential for people coming in right off the street. It was intense. After OTS, I never mocked "90 day wonders" ever again.

Officer training meant a trip back to San Antonio, back to Lackland Air Force Base, where OTS activities were spread across two areas. The largest, on Lackland proper, was home to two cadet wings. A third did business from a smaller adjacent complex called Medina Annex. In recent years, the school has relocated to Maxwell AFB, Montgomery, Alabama, a place slightly less hot but, if possible, even more humid. My theory is that the choice of sites like Lackland and Maxwell to train future officers is intentional: the level of discomfort tests candidates' commitments and challenges their convictions.

Larry McAllister, a friend from the Airmen Education and Commissioning Program, and I traveled to OTS together and were assigned to the same squadron. We had been prepped on some important aspects by other AECP colleagues who preceded us. For example, in the evening after details and other required business, we went to the classroom building to study. If trainees stayed in the barracks, upper classmen kept jumping in and out of their rooms. They couldn't do that in the classroom building so studying there was much more productive.

When we became upper classmen, we sometimes had off-base privileges from noon on Saturday until mid-afternoon on Sunday. We took our books and materials for briefings and research paper preparation and stayed off base. We got a lot done in those uninterrupted hours, and it was good to get away from the hassle. We usually wrapped up the respite with a sandwich from "Oscar's," our favorite greasy spoon near the base.

The OTS experience provided PhD-level instruction in budgeting time, planning ahead, and prioritizing tasks. It sometimes taught smaller, unexpected, lessons as well.

On one of my first days as an underclassman, I was assigned the garbage can detail. I didn't know it at the time, but that was the least preferred task: on a 1 to 10 scale of obnoxious duties, "garbage cans" scored an 11 or 12. It was a time-consuming chore and in an environment that placed a premium on spit and polish, uniforms sometimes got soiled as the large cans were carried to the outside dumpsters. Because the job was performed just before we fell into formation, a messy uniform could ruin an entire day.

I had done that task only a few times when an upper classman called me over and without explanation said that he had removed me from that detail and assigned me to another one that involved cleaning the hallway in the dorm. Later, not long before he graduated, he said that on my first day or two he had seen me help some of the new guys and decided that I "needed something better." I thanked him then, but it was only later that I understood the full consequences of his generosity. His gracious act had in a very substantial way helped me have a more successful experience at OTS. I do not recall the assistance to the "new guys" that had so fortuitously caught his eye. It was a random act from which something good happened. Sometimes you just never know.

/////

When I was commissioned that September in 1966, the monthly base pay for a brand new second lieutenant was $303.90. I was more fortunate; there was a separate pay scale for officers with more than four years of enlisted service. The six and a half years of enlisted time raised my monthly base pay to the near-kingly amount of $420.30. I was married the following year and drew an extra $110.10 for quarters allowance. As a senior officer told me when he discovered I was considering the military as a career, "If you keep score by money, find a different job." I do not keep score by money, and the Air Force turned out to be the right job for me. But, I often recalled his reminder as my bride and I stretched those second lieutenant checks from one pay day to the next.

Orlando AFB Florida

The Air Force has a propensity for closing bases at places like Orlando and Myrtle Beach and keeping them open at Minot and Grand Forks. This was pre-Disney World Orlando. The small base was in a nice location on the outskirts of what was then a rather sleepy southern city.

There were actually two Air Force bases in Orlando at the time. One, McCoy, was a Strategic Air Command base that shared a runway with the city's commercial airport. The other, Orlando AFB, was a few miles away on real estate mostly surrounded by the suburb of Winter Park.

There was a World War II-style Air Force hospital just off the perimeter of the base – separate wooden buildings each housing a specific ward, all tied together by covered walkways connecting every structure in the rambling complex. From there it was an ambulance ride across town to intersect with air-evac flights that landed at McCoy. A beautiful Air Force nurse from that hospital sometimes rode in those ambulances, transporting patients to and from the mercy flights that came into Orlando. I admired her from afar at base chapel services, was introduced to her at a mutual friend's house, and proposed to her 22 days later. Foolishly, she accepted. Nita and I were married that summer.

Orlando AFB was my first assignment as an officer. Although there were no flying operations, the base served as headquarters for both the Aerospace Rescue and Recovery Service and Aerospace Audiovisual Service. Both of those organizations were fully engaged in Vietnam, so despite its minute size the base was "busy."

I was assigned as Officer-in-Charge (OIC) of the Data Control Section: 57 people in five work units. That seemed a considerable load for a "butter bar" lieutenant, but in later life I came to appreciate the value of the experience that resulted from the "sink or swim" environment. I found myself knee deep or higher in supervision, discipline, performance reports, scheduling, and planning – the whole range of "in charge" responsibilities.

Not all of my junior officer contemporaries had the same opportunity. When I attended Squadron Officer School three years later it was surprising to find that so many lieutenants and captains had not yet supervised anyone, had never written a performance report, nor performed in a leadership or supervisory role.

That seemed particularly true of the "rated" cadre, the pilots and navigators. For many in that group the extensive training regimen, the structure of the flying squadrons, and the essential apprenticeship commitments excluded them from meaningful leadership roles. Much of that was unavoidable, but it was unfortunate nonetheless. Those were the people who would go on to command the Air Force's major operational units, yet they were getting a late start on learning how to handle and lead people. The good ones were very smart and most of them caught up. A few never did.

The NCOs at Orlando, at least those who worked in Data Control, epitomized to me what noncommissioned officers are supposed to be. Chief Master Sergeants John Ward and Dee Keller, and Master Sergeant Acie Causey set the standard. In later years in talks and mentoring sessions with NCO groups, I often used them as examples.

The three of them would have helped any new officer, but I sometimes wondered whether they subconsciously took special care of me because I was a former NCO. The "taking care" of young officers was an item of special importance to NCOs of that generation. To a good sergeant, a young officer became "my lieutenant" and the NCO went to considerable but subtle, non-usurping lengths to guide, teach, and mentor the rookie. When I retired 30 years later, I saw less NCO emphasis on "taking care of my lieutenant." At least that was my perception. I hope I was wrong. That unique responsibility is so important that it warrants special emphasis at NCO academies.

The NCOs who worked for me at Orlando were already spring-loaded to help, but some random actions might have abetted the process. A short time before I reported in, operations at Orlando were severely "pinged" by an Inspector General (IG) team. One of the harshest write-ups was in the personnel records area: records were lost and backlogged piles of updates and corrections were waiting to be filed and entered into the automated system. The fact that Orlando was a "mail order" personnel office for the hundreds of geographically separated units (GSUs) that were part of the Aerospace Rescue and Recovery Service and Aerospace Audiovisual Service exacerbated the problem. Thousands of documents had to be mailed back and forth from all around the world. Many came from units in the midst of the war in Southeast Asia. The people in those units had more important priorities than filling out personnel documents. It was a situation rife with chaos.

To help get a handle on the problem, expert teams were formed from throughout the base personnel organization. Under the supervision of a senior NCO, the rotating teams worked extra night shifts until the corrections were made and the backlog was caught up. One night soon after I signed in, I stopped by my office to pick up some papers. A team was hard at work, so on a whim I went out to buy coffee and donuts for them and then came back and worked with one of the groups. I wound up doing that with some frequency. It was a nice way to learn what was going on and to get acquainted with players from across the organization; it was one of the first actions I took as an officer that seemed to be appreciated by the people involved and to resonate across the organization.

A second was to quietly call aside a sergeant who ran one of the major work units in the organization. He was a pretty good guy and was well regarded as a technician. But, he also had the worst looking hat I had ever seen. It was a "wheel hat," soiled and unkempt. The cloth looked like it needed an oil change. His appearance was not the best example to set, especially for someone in a very visible position. I mentioned it to him when I visited his work area. The next day he came by with a smile to show me his new hat. No one else had been privy to our conversation, but when he showed up for work with sparkling new head gear, his colleagues immediately questioned him. Sheepishly, he said something like "The new lieutenant got on me about it." The word spread quickly and soon after, other new hats, chevrons, shoes, and uniforms began to show up around the squadron.

Playing on the unit's softball team also brought positive results. I was aware of the danger: "getting too close" or letting friendships lead to perceived favoritism. That was never a problem. The boundary was never crossed, thanks in part to the professionals who played on the team. In fact, softball turned out to be quite useful. Some of the youngsters, especially the newest or the shyest, sometimes had difficulty knocking on an officer's door in an "official" capacity during duty hours. Those kids found it easier or less threatening to talk about the job or their problems in the dugout or after a game.

A few months into my tour, events at Orlando precipitated a major change to the way the Air Force did its human resources business and affected my future as well. Orlando serviced nearly 200 GSUs (geographically separated units), predominantly Rescue and Audiovisual Service outfits scattered all around the globe. The records of every person in every one of those units were maintained at Orlando and all of the human resource actions involving them were transacted there. With Orlando AFB scheduled for closure, Headquarters Air Force decided to use the circumstance to test the concept of On-Site Personnel Service. The notion was to "disperse" the records to the bases closest to the GSU locations. The nearest installation would also transact all of the associated human resource business. On-Site Personnel Service made eminent good sense. The best auditors of an individual's files are the people themselves. With the documents at Orlando, most airmen never saw their records. Business was done by mailing pieces of paper back and forth. The time was right to change all that: emerging computer technology made the on-site concept do-able.

Still, there were considerable numbers of dissenters. Many senior commanders and personnel officials thought that dispersing the records would cause them to "lose control" of the individuals in their units. Then too, sending the records to the nearest bases would for the first time force extensive "cross-servicing" of personnel from other commands. For example, Strategic Air Command and Tactical Air Command organizations would be responsible for the human resource services provided to the Rescue and Recovery Service and Audiovisual units that were part of the Military Airlift Command. Traditionally, SAC units maintained the records of only SAC people, TAC units ran the human resource business for only TAC people, and so forth. It was manpower intensive and wasteful. On-Site Personnel service would significantly change the way the Air Force ran its personnel operations.

Because many of the actions involved in dispersing the records fell under the purview of the Data Control Section, on behalf of the Military Airlift Command I became the planner/project officer for the program. For a brand new lieutenant it was a stretch, but a healthy one. The last few weeks prior to base closure were the busiest of my career up to that point. Altogether, records would be sent to more than 125 bases. In addition to packing up and moving paper records, the technical plan had to be written for making the transfers in the automated system as well. With punch card technology, that was a sportier process then than it would be now. Finally, the status of actions on-going at the time of the transfer had to be identified and instructions provided.

One entire wall of my office became a status board as we tracked the progress of preparations, transmittals, and follow-up actions. Tasks varied base by base. Each of the 125 bases that would receive the records and the processing responsibility had a designated point of contact. I got to know many of them as telephone acquaintances as we worked through the transfer regimen. With some larger unit transfers, we sent teams to accompany the records and help with the handover responsibilities. Other bases sent crews to Orlando to do document checks and help "clean up" on-going actions before taking the records back to their "gaining" organizations. Transportation for people and records and finding "opportunity airlift" became persistent concerns.

Eventually, the project ended successfully. On-Site Service became a routinely accepted way of doing business. It was inevitable that it would. The closure of Orlando merely provided the occasion to accelerate the process. For me, the project officer role turned out to be a mixed blessing. The upsides were in the pleasure of seeing the plan work and in being a tiny part of a historic change in the Air Force's personnel operations. The downside was that it resulted in an assignment to Military Airlift Command Headquarters. I wanted very much to stay at base level where, to my thinking, the "action was," particularly in Southeast Asia.

Headquarters Military Airlift Command, Scott AFB Illinois

For me, the hype of being selected for a job at a major air command headquarters while still a lieutenant brought to mind the quote Abraham Lincoln attributed to the man being run out of town on a rail: "If it wasn't for the honor of the thing, I would just as soon do without it."

There were some great people at Scott -- and I was fortunate that two of the best NCOs from Orlando were assigned to my section – but overall it did not rank high on my list of favorite places. Situated about 25 miles east of St. Louis across the Mississippi on the Illinois side of the river and ringed by small tidy communities like Mascoutah, Lebanon, and O'Fallon, it is, by Air Force standards, a very old base. At the time it was a drab, run-down installation with poor facilities, its appearance mostly unchanged from the time balloon training was conducted there in World War I. In more recent years, a new headquarters building and other modern structures have rejuvenated its appearance and spirit. The mission of the 1969 version of Military Airlift Command (MAC) didn't seem to have the have the pizzazz of the "war fighting" commands. Now, reincarnated as Air Mobility Command, it is a highly valued, full and essential partner in our nation's military operations.

My office at MAC headquarters was deep in the basement of a 1920s building. Water and goodness knows what other sorts of pipes ran immediately overhead. The noises were interesting. Still the 30 or so people that worked with and for me were a good group, and our collective efforts helped make MAC's personnel system better.

For sure, we gave the command a more current and accurate data base. The Air Force was just then stepping heavily into automated, computerized operations. "Punch cards," key punch machines, and main frames were the gee-whiz equipment of the day. In that computer sunrise, MAC's data base was one of the dimmest in the Air Force: "purged" items (data elements overdue for correction or update) and errors numbered in the thousands. Acie Causey, a superb master sergeant who had come with me from Orlando, and I worked that problem day in and day out for the 20 months I was at Scott. Eventually, using repeated follow-ups, staff visits, and getting wing commanders and staff officers engaged, we whittled the numbers of errors down to a tiny fraction of their original size. In part it was a matter of educating commanders about the importance of those mysterious electrons in the lives of their people and the operations of their units.

As usual, the NCOs carried an enormous load as we transitioned into the main frame era. Most were "good people" and excellent technicians. They were fine teachers, too, although their patience was often tried by foot dragging throughout the headquarters by those – early on, the majority – who were not comfortable being around computers much less ready to use one.

Many of those fine NCOs labored in dingy conditions: the water pipes in their work spaces were far worse than mine. When at last some money trickled down to our building, all of the initial funds went toward renovating the headquarters suites on the top floors. I went to see the boss and asked him to throw some of that cash in our direction. His new carpets looked fine, but my folks' offices had concrete floors and vibrating pipes. He turned me down.

On the way out of his office, I picked up a four inch by four inch piece of carpet that had been trimmed from the roll. I took it downstairs and dropped it by my office door, announcing that we'd have to wait awhile for the floor to be totally covered because this piece was the only size authorized for lieutenants. The troops thought that was neat. The carpet fragment remained there for weeks until a custodial crew, not realizing the shrine it had become, mistakenly threw it in the trash.

My time at headquarters was not all spent in that office with its harmonious pipes. I was frequently on the road on assistance visits to MAC units that directly supported the conflict in Vietnam. There were lots of those because in addition to its airlift and passenger support elements, Aerospace Rescue and Recovery Service and Aerospace Audiovisual Service were also part of MAC. The latter two organizations had detachments all over the landscape. As a result, I got my first look at places like Guam, Japan, the Philippines, and Hawaii.

Thirty-five years later, I still remember part of a briefing I sat in on at Pacific Air Command Headquarters, at Hickam AFB, Hawaii. The briefer commented that at the moment there were "700 casualties in the air" coming out of Vietnam, and the air-evac system was "stressed." At another stop along the way, a group commander was showing a senior officer and me around the base – neither of us had asked him to do that; the demands on a commander's time, especially in that environment were so extreme – when he mentioned, almost casually, that his wife had left him two days before and had gone back to the States. The commander, I think, just wanted someone – some outside party – to talk with for a few minutes before getting back to his grinding, and now lonelier, chores. It is not a life for everyone.

Scott AFB had a ten-space officer trailer park. Nita and I bought a new mobile home when we arrived there. Unsure of how long the assignment would last with a war on and having very little furniture, it turned out to be the right decision. The size was an ideal fit for the two, soon to be three, of us. Plus, we could afford it. The interior was beautifully wood paneled; the place was "user friendly" and comfortable. The nine other slots in the officer trailer court were mostly filled with junior officers with young children and not much money. Just like us. Lots of Midwest evenings were spent outside playing with kids and talking with neighbors. It was a fun crowd.

/////

A secretary sat right outside my office door in our basement work space. Lucy always kept a supply of lollypops on the corner of her desk. It became my habit to grab one frequently when I came into or out of the office. As would soon become clear, that fact had registered on my co-workers.

When the date rolled around for our aerobics fitness test (a mile and a half run at the time), one of my fine NCOs challenged me to a race. It was a friendly challenge; he was one of the two outstanding sergeants that had been assigned from Orlando. Still, like Eddie Moran's subaltern in the desert, I knew I had to "set an example for the men." Surely the challenge could not go unanswered; especially with the entire staff looking on. So, I accepted. I was worried immediately. As a runner and a softball player, my forte was as a sprinter; I was not a "distance" person. The timed aerobics run was still a month away, so I spent that time practicing at a nearby track.

My theory was to train myself to run a steady first mile, begin accelerating at the fifth quarter, and then essentially sprint the last quarter. That strategy sounded fine in concept but on "race day" it appeared more dubious as my "steady" first mile succeeded in getting me behind by about half a lap. Finally, fortunately, I caught up and with the final sprint prevailed by about 20 yards. I felt like I swallowed both of my lungs; it would always remain the fastest mile and a half I've ever run.

What brings us back to the lollypops is that on the day I "PCSd" from Scott, my office mates formed up for a "formal" award ceremony. There in an official beautifully embossed presentation kit, just like the ones used for medal programs, was my "Giant Sucker Award." Inside on the left there was an enormous lollypop, at least a foot in diameter. On the right side, the "citation" to accompany the "award" noted that I had mastered the art of placing one foot in front of the other ("a rare quality in a lieutenant") and had remembered how to do that for an entire mile and a half. There was a full page of other droll, nicely crafted teasing that recalled the "carpet" and several accomplishments together.

I have always thought that the "Giant Sucker" was one of the finest "awards" I ever received. I have never forgotten it or the thoughtful, classy bunch of people who formed up in my office that day.

It was the lesson of Minot all over again: it is the *people*, not the *place*, that make an assignment.

Squadron Officer School

Squadron Officer School was the worst of times and the best of times. The beginning was horrific; the finish was exquisite.

I was selected for the 13 week course at Squadron Officer School while assigned to Headquarters, Military Airlift Command at Scott AFB, Illinois. Nita and I packed our color TV set, a cat, and our soon to be one year-old daughter in the back of our 1965 Mustang and headed for Montgomery, Alabama, home of Maxwell AFB, stopping the first evening at a Holiday Inn in Memphis, Tennessee.

During the night our car was robbed. Uniforms, insignia, civilian clothes, other items -- all gone. Devastating. The car was parked in front of a light pole outside the main lobby, but no one professed to have seen anything. In my naiveté, I asked the police that answered our call if I should wait a day to see if anything would be recovered. They seemed to have a hard time suppressing their laughter. I didn't come away with a warm feeling that the Memphis police typically expected to catch anybody, anytime.

It was all rather incongruous. Somewhere in Memphis there is probably a well dressed thief; although I don't know where he or she is going to wear a formal mess dress with medals and shoulder boards affixed.

The only uniform I had left was the wrinkled set I had worn just before leaving on the trip. It was folded up in a corner of the trunk and missed the thieves' search. I would need that set to report in. Nita immediately pressed it with a hotel iron. In the meantime, scurrying around, we began the process of recovery. I called a neighbor at Scott with keys to our trailer and asked him to "send everything left in the closet." Then I phoned a friend recently separated from the Air Force and asked if he would mail his fatigue uniforms to me.

Things didn't get any better. On the drive from Memphis to Maxwell AFB, we discovered that all the uniform insignia had been taken. I was a first lieutenant when selected for Squadron Officer School, but about a week into the course I was due to be promoted to captain. In preparation for that, I had bought two sets of captain's "tracks" and slipped them into a jacket pocket. We found those when we reached Maxwell. I cut the "tracks" in half with a pair of pliers and put the halves on the uniform Nita had ironed: each half "track" became a first lieutenant bar. I reported in and then hustled over the Military Clothing Sales Store just before it closed and bought enough uniforms to get past the first couple of weeks of school.

That led to another problem. The Clothing Sales Store could not alter the uniforms in time for several early school functions. I grabbed a Montgomery phone book, sorted through the yellow pages and found a name: Cunningham the Tailor. I called, explained my problem, and Mr. Cunningham agreed to stay open until I got there.

Nita and I hadn't even seen our apartment or unloaded our car yet, but I repacked her, the cat, and our daughter back into the Mustang and set out for the tailor shop. God must surely have a special place reserved for people like Cunningham the Tailor. Perhaps he took pity on our plight, or on my beautiful wife, or our infant daughter; at any rate, he set his other work aside and had my uniforms done the next day. Nita and I have always remembered his act of kindness. We hope life has been as gracious to him as he was to us.

Still, we weren't quite out of the woods. Mr. Cunningham had tailored the mess dress uniform that I would need for the formal

Dining In ceremony scheduled for the first week of school. But, the thieves had stolen the shoulder boards that went with it. As Nita and I quickly discovered, there were no lieutenant shoulder boards to be had at either Maxwell AFB, or Gunter AFB, a smaller installation across town. What to do next? After everything else we had been through and the problems we had overcome, this could be a showstopper. Then on a whim, I went to the Base Thrift Shop. There, miracle of miracles, I found one set of *second* lieutenant shoulder boards. I bought a small jar of silver paint for airplane models, painted the gold mess dress bars silver and survived the first week.

Several days before leaving for Maxwell, we had made arrangements to rent a small apartment in a place called Lanier Court. The grapevine said that other SOS students often stayed there because the apartment complex was inexpensive and convenient to Maxwell.

That scuttlebutt was certainly true; almost every apartment in every building around the three-quarter oval was inhabited by SOS student families. What the latrine rumors didn't describe was the condition of the apartments and the furnishings in them.

Lanier Court was located in a neighborhood in transition. In this case, the spiral was decidedly downward. Once no doubt very pleasant, the facilities were now shoddy. Furnishings were sparse and poorly maintained. Still, after having our car robbed and surviving the uniform crisis, it was hard to get upset about what the furniture looked like.

In fact, it was *funny*. We ate on only the left end of the table because the right side slanted down and the dishes slid off. There were no end tables of any kind, so we turned two large cardboard boxes end-wise and draped them with white sheets. Those became part of our living room furniture. We slept in the middle of the bed because the mattress bowed so much there was a natural downhill rotation in that direction. Nita went by the Thrift Shop to pick up silverware to complement the sparse assortment we inherited with the apartment. One utilitarian pot served as cooking utensil, food transporter, and serving dish. Our other SOS mates around the oval were in much the same situation, so tales of Lanier Court served as grist for lots of conversations.

Our daughter Laura learned to walk in that apartment. We spaced the few items of furniture – couch, coffee table, kitchen table – at distances where she could easily reach from one to the other after a couple of steps. For Laura, SOS was a momentous time. She said her first word on the way to Maxwell on the day we were robbed. Somewhat to Nita's chagrin Laura said "kitty" or a reasonable facsimile (she was sharing the small back seat of the Mustang with the cat). Nita was a little perplexed that "Mommy" or "Daddy" was not the first thing Laura said. "Daddy" was her second word, though, which exasperated Nita a little more.

Once past the tribulations posed by the robbery and the apartment, SOS turned out to be a fantastic experience. Our section consisted of a munitions offer, a weapons director, a communications officer, an intelligence guy, an auditor, a manpower specialist, a JAG, a maintenance officer, an F-111 navigator, a C-130 pilot, two F-4 pilots, and me with a touch of personnel, computers, weather, and some fill-in time as a commander in my background.

The school had done a nice job of mixing and matching. Talk about an Air Force 101 learning opportunity: it was the first time I'd really had a chance to get immersed with an entire cross section of the Air Force all in one setting. There were daily discussions and insights packaged in easy conversations between close friends. All the rated guys plus the munitions, intel, and maintenance officers had recently completed tours in Southeast Asia. Those fresh experiences evoked spirited discussions about the war and opinions about how it was progressing.

"Bonding" is a much overused term. But, there, within that 12 person section, it was exactly the right description for what resulted. We saw each other everyday for 13 weeks, sat next to each other in class, worked projects together, and played volleyball, soccer, and flicker ball (an SOS innovation: a combination of football and basketball) as a team. The families gathered together and shared picnics and evenings out. In the process, we bonded indeed.

I learned an immense amount about the Air Force from my colleagues. Outside the seminar room, I enjoyed the heavy hitters who journeyed in from Washington to speak to us. The leadership exercises and planning and execution projects were top notch. Simply by virtue of having a job at a major command headquarters, I had done considerable briefing and writing before attending SOS. There was always more to learn and skills to improve though, and despite class-wide grumbling about this part of the curriculum, I thought the school did a nice job of teaching and reinforcing the basics. Because a surprising number in the class had not briefed, supervised, written performance reports, or any of the myriad tasks all of us would eventually be called upon to do, instruction in those areas certainly filled a valid need.

It was a group that learned to work easily and successfully together. In particular, the results of one of our war planning exercises drew special note from the school.

But it was not all treated as serious stuff. Our faculty seminar leader was a staid, sober, senior captain handling his first class and determined to set a proper example. One of our seminar exercises was to design an air base from scratch. We were given a certain amount of "money," equipment, time, and other parameters and were turned loose to build an installation. Primarily at the instigation of the rated guys, the seminar created a base that had only a runway, a golf course, an officer's club, and a house of ill repute. When one of the straight-faced pilots briefed the faculty representative on the plan – noting carefully that the money had been allocated to the penny and the base had been completed within the timeline – I could see the captain blanch. His eyes widened; he was clearly at a loss for words. Uncertain as to the seriousness of our effort, he was left in stunned silence for a moment until eventually we showed him our "real" base, which actually had hangars, barracks, a control tower, and other somewhat useful structures.

My eleven seminar mates became close friends and colleagues. I recall those weeks with them as being among the most interesting and important of my career. After a truly horrendous start, SOS had the best possible ending.

Mnemonics? ... and Principles of War

"Oh, Lord," I thought as I checked the schedule for that day's classes at Squadron Officer School, "*Principles of War*, what a way to start the day." Presented as a lecture, too. Were they *trying* to make it painful?

I had a mental image of half of the 550 people in our class sound asleep in the "blue bedroom," the large auditorium where lecture presentations took place. I eventually summoned up courage to walk to the auditorium, wishing I could take my coffee with me. During one previous less than inspiring lecture, I had counted the tiles in the ceiling. Light bulbs, too. My classmates and I settled in, anticipating that time would move slowly in the hour ahead. Instead, we were disappointed when it was over.

The school had wisely asked a member of the attached faculty, an RAF wing commander, to present the lecture. Our attention was immediately riveted by the wry humor and the British cool.

He began by saying that as a young officer during World War II he served as Squadron Censor; his job was to read the out-going mail of his squadron mates and delete any hint of operational information. In the course of his duties, he noticed cryptic messages affixed to the front of envelopes. These notices changed as the war went on. After all, Britain was at war for nearly six years and some of the Brits made it home only rarely during that time. Understandably, the emotions and anticipations changed as months and years went by.

At the beginning of the war, the wing commander said that the most common message on the envelopes was "SWALK": "Sealed With a Loving Kiss."

Then with the passage of seemingly endless months the tide slowly turned and there began to be the glimmerings of hope that eventually it would all be over. On envelopes then appeared "NORWICH": "Nickers Off Ready When I Come Home."

Finally, with the end at last in sight, the passions clearly building, and his squadron getting ready to ship back to England, the code on the envelopes changed to "BURMA." That meant "Be Upstairs Ready, My Angel."

There would be no sleeping that day: the wing commander had

us in his hand. He told a few more "war stories" and then mentioned that "SWALK," "NORWICH," and "BURMA" were "mnemonics" – arrangements of letters or syllables as a memory device to help in the recollection of lists or longer phrases.

With a smooth shift of gears he said that he recalled those envelopes when he was studying for promotion (in the RAF, officers had first to pass a written examination in order to qualify). The study materials were voluminous and he had found mnemonics useful in helping recall the numerous lists of items he was accountable for on the test.

"Principles of War" was one such example, and because the RAF "recognized" so many, the list was a long one. Nonetheless, the mnemonic he developed – "AMOSSCEFCA"; pronounced "Amos Sefca" – had made it easy for him to remember the principles which were:

Aim
Morale
Offensive
Security
Surprise
Concentration
Economy
Flexibility
Coordination
Administration

I heard that lecture in 1969, and thanks to the wing commander's mnemonic, I still recall his principles. It was a superb presentation and a wonderful way to remember things. I have used it many times in briefings, studying, and teaching.

In fact, two years later I found myself teaching Air Force ROTC at the University of Nebraska. The year was 1971 and Nebraska and Oklahoma had two of the finest college football teams ever assembled. Nebraska was the defending national champion and the teams were about to meet in the much anticipated "Game of the Century" on Thanksgiving Day.

Ironically, an introduction to Principles of War was part of the sophomore curriculum that I taught. At the time, the Air Force recognized eight principles: control, coordination, economy of force, flexibility, objective, offensive, security, and surprise. I rearranged those into "CECFOOSS" – pronounced "Seck Foose" – then, with an eye toward the upcoming football game (and with a sincere apology to my many friends in Oklahoma), I gave my students an optional phrase to help further jog their memories. They could either remember "CECFOOSS" or they could recall it as "**C**ornhuskers **E**arn **C**onsecutive **F**irsts **O**utplaying **O**klahoma's **S**orry **S**ooners."

Okay, so it was a stretch.

But, on the final exam that was the only question that every kid in the class got correct.

Air Force ROTC

It was the only time I ever wrote a letter bitching about an assignment. Teaching ROTC was not going to be my cup of tea. No way. No sir. None of that banker's hours no challenge stuff; send me where the action is.

The orders for ROTC were a major disappointment. I had just wrapped up 14 months at a university under the auspices of the Air Force Institute of Technology (AFIT) while completing work on a master's degree. I was sure the follow-on assignment would be to Southeast Asia. In fact, the AFIT package even stated that the majority of graduates who had not yet completed a "SEA Tour" would receive one when their Institute of Technology schooling was finished. That was one of the many reasons I had applied for the training: it enhanced the possibilities of going to Southeast Asia. The war was creating enormous cross-currents throughout our society; but, the military was my profession and I wanted that personal experience. At Military Airlift Command headquarters, I traveled through Asia assisting units that supported our operations in Vietnam, but I had not set foot "in country." Taking part from a distance was not the same.

My disappointment was obvious to all. An Air Force friend tried to humor me by saying "Look at the typical college campus – shootings, fire bombings – you'll probably see more action there than you would as a personnel officer (the work that I was mostly doing at the time) in Vietnam." My smile must have been grim because we never had that conversation again.

Downcast, I felt sorry for myself for a few days and then wrote a letter asking that the assignment be changed. My request was denied: "The needs of the Air Force are compelling." I thought it was strange that the Air Force needed ROTC instructors more than volunteers for Vietnam, but now having been officially refused – I regarded the turndowns from three phone calls I had made as *unofficial* – I reluctantly decided it was time to shut up and color.

I grudgingly prepared to move, expecting that when I reported in my situation would conform to the stereotype I had formed regarding ROTC duty: eight to four, lots of idle time, certainly nothing like the excitement, interest, or importance of any number of other jobs I really should be doing.

I was wrong.

What I found instead was a busy schedule and the enjoyment of working through a continuing series of challenges. Most important, I found a great bunch of young Americans. Somewhat to my surprise -- but seemingly confirmed by student, university, and Air Force evaluations – the experience uncovered a heretofore unsuspected knack for teaching. Often overlooked is the fact that the military is a young people's organization. I have always enjoyed working with that age group. Teaching AFROTC illuminated those feelings. That sense of satisfaction contributed to the continuing series of decisions to "stay in" for three and a half decades.

The longer I was around those young people, the prouder I became of them. It took an act of courage to be an ROTC student at that time. On the campus where I received my master's degree, the ROTC offices had been fire bombed and Air Force students were not allowed to wear uniforms on the university grounds. At the institution where I taught AFROTC, several buildings had been taken over and protests occurred almost daily. Pressure from student peers was enormous; signing up for the one hour elective credit (freshmen and sophomores) or three credit hour course (juniors and seniors), required an exceptional level of commitment. For a 17- or an 18-year-old kid to make that choice and for whom wearing that uniform obviously meant so much, was rather extraordinary.

At work, so much for the eight to four stuff. The detachment's four officers and four NCOs essentially ran a mini air base that included a flying program at the local airport. In addition to teaching the sophomore class and holding down several other additional duties, I also served as the detachment exec. That job was sporty in itself at times. The unit received money from three different pots: the university, the state, and the Air Force. The lights were sometimes on late in my office as I worked to keep track of the dollars and shift them to cover our needs without going to jail.

In the classroom, contrary to the letter I wrote and the calls I made, I found that the assignment was indeed "my cup of tea." I especially liked my part of the curriculum, a national power potpourri that included international relations, spectrum of conflict, principles of war, some Air Force history, organization of the defense establishment, and several other areas. I was free to change the course, so with Vietnam going on I added considerably to the insurgency-counterinsurgency block.

During my first academic year, I felt like I was, charitably, about one week ahead of my students. There were eight days between the completion of my master's degree assignment and the beginning of ROTC classes 500 miles away. Getting a handle on my executive officer duties and building lesson plans, while talking with the flow of students that began almost immediately, made for a lively time. By the second rotation, order was restored and the opportunity presented itself to add several innovations to the classroom work: a meeting of the "presidential staff" and a subsequent conflict in the Middle East, an exercise centered on the Panama Canal, and a "football game" Q & A course review for the final exam. I enjoyed adding the pizzazz to the course and the cadets seemed excited by the changes. Retention from one semester to the next improved steadily. Eventually, in my last year, we hit the jackpot: every kid returned.

All of us, students and faculty alike, benefited from the fine commander who arrived a few months after I did. Colonel Dan Babcock was a former Senior Controller at the SAC Command Post. He brought a level of interest, commitment and willingness to innovate that served the program very well. Unlike some colonels who thought that an ROTC Detachment Commander/Professor of Aerospace Studies position was a dead end job unbefitting their high station in life, Babcock was energized by it: he saw it as a chance to grow and influence a new generation of officers.

Colonel Babcock assigned me three additional duties that I came to value very much, although from time to time all of them caused me to burn considerable amounts of midnight oil. I think he read me well enough to know that busy was better; I'd be more satisfied and would pester him less when I had lots to do.

The first was to develop a recruiting plan. Nothing systematic had previously been done in this area – nary a document that would trigger information on advertising campaigns that were time-specific, depending on which category of recruit we were after. There were indeed several populations to target: high school juniors and seniors, the university student body at large, college sophomores specifically (potential candidates for entry into the two-year program), students from nearby universities with whom we initiated consortium agreements, and veterans. We also developed special campaigns that landed us the school's first scholarships for women and minorities. For most of these groups there were time sensitive "windows" for receiving and reacting to our information, yet in the past the entire effort was done on an ad hoc basis, improvised from year to year.

Nor was there anything approximating a statewide advertising campaign. When I called ROTC headquarters and explained what I was trying to do, they released enough advertising money to test it for a year. We placed small ads in every newspaper in the state, including the little once a week publications that touched the tiniest communities in our predominately rural area.

Once I had a handle on where all the papers were located and the specific areas they served, I started sending small "news releases" that informed the readers that "Johnny Jones of Corn Crib Township has enrolled in/completed his ___ semester of Air Force ROTC at the State University"; or, had been promoted to a higher cadet rank or earned some award through the program. The papers appreciated these "fillers" and in retrospect I think the small announcements in the miniscule weekly newspapers were one of our most effective tools.

During school breaks, we asked current cadets to contact students in their hometown areas that had expressed an interest in the program. To reach broader audiences, with Colonel Babcock's approval, I assigned officer staff members to nearby radio and TV outlets. We visited the stations, requested the station manager's kind indulgence in playing Air Force ROTC public service spots, and made ourselves available for interviews about the program and the Air Force in general.

That year our cadet population climbed from 85 to 129.

The second major additional duty was to streamline the scholarship program. That project went quickly. Staff members and university officials assisted in upgrading our application packages. Among other things, the quality of writing in the narrative justifications was measurably improved. With Colonel Babcock's direct involvement we strengthened the scholarship boards that were held each year to prioritize the application packages prior to submitting them to ROTC headquarters. The boards included local university officials, and with Babcock's assistance, we got the true heavy hitters on campus to participate. The effect was two-fold: our packages had more punch at ROTC headquarters and the credibility of our program was enhanced university-wide. Colleges in the university system that had not previously awarded our courses full credit began doing so.

It was a tribute to Colonel Babcock that he was able to look at things like recruiting and scholarship boards – areas that others regarded as routine, pro forma activities – and modify them in ways that had ripple effects of major consequence.

The third additional duty he assigned me turned out to be a labor of love: he asked me to build a running history of the detachment – pictures, clippings, important events, names of staff members, important documents like commissioning program brochures – everything. I enjoyed it immensely and the project grew in its contents and ambitions as the months went by. The history became a frequently used reference by staff members, cadets, and university officials. Colonel Babcock rightly realized that even in the tiniest military units, legacies are important.

A large university can be an impersonal place for many youngsters. It was a compliment to my colleagues that the "guys at the detachment" became known as somebody to go to when the students just needed someone to talk with. We found ourselves listening to academic problems, financial difficulties, and boy friend/girl friend issues. We listened, helped when we could, and interfaced with university agencies as appropriate.

I started an informal session on "how to study/how to take notes" that at the time was not being offered by the university. It was easy to see that there was nothing academically or intellectually wrong with many of the kids who were having trouble with university course work: it was just that they didn't have a clue about how to prepare for college classes. These sessions wound up supporting a broader service – helping "personalize" a sometimes tough and lonely environment – that went beyond the modest goal that I had visualized at the outset.

One of the finest compliments that was paid to us occurred when one of our students brought in a friend, not a member of the cadet corps, "because he/she needs someone to talk to." That was a not infrequent event. We came to regard it as high praise. Although we wished the university was better equipped to cope with these issues, we were pleased to be able to help, even if in a small way.

One evening soon after I received orders to my next assignment, I came home from work and knew immediately that something was afoot. First, there was sort of a bemused, quizzical look in Nita's eyes. Second, she turned down my invitation to go to a nearby restaurant. Third, she was obviously reluctant to let me leave to pick up Chinese takeout even though she didn't "have anything planned for dinner."

A few minutes later almost the entire sophomore class showed up to say goodbye, carrying appropriate quantities of pizza with them. They had kept it all quiet. Clearly, this group was not going to have trouble handling classified material later in life. It turned out to be a terrific night. Some of those sophomore cadets were lieutenant colonels when I retired, but I think my favorite recollection of them is from that evening with all of them sprawled over my lawn, porch, living room, and basement, eating pizza and

talking together.
One of my favorite general officer bosses had a maxim that he frequently repeated to young officers: "Bloom where you're planted." "Yeah, right," I thought, "easy for you to say; look where you're at."

In later years I sometimes recalled his words when I thought about the letter I wrote complaining about the assignment. I had wanted desperately to get out of it; yet, in retrospect it had become one of the best experiences of my life.

Possibly, just possibly, he may have been correct.

Air Force Military Personnel Center

The main gate of Randolph AFB is across a highway and railroad tracks from Universal City, Texas, on the northeast outskirts of San Antonio.

Travelers crossing the highway and railroad tracks and entering through the main gate are confronted by a truly extraordinary sight. At the end of a long, broad "avenue of flags" there stands a building known throughout the Air Force as the "Taj Mahal." The name is rightly bestowed: shimmering white, majestic, with an exquisite facade, it soars over and dwarfs the surrounding landscape. For years the building has been on the National Register of Historic Places.

"The Taj" serves as Randolph's base headquarters. It is a well kept secret that the purpose of the tall central spire in this, one of the country's most beautiful public buildings, is really to encompass and hide the base water tower!

Randolph is an Air Force showplace, one of the world's most attractive military bases. Built in the 1930s, it was among the first installations designed specifically to accommodate flying operations. Runways and a connecting taxiway bound three sides and form a horseshoe around the facility. Inside the horseshoe the post is laid out in concentric circles with spokes radiating from a central hub containing Education and Training Command Headquarters and the officer's club.

Nita and I drove through Randolph's main game and I saw the

Taj Mahal for the first time in August, 1974. A short distance from it, located on one of the base's outer rings was the site of my next assignment: the Plans, Programs, and Analysis Directorate of the Air Force Military Personnel Center. "MPC" as it was usually called (the full name has subsequently been shortened to "Air Force Personnel Center" to account for the inclusion of the civilian workforce as part of its business) is the Mecca for personnel operations in the Air Force. Accessions, assignments, classification, promotions, awards and decorations, morale-welfare-recreation programs, retirements and separations – the entire range of military human resources activities – are handled from the Center. Its impact on the Service's personnel business in many ways mirrors that of the Pentagon on other Air Force operations.

There is a spectrum of quality in every organization. A statistician would portray it as a bell-shaped curve with the highest achievers shown at the small tip of the arc at the right end, the great mass of "average" troops in the tall bow in the middle and a smaller group of less capable individuals on the extreme left sweep of the "bell." A spectrum of quality existed in the Plans, Programs, and Analysis Directorate also, but the shape of the curve would have puzzled statisticians: the "bell" was skewed far to the right. This was a unit of hand-picked, type-A, caffeine-energized over-achievers. The organization got a tremendous amount of important work done – correctly and *very, very* fast. Everyone ran hard. It was my first experience in that type of company.

On my annual records review, my "career brief" showed that at the time the organization level was Headquarters Air Force-equivalent. It was easy to see why. The directorate teemed with "below-the-zone" promotees, academy grads, and officers with exotic degrees from renowned institutions. A person could get spoiled in that environment. In fact, I found myself having to guard against being spoiled when later I went to command a detachment in northern Italy. We got along fine, even though unlike the staff at Plans, Programs, and Analysis, none of the kids in the detachment had a master's degree in Operations Research from RPI! Still, what a unique experience it was at AFMPC to ask a colleague for help with something and to know with absolute certainty that the task would be done accurately and at warp speed.

My job mostly involved officer evaluations. For two or three years a team of officers had been at work designing a new system to replace an existing program that had become "inflated" to the point that its credibility was being called into question. Most officers received top block ratings: everyone "walked on water." Promotion selection boards and assignment managers reported increasing difficulties in picking the best officers. Job performance was intended to be the main predictor of potential, but because so many records looked about the same in that area, factors like academic degrees, professional schooling, awards and decorations – normally somewhat peripheral to the decision process – assumed a larger influence on selection choices.

There was general agreement throughout the Air Force that a change was needed. There was less than general agreement that the proposed system was the right way to proceed.

The key component of the proposal was a "controlled" rating system intended to address the inflation problem that plagued the existing program. The concept restricted the number of marks that senior evaluators could assign in the highest two rating blocks on the assessment form. These rating "quotas" immediately became the most contentious part of the new system.

"Rating controls" drew flak from all quadrants. Originally, there were intended to be three "rating curves" to help account for selective assignment patterns. Higher percentages of top ratings were allowed for officers in organizations such as the Office of the Secretary of Defense, Office of the Secretary of the Air Force, and Air Staff that were 100% hand-picked. Analysts had determined that there was a mid-level degree of selectivity for officers chosen for assignments to the United States Air Force Academy and for duty as Air Force ROTC instructors. Officers in those organizations warranted a separate rating curve. The third rating curve, the one in which the lowest percentage of top ratings was allowed, was for everyone else: the officers assigned to Air Force wings, base level organizations, and other units.

From that latter population, which accounted for more than

90% of all Air Force officers, there instantly arose the cry of "unfair." Allegations of favoritism towards officers assigned to the higher headquarters organizations grew increasingly shrill. To these claims of bias, the system designers replied that the three rating curves simply mirrored historic promotion board results. Wing commanders countered by noting, not without reason, that the officers in the wings and at base level were the "war fighters." In their view the institution should not limit the group that would carry out the service's combat mission to the lowest rating curve. That would be bad form. They were not amused.

They won the argument. The war-fighting commanders' concerns were recognized by a decision to adopt a single rating curve for the entire Air Force. Ratings in the top two blocks would still be restricted, but the same limitations would apply across the Air Force. The rationale was that selection boards, as they had been charged with historically, would account for quality differences between organizations. The presumption was that when viewed in the context of an officer's entire record, board members could correctly interpret the value of a '2' rating assigned to an individual at the Pentagon compared to a '1' (highest rating) given, for example, to a Fuels Officer at Mountain Home AFB, Idaho.

The single curve decision momentarily abated the fury of the wing and base level officers only to provoke the wrath of the officers in organizations that had originally been assigned the two higher rating curves. Their argument was that had they been at Mountain Home AFB, instead of on the Air Staff, they would have received a '1' also. They were wary that the selection boards could sort all this out, a worry that increased when it became obvious how powerful the new 'controlled' rating would be in selection decisions. Absent other serious glitches in an officer's record, a '1' rating on the most recent effectiveness report almost guaranteed promotion.

The decision to change to a single curve was about where things were at when I was assigned to the program office. The design cadre left those of us tasked to implement the new system with a proposal that appeared okay as a theory and as an intellectual construct but created enmity in practical, "real life" application.

The controlled rating system with further modifications lasted about four years. For the remainder of the system's life, it was the task of my office to provide information to the officer corps, educate evaluators, and adjust the program when required. The most significant intervening change was to apply rating controls only to the highest block on the assessment form. After a couple of years operating in that mode, controls were removed completely. In the meantime, we got lots of practice briefing skeptical audiences.

Whenever we saw them, my office mates and I kidded (or harassed, depending on the fire the program was taking at the time) the guys who designed the original system. The usual banter was something to the effect that anointed as heroes for designing the wondrous new system that would save the Air Force, they had chosen to take their medals and get the hell out before the shelling began.

Not helping at all with the program's approval quotient was a series of poor decisions made soon after implementation. To increase acceptance of the system and concurrently dispel a major concern that officers with less than top block ratings would not be promoted, we recommended that the new system be used first on a board such as selection to captain, where the promotion opportunity was high. That would assure large numbers of officers with '2' and '3' ratings ('3s' were the real concern, initial limits were on the top two – '1' and '2' – rating blocks, and half the officer corps would receive '3' ratings) would be promoted; and the board mechanism would gain some practical experience in handling the powerful new evaluation tool. Instead, the system was employed for the first time on a colonel's promotion board where the overall selection opportunity was quite small.

As a consequence, few officers who met the board with a '3' rating on their most recent effectiveness report were chosen for promotion. The results had a chilling effect. Instead of building confidence in the new system, the outcome added to the anxieties regarding it.

Conversations regarding "the system" were non-stop.

Consternation regarding it continued to grow. In some units competition for the limited number of '1' ratings – seen as assuring promotion – was so intense that commanders worried about sustaining esprit in the organization. In a profession in which an ethic of "all for one and one for all" and "trust your buddy" is imperative almost above all other things, the steadfast cohesion so essential to mission success was threatened. Senior leaders worried about the effect on officer retention as well.

After a series of modifications that attempted to soften the sharp edges and make the program more palatable to the officer corps, rating controls were eventually removed completely.

"Psycho-socials" were a major factor. Controlled ratings were cold water in the face of an officer corps accustomed to a system where a top rating had become almost an expectation. Conversely, with rating control limits, half the officer population received '3' ratings or below every rating cycle. Even that program decision was unfortunate. Setting the break point at exactly 50 percent between the top two "controlled" ratings and all others created what came to be known as the "bottom half syndrome." Had the approach been introduced in an organization just starting from scratch, the concept might indeed have taken hold. In the real world, however, it was imposed on a mature institution that had grown up with different experiences and anticipations. Decisions regarding the initial use of the new evaluations in "live fire" board deliberations did not serve the program well and a continuing series of changes following implementation further eroded its credibility.

I came away from the experience thinking that we really needed to design a system that would allow everyone to get 'A's (thus forcing no ego deflating lower ratings), while some select few (the true "fast burners") could be identified with 'A+'s. For sure, the commanders needed a strong voice in the process. In an inflated system, promotion decisions were too easily swayed by factors other than performance. It was also clear that the officer evaluation program carried a lot of baggage with it: the Air Force used it to document performance, assess potential, and make assignments. Because the system directly effected promotions, it ultimately influenced attainment of retirement eligibility. Every one of those things hit officers where they live. Each induced a *lot* of pressure on a system intended to accommodate so many things. Because of those pressures, in my musings I believed we should separate, as much as possible, the promotion component from the rest of the system.

All in all, it was a busy and interesting time for me. When I later attended Air Command and Staff College, I used the history of the controlled rating system and the lessons learned regarding it as the focus of my major research paper. Several years later in a small way the "lessons learned" assisted my friend Rex Klaurens and a superb team he assembled in creating a brand new concept for evaluating officers. Rex and his group did indeed find a way to give everyone an 'A' and a select few an 'A+', and to essentially separate promotion-related assessments from the rest of the evaluation program. It was masterfully done. The system continues in use to this day.

In Praise of Chiefs ... and Indians: Part I

I first met Jim Lloyd when I was a young captain. We were part of a team from the Air Force Military Personnel Center that spent five or six weeks traveling to bases in the Pacific, briefing audiences about new programs and trying to solve human resource problems on the spot. Before the trip I knew Jim only by reputation; he was a highly respected chief master sergeant. As the journey progressed, I quickly began to understand why he was held in such high regard by his contemporaries. I've seldom seen anyone work so hard or so successfully. After full days of briefings and meetings, Jim would go to the flight line until two or three each morning to talk with the young one- and two-stripers working midnight shifts. He listened to the young airmen, counseled them, solved some of their problems immediately and took others back with him to fix when we got home.

Years later, when I returned to the Military Personnel Center as Director of Personnel Operations, Jim, now a retired chief, worked as a civilian employee in one of the divisions that came under my umbrella. He was as wise as always and worked just as hard.

A day or two before I left the organization to move on to a

command job, we had lunch together. Afterwards, as we were getting ready to say our farewells, Jim slipped a small, carefully wrapped package into my hand. Too stunned to do anything except look surprised, I fumbled to open the box. When I removed the lid, inside was a beautiful silver eagle tie tac. Jim said some gracious words as I stared at that incredible remembrance. I was probably too dazed to do much except mumble "thank you": my usual eloquence. That act of graciousness was typical of Jim's concern for those he worked with. For me, he needn't have said nor done anything out of the ordinary: knowing him was honor enough ...but I've always kept that tie tac.

R & R

A MORAN STORY: THE FIVE-STAR RESTAURANT

It was the Aggie cadet's first visit to New York City. As the guest of a classmate he made the long journey from Texas A & M and now found himself enthralled with the sights and sounds of the big city.

On his first night in town his friend introduced him to the most beautiful girl he had ever seen. On an impulse, he asked her for a date the following evening. Much to his surprise, she accepted.

Immediately, he recognized his quandary. Being an Aggie, he was totally lacking in social skills and sophistication. For one thing, he didn't have a clue about how to order a meal at a fancy restaurant. Still, he was determined to impress the dazzling beauty who had so astonishingly agreed to accompany him the next night.

Early the following morning, he phoned a French restaurant and explained his dilemma. A kindly maitre d' took pity on his situation and talked him through an entire multi-course extravaganza. The cadet took furious notes and spent the remainder of the day committing the process to memory. Convinced that he had it down pat, the Aggie confidently went to pick up his date.

As they journeyed together into the city, their first moments together surpassed his fondest expectations. *Everything* went just right. He said the right things, did the right things: the young lady was obviously impressed.

When they reached the city, eager to keep a good thing going, he began looking for a place to dine. Spotting a promising appearing establishment, he took his date by the arm and led her to it. With perfect decorum, he introduced himself and his lady to the proprietor who was standing out front.

Then, eager to demonstrate his newly acquired social skills, he carefully recited the order he had worked so hard to memorize.

"Let's begin," he said casually, "with an appetizer of Aubergines with tomtes farcies." "That is stuffed eggplant with tomato sauce," he quietly explained to his date, "I think you will enjoy it." "Please serve it with well-chilled champagne," he instructed the proprietor.

Then, smoothly, almost majestically, he ordered course after following course of magnificent French cuisine, thoughtfully translating each portion of the menu to the beauty on his arm. "After the appetizer, we'll have Soupe aux herbes – "herb soup made with sorrel," he said as an aside to his date, then followed a fish course "with wine from the Alsace region," an entrée of baked chicken with mushrooms, garlic potatoes, and asparagus ("and for our dinner wine a Voignier'), then a salad of mixed greens with vinaigrettes, and later, cheese ("room temperature Brie avec du pain'). Finally, the dessert: "a Souffle a l'abricot served avec sauterne."

There! He'd done it! With considerable flair, he'd made it through the whole thing ... and he'd gotten it entirely correct!

When he finished there was a moment of silence. The owner looked at him rather quizzically. Finally, the proprietor said, "You're from Texas A & M aren't you?"

"W-why, why y-yes," the startled cadet responded. "How did you know?"

"Because," said the proprietor, "this is a hardware store."

GOLD AND SILVER LEAVES

Air Command and Staff College

    I was selected for Air Command and Staff College (ACSC) concurrent with promotion to major. Focused on preparing officers for command or staff officer slots at major air command or higher headquarters, ACSC is the Air Force's "graduate school" for mid-level executives.

    The school is located at Maxwell AFB, in Montgomery, Alabama. Like Randolph, Maxwell is one of the Air Force's historic bases. In its distant past, Claire Chennault and other luminaries, assigned there as faculty in an organization called the Air Force Tactical School, devised operational tactics later used in World War II.

    ACSC shares a position of honor on "Academic Circle" along with the Air Force's two other major institutions for professional military education: Squadron Officer School (junior officers) and Air War College (senior officers). More recently, Air Force Officer Training School, moved from Lackland, has claimed a place on "The Circle" as well. Positioned in the exact center, like the hub of a wheel that has the schools circling it around its rim, is the Air University Library. The Library houses one of the world's finest collections of military publications.

    As a Squadron Officer School student I had gone there for the first time years before looking for a map of Haiti to use in a class presentation on the Duvalier regime. I trucked up to the Library's second floor Map Room and stated my need, not realizing what was about to be perpetrated on me. A stunning number of maps of different sizes, types, and varieties, all on that one small less than cosmically significant place, were immediately made available to me and soon loaded onto my arms. I remember walking out of the

Library thinking I was lucky I hadn't asked for maps of a place that was really important. I would not have been able to carry them. I have been fascinated by the place every since; it is a national treasure.

The ACSC experience was a mixed bag. I enjoyed, immensely, the blocks covering international relations and military issues in general. Excellent speakers endured the long trek from Washington D.C. to Montgomery, Alabama ("Gateway to Downtown Wetumpka") to speak to us.

As usual, I learned as much from my classmates as I did from instructors at the lectern. One of the best parts of ACSC was the opportunity to interact with sister service officers and colleagues from the more than 30 countries that sent officers to the course.

Those were certainly positive features, but there were areas where the curriculum desperately needed an oil change. Although one purpose of the school was to serve as a precursor experience for staff officer duty, by the time I attended ACSC I had already completed a tour at a major command headquarters and one at Headquarters Air Force level. Possibly swayed by those experiences, I came to regard the management area as the weakest block of instruction in the entire course. It lacked depth and sophistication. There were too few "real world" situations, and too much out-dated material. I felt badly that we were subjecting the allied officers to that sort of simplicity. Many of them had long service records and experiences in tough, complex jobs. They – and we – deserved better.

Nor did the curriculum do much to differentiate leadership from management (there *is* an enormous difference) or, indeed, to present much food for thought about leadership in general. Considering the mission of the school and the profession of the people attending it, that was a major failing. In 1978-79, ACSC was not yet deeply immersed in computerized war-gaming. Class exercises reflected the program's infancy; it had considerable growing up to do. Certainly a reflection of the time was that the major war game involved a large scale nuclear exchange between Warsaw Pact and NATO forces.

The history portion of the curriculum, more specifically the lack of one, was troubling. I remember writing on my final critique how disappointed I was that a history component to the course – either Air Force specific or general military – was almost nonexistent.

The Air Force is the youngest of the U.S. military branches. It has had less time to "build" a history and for that reason as well as its embedded relationship with technology – and the imperative need to recognize and adapt to rapid technological change – it gets less mired in precedents, protocol, and "history" than do the other services. That's as it should be, but to teach almost *no* history was short-sighted. The same principles of war apply even though the Air Force fights in a different medium. A knowledge of history can build pride in an organization with all kinds of positive influences: retention, personal commitment, "service before self", and on and on. "Bragging rights" are important. That part of ACSC needed to be made better.

August 1978 to June 1979 was an interesting time to be at ACSC and be immersed in studies with an international cadre. "Red" China received "Nationalist" China's seat on the United Nations Security Council; the Camp David Peace Talks took place; Iran was falling apart – the Shah would soon leave and the Ayatollah would take over; the Marcos regime in the Philippines was the target of increasing criticism; Prime Minister Thatcher was in the initial stages of transforming Great Britain; and there were flare-up episodes in Central America and Africa. No visible cracks in the Soviet Union had yet appeared. The Warsaw Pact looked as formidable as ever.

It was an eventful ten months filled with several poignant moments.

My good friend Tao-Chien "Harry" Chen from the Republic of China, who sat next to me in auditorium lectures, was devastated when the UN voted to seat the Peoples' Republic in Taiwan's place on the Security Council. So distraught that he initially considered going home, "Harry" was eventually persuaded to stay. I'm glad he did; the relationships he formed with others in the class were lasting and important.

Yohanon Or, an Israeli helicopter pilot, and an Egyptian officer who flew a MIG became acquaintances as the weeks went by. Tracing their experiences in the October War of 1973, they found that at least on one occasion they were in the air over the same general location at about the same time. Interestingly, their relationship became strained only during the Camp David Peace Talks. It was as if each felt the pressures and personalized the arguments and negotiating stances of their national delegations.

There were three Iranian officers in the class, a manifestation of how closely Iran was aligned with the U.S. at the time. They represented all shades of the political spectrum: one increasingly tilted toward the Ayatollah Khomeini, one was pro-Shah, and the third was somewhere in the middle. When conditions inside Iran continued to deteriorate, the latter two officers were especially conflicted. Both were reluctant to return home, but were wary of what might happen to their families if they did not. It was a sad, dangerous, and difficult time. Those that did return would soon find themselves in the middle of an eight-year war with Iraq.

I've also pondered the fate of Ronny Benedicto, a major in the Philippines Air Force. Ronny was a member of one of my seminars and other than "Harry" Chen, he was the international officer I got to know best of all. Ronny and his family represented their country very well. Whether by conviction or personal loyalty, or both, Ronny was an articulate defender of the Marcos regime. He spoke about it only when obliged to do so, and even though our families became fairly close – we had a lot in common to talk about as my wife had grown up in the Philippines while her dad, a First Sergeant, served two tours at Clark AB – I was never totally sure how much of the party line he really bought into. It is doubtful that at the time any Filipino could have gotten a posting to ACSC without some political connections, however, so there was undoubtedly a sense of obligation. Whatever transpired later, I hope Ronny and his beautiful family are well.

Perhaps the most poignant of all cases was that of a major from Bangladesh. He initially declined the prestigious assignment to ACSC so his impoverished country would be spared the cost of sending him. Eventually, his seminar mates "adopted" him to the extent of helping ease his way through the school

The craziest of our classmates were the Aussies. I hope they will always be on our side: we need them for comic relief. International officers were given blocks of time to "brief" the class on their countries. As a way of illustrating that they were from "down under" and things were reversed on the other side of the world, the Aussie presenters began with a picture of two topless women standing on their heads! Their time slot was supposed to be limited to 15 minutes; they cheerfully rambled on for 40. They always had a good time.

I never met the officer from Kuwait. My recollection of his platform presentation is how casually he mentioned that the school kids in Kuwait had their lunches flown in on Air France jets from Paris everyday. Conversely, the Jordanian officer introduced himself to the class by saying that he was from the Arab country that had "no oil ... and no money."

My wife Nita got an up close and personal look at the affluence of one of our Arab classmates. A Saudi prince was a member of the class. With him, he brought a dazzling wife and an entourage of 34 people. To house them the Saudi government rented a walled compound in a small town near Montgomery. Nita was invited to a luncheon hosted by the prince's wife. The princess was a gracious hostess, the cuisine was excellent, and the décor was a tad more toney than that in our government-supplied quarters on Gunter AFB. Standing behind the princess's chair at all times was a servant/body guard. My wife was duly impressed.

Bob Van Houten, a U.S. Marine major, became a special friend. On one occasion, Bob enrolled me in a Johnny Carson – Ed McMahon routine to lead off his seminar presentation. He began by holding up a lone sheet of notebook paper and casually announcing that it contained all we would ever need to know about the subject he was going to talk about. I then interjected as Ed McMahon: "Wait a minute! Do you mean to tell me that on that one small bit of paper, that one tiny 8x11 inch piece of processed lined, that you have distilled the entire ..." And on and on. After I had run down, Bob said "Right, airplane breath ..." All of this drew groans from the crowd -- which was exactly what he had intended.

At that time, no Marine had ever been designated a Distinguished Graduate at ACSC. It was a point of pride with them. I think Bob could have easily done it, but chose not to be the first to sully their record.

For our international colleagues, an assignment to ACSC was considered a prestigious posting. Countries generally sent very good officers, "comers" destined for high rank, to attend. There were two notable exceptions.

One was an officer from Afghanistan. Lieutenant Colonel Parwizi was about as far from a tall, lithe Pathan raider that formed my mental image of a typical Afghan warrior as could possibly be imagined. Short, stocky, almost obese, he affected an obsequious manner that didn't play well with his colleagues. He invariably asked questions during the Q & A periods that followed major presentations. Many of his queries were inane, divorced from or only marginally related to the point of the lecture. His gaffes embarrassed the other international officers, including my friend "Harry" Chen. "Harry" mistakenly thought that Parwizi's performance reflected poorly on the entire group of foreign officers.

That was not true. The USAF students recognized that "Harry" Chen and most others would have been assets to any nation's air force. My close friend and classmate Rex Klaurens took a computer lab with one of the Iranian officers and remarked that the Iranian was "one of the smartest guys I've ever met." Usually with Rex the absence of criticism constituted praise, so that comment was a high compliment indeed.

At any rate, Parwizi was an exception. His seminar mates said that he had already been in the U.S. for several years mostly on assignments in the Washington D.C. area. Their view was that he would try to stay in the United States indefinitely. His officially stated forwarding address from ACSC was Bagram Air Base, a name much in the headlines a quarter century later, but he did not seem anxious to return to Afghanistan any time soon. It is problematical that he went back. If he did, his return would have placed him directly in harm's way: the Soviets invaded Afghanistan the following year.

The other international officer who marched to a different drummer was Major Kimani from Kenya. No matter what the project, Kimani claimed not to have the background, experience, training, or time to do it. Others in his study group had to prop him up and carry his load. Almost always he announced his lack of background, experience, training, or time in a mincing voice that declared himself congenitally incapable of doing the work. His standard pitch made it clear that the task would only get done if someone else did it for him or, essentially the same thing, dropped what they were doing and led him through it. The former was usually a better option than the latter, because, truth be known, Kimani did not seem terribly eager to learn.

One good thing resulted from Kimani's antics. My colleague Ed Petersen developed such a well-practiced shtick for mimicking Kimani's usual fawning plea to be exempted from work that in otherwise quiet moments, Ed kept the seminar in stitches.

/////

It has been interesting to observe how many of my USAF and international colleagues went on to hold very high positions in their military services. ACSC did a nice job of providing the opportunity to grow and sustain important linkages between them.

Vicenza, Italy

It was the first, and maybe the only, "dream" assignment I ever received: Commander, Detachment 9, 1141 United States Air Force Special Activities Squadron, Vicenza, Italy. Professionally, the job filled the deepest of all career goals: *commander* of a unit. For my family and for me personally a tour in Europe was a prayer answered. And at *Vicenza, Italy* no less: 45 miles from Venice, the Dolomites visible in the distance, Rome and the other great cities of Europe all within reaching distance. It was indeed a dream come true.

The distant hope began to take shape more than a year earlier, while I was assigned to the Air Force Military Personnel Center in San Antonio. When I finished briefing a promotion board, one of the panel members followed me back to my office. He introduced himself as "Colonel Bob McCartan, Commander of the 1141st USAF Special Activities Squadron." That was followed by: "How would you like to command a detachment in my organization?" I was flattered by his offer and told him so. Then I admitted, "I'm not sure I know what the '1141st USAF Special Activities Squadron' is." Colonel McCartan explained that his outfit "takes care of the personnel business and various other things" for Air Force people assigned to international organizations "like NATO, for example," throughout Europe, Africa, and Southwest Asia. He said that his headquarters, at Stuttgart, Germany, was "just down the street from Headquarters, U.S. European Command," and there were major detachments at places like SHAPE Headquarters in Mons, Belgium; Brunssum, Netherlands; Naples, Oslo, and Teheran. Nine total. Vicenza was one of them.

The more he talked, the more intriguing it sounded. I told him that I would like to be considered for one of his jobs, but there was a major glitch: I was already "on orders" to attend Air Command and Staff College, a ten month course. To which he replied, "I'll wait if you will." He was as good as his word. Several weeks prior to ACSC graduation he contacted me to see if I was still interested. I was. Orders to Vicenza arrived soon after.

A three-day orientation stop at squadron headquarters in Stuttgart on the way to Italy confirmed there would be work to do. The detachment was ranked rather low in some of its operations. Still, it promised to be a great job at an incredible location; my family and I were eager to get there and get started.

If anything, both the job and the place exceeded our expectations. With the help of some superb NCOs the detachment improved quickly and dramatically. The unit was soon at or near the top of the leader board in nearly every category. Like every commander, I never felt I had enough time, or money, or people to do all I wanted to get done. Nonetheless, moving an organization forward and taking it places it had never been before brought some of the most satisfying moments of my life.

Nita and I found a home in a nearby village – #1 Via Carducci, Villaggio Monte Grappa – and settled in. We loved it immediately. The place was typically Italian: balconies on three sides off the upper floor, flower boxes all around, incredible tile floors. The house was heated by fuel oil. Because fuel was expensive and there was often a shortage, on the coldest days of the winter, like our Italian neighbors, we closed off the rest of the house and lived in the kitchen. American television did not reach us so we read, played games, and listened to records or to the old time radio shows broadcast over a small Armed Forces Radio station.

Our landlord, Mr. Benetti, a wonderful old gentleman with courtly European manners, had a crush on Nita and doted on our two small daughters, so the place did not lack for attention or maintenance. To get around, we bought a used Fiat. It was a station wagon and it was orange. Both features embarrassed my daughters no end, but the little vehicle took us everywhere and as the "national car" of Italy, repairs and parts were always close at hand.

Nita shopped often in the village. There was a bakery, a meat store, a cheese store, a vegetable store, each separate and distinct from its neighbors. The clerks soon came to recognize her and with a twinkle would "refuse" to sell her anything until she pronounced the name *just right* in Italian.

Our five-year old, Karen, learned the language best of all. She played back and forth, over the walls and up the street with Italian friends much of the time. She absorbed Italian like a sponge. It was a bit embarrassing to be at a store downtown and find it necessary to have a five-year old translate for me, but at times it turned out that way.

One Halloween we took Anna Marie, one of Karen's friends, trick or treating with us to some American homes. Halloween is not celebrated in Italy (in fact, an Italian farmer in the Po Valley grew pumpkins specifically for the occasion), so this was a new and different experience for Karen's small buddy. Anna Marie spoke no English, so we coached her on what to say. It turned out to be a memorable evening; we have never before or since heard "trick or treat" pronounced quite the same way Anna Marie said it that night.

Living 45 miles from Venice turned out to be a mixed blessing. Seldom have we been so popular. At times, Nita felt like a tour guide, escorting various friends and relatives – many of whom we hadn't seen or heard from for years – back and forth to the city. But, as long as the crowd did not get too large, we rather enjoyed being a favorite destination.

All of the U.S. Air Force families assigned to the Fifth Allied Tactical Air Force (usually abbreviated "5ATAF" and pronounced

"Five A TAF") – that was the international organization my detachment supported – lived "on the economy" in Vicenza and the villages and towns around it. American television was not available to any of us. The only convenient places that had access to it were at the officer and NCO clubs at the nearest U.S. Army post. All of us would often gather in the TV rooms in those places to watch a stateside sporting event, eat, and converse. Softball games were also a staple; when we played it was, as one spouse said, "Like 5ATAF night at the ball park."

We now realize that we became closer to that special collection of families than to any others at any other place. They were neat people who looked out for one another in an environment that was already conducive to drawing people together.

Then, after two years in Italy, an event happened that brought us closer together still.

A Different Kind of Courage

In the evening of December 17, 1981, Red Brigades terrorists broke into an apartment in Verona, Italy, and kidnapped U.S. Army Brigadier General James L. Dozier. Additional threats came quickly in the hours and days that followed. The isolated Air Force community was especially vulnerable; work sites were widely separated and families were scattered throughout numerous small towns and villages. The security problem was way "outside the box," not anything like the "normal" situation. Families would have to be involved. It was clear from the outset that keeping everyone safe would take a community effort.

Briefings and checklists covering residence and vehicle security, driving tips, points of contact, incident reporting, and general do's and don'ts were immediately provided to spouses and children. They welcomed the information and then at community meetings went further by helping create a series of "check in" procedures that allowed us to verify the safety of everyone, everyday.

Many families supplemented these measures with their own individual signals that, for example, by positioning window shades or configuring outside lights, relayed the presence of anything suspicious to neighbors and to military members coming home from work.

When General Dozier was freed 42 days later by elite police units and Red Brigades cadres were taken into custody all over Italy, there was understandable rejoicing throughout the community. But there were also feelings of enormous pride that the small group of families had stayed, held each other together, and persevered through the peril. No one panicked. No one left or asked to leave.

The recollection of the quiet courage shown by those families, and their exceptional grace under pressure has always remained with me. Even in the cold and darkness of a menacing Christmas Eve when they were told they were under specific threat, the typical reaction was "Appreciate your coming to tell us. We're staying. See you at work."

If I could have handed out medals to spouses and children that night, I would have done so. It was an honor to have been part of such a special group of people.

The Dozier Kidnapping: Confronting the Red Brigades

On December 17, 1981, Red Brigades terrorists kidnapped U.S. Army Brigadier General James L. Dozier, the senior American officer at a NATO headquarters in Verona, Italy. That action broke the pattern of previous terrorist activities in Italy; until that time terrorists had targeted senior Italian politicians, industrialists, jurists, newspaper publishers and police officials. In the days that followed, a series of warnings identified other Americans as potential victims. The information came through many channels, from several sources, and differed greatly regarding its specificity and assessed reliability; nevertheless, the overall picture portrayed a period of jeopardy for Americans in Northern Italy.

News of the kidnapping reached commanders in the area early the following morning. When the call came, I took one last sip of coffee and headed for my office at a nearly airfield. I had been Commander of Detachment 9 for two years. I knew General Dozier well and worked closely with him on matters associated with the Verona American Community where the General was based and where about half of my troops were assigned.

My detachment was an unusual organization: we did not "own" any base facilities, had no integral security assets, and the American service members we supported were intermingled with allied forces as part of a NATO organization. The detachment's orderly room was located on Dal Molin Aeroporto, an Italian Air Force base on the outskirts of Vicenza; the nearest American facility was a U.S. Army Post (Caserma Ederle) located several miles away. The closest U.S. Air Force support was from Aviano AB, about 100 miles distant.

At the time of the incident, 110 U.S. Air Force members and families depended on the detachment for support, as did some U.S. Navy, U.S. Army, and assorted German, Turkish, and French personnel assigned to international units strewn across Northern Italy. About half of the Americans were stationed at a NATO headquarters (Fifth Allied Tactical Air Force) in Vicenza, Italy, while the remainder was assigned to Headquarters Land Forces Southern Europe (LANDSOUTH), at sites in and around Verona, Italy, 55 miles away. The Verona locations were in turn separated from one another by distances of 25-30 miles. There was no military housing for detachment members. Everyone – married and single members alike – lived "on the economy," widely dispersed in towns and villages surrounding the two larger cities. At the beginning of the threat period, only 19 of the 100 assigned personnel had telephones in their residences. (Due to a shortage of phones and circuits, telephone installation in Italy was a cumbersome process involving a high initial deposit fee and a waiting period often lasting a year or more.) Thus, the security environment was far from ordinary; it was instantly evident that the "standard" approaches to security would not apply.

A large contingent of officers and NCOs hurried to the headquarters after hearing the news and quickly congregated in my office. Huddled around a small conference table, seated in chairs along the wall, or standing near the doorway, we discussed the information that we had – sketchy as it was – and began plotting steps aimed at keeping our families and colleagues safe. The first action was to build an emergency fact sheet containing points of contact and "things to look for," "things to do" precautions. This package was written, produced, and put in the hands of every service member and family by mid-morning. We expanded the checklist considerably in the following weeks, but the rapid availability of the initial version struck the right chord. Most families kept copies posted in their homes and cars.

Second, the First Sergeant and I visited, face to face, every member of the unit, answering questions and addressing concerns. We quickly learned that any worries about "over informing" people were unfounded. There was an enormous thirst for news. We chose to release everything allowed by security constraints. Even when the news was "bad," it was clear that the comfort level was higher when people felt they were fully informed.

Terrorists abduct high-ranking officials for several reasons, propaganda and media value foremost amongst them. We believed that terrorist acts would focus on senior people and we said that in our conversations. That assessment was based on available information and an analysis of past terrorist actions -- and was later corroborated when Italian police began rounding up suspects.

Thus, there was no indication that family members would become terrorist targets. Deliberate violence against family members is antithetical to the Italian culture; the backlash resulting from damage to family members would be counter-productive to the terrorists' aims. However, in the next breath we urged everyone to avoid providing terrorists with such easy "targets of opportunity" that they could not afford to ignore them.

At Verona, during those same early hours that first morning, supervisors contacted everyone, including off duty shift workers. Security information was hand carried to the three operating sites and standard telephone conference times – which continued through the crisis period -- were established between detachment members at Vicenza and Verona to share information and coordinate actions.

Because the Verona operations were dispersed over a large area and Americans were scattered through several communities, "check in" procedures were developed to account for service members and families. This was particularly important because the majority of the GIs were shift workers whose duty schedules kept them "out of pocket" for varying periods and the absence of telephones prevented status checks from being made by phone. The detachment's "audit" procedures involved a combination of private telephones where available, visit contacts by one neighbor with others, a "deposit slip" certification by family members at a safe location during prescribed intervals, and "patrols" on a rotating basis by designated individuals to confirm the well-being of other Americans living nearby. This menu of techniques allowed us to verify the safety of everyone, everyday.

Meanwhile, the detachment arranged with other U.S. sister services to install a temporary "no uniform" policy for Americans working at the NATO complex in the center of the city. This reduced the visibility of U.S. service members and shielded them from the massive numbers of news media representatives that saturated the city.

These first steps were admittedly stop gap in nature. We soon followed with expanded checklists, briefings, and training in areas such as residence, vehicle, and office security, and defensive driving. We met frequently with families. Several common sense measures came from these community sessions. None in itself was of cosmic importance, but each contributed an additional layer of informed protection for military families who "bought into" the process and became its strongest adherents. For example:

- The importance of no lost dependent ID cards was repeatedly stressed. An ID card was an entry ticket to a U.S. or NATO installation. Lost cards were reported immediately.
- Families were counseled against being drawn into discussions that would reveal the locations of American residences in the local community.
- Tighter controls were placed on the availability and distribution of organizational listings and "social rosters" that revealed names, ranks, duty titles and addresses of people assigned to the unit.
- Families with telephones answered their phones in Italian. No indication of name or rank was given until the identity of the caller was confirmed.

- Name designations or displays showing affiliation with U.S. forces were removed from door bells and mail boxes.
- When maintenance, repair, or utility company personnel were called to a home, their arrival was requested at a specified time and their dispatch confirmed with the company when the employees arrived at the door. (Terrorists had entered the Dozier's apartment under the guise of being plumbing repairmen.)
- Since many Italian dwellings had utility or "extra" rooms on the ground floor and living quarters on the upper levels, families were reminded to lock interior doors as well as outside entrances. The same guidance applied to windows and doors opening to outside balconies, which are common features on Italian homes.

Like all commanders of overseas units, I often "preached the sermon" about being sensitive to the image portrayed by Americans. The need was now even more compelling. Embarrassment-free conduct enhanced the good feelings increasingly coming from the Italian populace, and a "low profile" was exactly what the situation required for the security of the detachment's people. The last thing we needed was for someone to provide terrorists with such visible targets that the group could easily exploit them. And, given the circumstances at the time, it made especially good sense to avoid alienating Italian friends; few things could contribute more to the security of our people than the presence of "good neighbors."

Basic precautions were reiterated at every session -- varying routes to and from work, keeping doors locked at all times, allowing no unidentified individuals into the residence complex. The track record of the Red Brigades and similar groups indicated that they preferred to gain access through subterfuge, or through an unlocked door, or capture the target on an open road, rather than attempting to batter their way in to a locked and secured facility. One – notable – apparent exception to the usual modus operandi occurred during the crisis. On January 4, 1982, terrorists with probable sympathies to the Red Brigades blew away a portion of a prison wall and freed four convicted group members. It was a meticulously planned operation that killed one prison guard and wounded six others.

For the first week of the crisis, our actions were concentrated against a serious but somewhat generalized threat. That situation changed late on Christmas Eve 1981 with the arrival of several additional warnings. Received from credible sources, these communications focused the threat much more directly against specific members of the Detachment 9 community. The initial warning notice was relayed to me by the Italian *carabinieri* (national paramilitary police) through *Colonnello* Guido Cutry, Italian Air Force, commander of the airfield where the detachment's orderly room was located. Detachment "circuit riders" immediately set out to inform those whom the message placed most at risk. We assessed security needs and individual reactions during these contacts as well. If any family became "unraveled" by the news, we would need to deal quickly with the problem. Fortunately, that was never necessary. Some individuals and families required more information than others, but none reacted in anything but the most responsible manner.

Like a chess match where every move and countermove had lethal overtones, we reacted to the altered, intensified threat by putting different, additional measures in place. The detachment staff arranged with the military police at the nearest U.S. Army Post, local Italian police, and *carabinieri* for police patrols around the residences of Americans most at risk. Because of the absence of telephones, we provided "strip maps" to police officials showing the locations of American homes. The strip maps were placed in the cruisers of American military police and enabled patrols to respond more quickly to threat notifications. Local police made frequent checks of the homes or posted guards outside them.

Soon after, detachment and NATO officials acquired radios for members of the target group. With the assistance of some skilled Air Force communications technicians, ranges were boosted sufficiently to enable Detachment 9 people to be in direct contact at all times with both the military police desk on the U.S. Army Post and the switchboard at the NATO headquarters.

Communications help was also received from high-ranking Italian officers in the NATO unit who intervened with local civilian authorities to expedite the placement of telephones in the homes of the threatened individuals. This was a most appreciated effort. Families that had waited more than a year for a telephone now found one installed within a week.

At Detachment 9 work sites, Explosive Ordnance Disposal briefings addressed the possibility of explosive devices being placed in our facilities. On the same briefing program, counterintelligence personnel provided information on terrorist groups and methods.

Meanwhile, detachment NCOs worked with Italian counterparts to address after hours security of the detachment's buildings. Italian technicians did an excellent job of surveying the installation from a security standpoint. Several U.S. offices were "sealed off" after duty hours. Italian officials augmented the installation's perimeter security, instituted roving patrols, and placed machine gun posts at base entrances. All cars entering the compound were checked and personal ID inspections were made thorough and intense. These were significant steps by our Italian allies. Prior to General Dozier's kidnapping, the environment was regarded as benign and security measures reflected that casualness.

To assist the Italian national police in screening people and vehicles entering the NATO complex, the detachment provided NATO security personnel with lists of vehicles stolen from U.S. personnel and license plates missing from American-owned cars. (In Italy, automobiles of American military personnel were identified with distinct "Allied Forces Italy" license plates.)

The "worst case scenario" was, of course, a direct attack on U.S. facilities. Intelligence reports regarding the Red Brigades' intentions were ambiguous, but it was clear that the group had the *capability* to launch attacks if opportunities presented themselves. On January 10, *carabinieri* raided a Red Brigades' hideout in Rome and found, in addition to an impressive array of small arms and ammunition, surface to air missiles, rocket propelled grenades, and bazookas. Six days later, at another Red Brigades' safe haven in Biela, police discovered 1,000 sticks of explosive gelignite, 764 detonators, and 750 yards of fuses and cable. Precautions were immediately taken. Weapons for unit members assigned to the headquarters and remote sites were tested, ammunition was placed adjacent to the weapons, weapons qualifications were checked, training was conducted, and weapons release procedures were rehearsed. These were necessary steps given the detachment's operating environment. Italy has some of the world's most restrictive and stringently enforced weapons laws. The detachment's weapons – M-16s and .38 revolvers – were kept in an armory at the NATO headquarters. In normal threat conditions, ammunition was stored in a separate bunker located a considerable distance from the weapons. With the assistance of *Colonnello* Cutry, the base commander, ammunition was collocated with weapons and release procedures were accelerated.

To many families, terror now seemed to blanket Northern Italy like a malevolent fog. Security techniques at the nearest American installation (Caserma Ederle, a U.S. Army Post) also addressed this new threat, so different from that faced by most Americans in the past. The most visible response was the massive presence of heavily armed guards at all entrance gates, posted at vantage points that offered unrestricted fields of fire. These marksmen provided a tangible presence, and their psychological impact on the minds of persons contemplating shooting their way into the post had to be impressive. The number of access gates was reduced, and the hours each was open were changed frequently and on short notice. During the most intense period, every car was stopped. Hoods and trunks were opened to search for explosive devices; mirrors were placed under vehicles for the same purpose. Bomb disposal experts were always available, close at hand.

The perimeter of the installation was heavily patrolled 24 hours a day. The post boundary "wire" fronted on everything from a congested residential area to cornfields and open ground; night vision devices proved invaluable. Roving quick response teams cruised at random around the base. At the height of the threat period a mobile strike force was kept on alert in a barracks area to respond with firepower and numbers to a "suicide squad" attack such as had occurred at Lod Airport at Tel Aviv. Top priorities were given the dependent school, hospital and headquarters. Rehearsals to move to, guard, and defend these and other key locations on the installation were frequently held. (Interestingly, although a possible terrorist attack on the detachment's support post was a grim subject, when family members were told about the precautions most emerged from the briefings more reassured.)

Full vehicle searches slowed traffic attempting to enter the post. On most entrances, however, after search personnel became proficient, the worst delays approximated only 15-20 minutes during peak periods. Army officials addressed the situation by staggering duty hours for various units and by Public Affairs "spots" broadcast by the Armed Forces Network radio station, urging patience and explaining the need for the checks. At Commander's Calls and group meetings, local commanders reiterated the need for patience, counseling troops that the searches were necessary to insure maximum protection for themselves and their families. There were few complaints.

Where reasonable security could be provided, organizational activities were continued – and expanded. We believed it important to draw the tiny community even closer together and we developed a questionnaire that matched interests and hobbies, so families that shared mutual leisure pursuits could, if they wished, join together in the activities. With great care taken for security, holiday parties, ball games, and social activities were continued.

A small Armed Forces Network radio station located in Vicenza provided the only English language broadcast service available to detachment families. The American communities in Vicenza and Verona depended on it for current U.S. and local news. The station was especially important in providing information to people in outlying areas; families relied on broadcasts to "keep in touch" with events. Because it also broadcast stateside information, American music, sporting events, etc., the station served as a continuous and comfortable link with "home."

How much they relied on the station was made clear when, during the height of the crisis, difficulties impaired reception in distant areas. While these problems lasted, they isolated remote site families and caused considerable consternation. A great deal of time was spent with the station manager, chief engineer, and network director, working to pinpoint difficulties and advising them of the locations and extent of reception difficulties reported by detachment families. The unit provided Air Force communications technicians to help resolve transmitter, cable, and antenna problems. "Pirate" stations operating illegally on or near the frequency assigned to the American station posed a broader difficulty. Eventually, we requested assistance from U.S. embassy officials who interfaced with Italian government representatives and eventually shut down the "pirates."

In a tense and fast moving environment, with daily changes in threats and hourly changes in rumors, dealing with the public is not an easy task. In the military these interactions are handled by representatives from what are usually labeled "Public Affairs" offices. The actions of these offices during the crisis both helped and harmed our efforts. Particularly useful were the radio "spots" developed by the Public Affairs office at the U.S. Army post. These brief announcements counseled patience during delays caused by car searches, described precautionary measures for the homes and vehicles, and indicated where to go and what to do in event of an emergency. These spots aired several times each day and helped educate the American communities. Articles in the post newspaper were similarly helpful.

Other actions missed the mark. Soon after General Dozier was kidnapped, one Public Affairs office released a picture of the General with a group of officers. The picture appeared in major newspapers and had the potential effect, through their clear identification, of placing the safety of other individuals in jeopardy. Conversely, several photos of General Dozier were of such poor quality that they would have been of little use in helping identify the General even if by chance someone caught sight of him.

Public Affairs people performed yeoman service, however, in handling queries from the media. Guidance given to detachment families in Verona, where the media presence was most intense, was to refer press queries to the Public Affairs office. This eased pressure on the families and helped assure that the media received factual information, not rumor and conjecture. It seemed to those on scene at the time that articles in the press often reflected comments and reactions representing the most extreme and quasi-hysterical viewpoints. When press queries were referred to the Public Affairs offices, their efforts were helpful in presenting a more balanced perspective.

On January 28, 1982, an elite *carbinieri* team freed General Dozier from a so-called "people's prison" in Padova, Italy. We certainly welcomed the enormous sense of relief that came from his release, but on the other hand we were concerned that people would let their guards down at a time when precautions remained in order. Follow-on terrorist threats were still operative and there was a danger of a backlash by the Red Brigades or sympathizer groups to recoup the prestige lost with General Dozier's safe return. Indeed, threats of revenge came almost immediately. Therefore, we spent time addressing the need for continued security measures. Two things helped us. The first was the credibility of previous communications. The second was that by this time people had become so accustomed to taking security precautions they no longer felt burdened by them.

The six weeks of the episode – from kidnapping to release – were one of the most intense periods in my life. The days, and nights, were filled with planning meetings, visits to work sites, and sessions with families all aimed at keeping people safe from harm. When the chaos settled down and there was time for reflection, I came to believe that several keys were significant in reacting to the threat. Communication was foremost; specifically, the consistent flow of candid information. Frequent face to face meetings created a sense of trust and helped stabilize the situation. Briefings – available to all comers -- supplemented the stream of guidance and training in personal, family, residence, vehicle, and work place security. In combination with the visible measures taken at all locations, these steps increased the "comfort level."

The second item, an extension of the first, was the availability of the unit's entire leadership. Senior enlisted personnel and officers logged miles on the road and in hallways, offices, and work sites, being "seen" and talking with members and families. In addition to dropping in at work areas, members of the staff were at all group gatherings, athletic events, and special occasions. Their visibility was conspicuous and reassuring.

The final item of the three was the proper sense of awareness created by the first two. The detachment community recognized the reality of the threat and understood the measures most likely to be effective against it.

Throughout the crisis, my staff and I were reassured by the spirit of American service members and their families. Their examples of professionalism, courage, and fortitude provided daily inspiration in large and healthy doses.

The Dozier Kidnapping: A Personal Story

Two weeks after General Dozier was kidnapped, my wife and I and our two small daughters were traveling to our home in a small village on the outskirts of Vicenza when a car raced along side, matched its speed with ours, took a flash photo, and sped away. Although I took a zigzag course home, a second car attempted to follow us into our driveway. I slammed the gate shut, locked it, and after hurrying the family into the house, reported the incident.

To this day, the episode remains ambiguous. However, because of my professional tie with General Dozier and because documents taken from his apartment identified my position as commander of a unit nearby, U.S. military and Italian police decided to take no chances. After sifting through the possibilities, early the next morning the entire family was moved on 30 minutes notice.

When I called from work to tell my wife that she had a half hour to pack for a move of an indefinite duration to a place not yet determined, she asked the girls to help choose the items they wished to take with them. It has become part of our family legend that Laura, the 12-year old, packed only her phonograph records. Fortunately, my wife did a last minute logistics check and suggested that things like clothes, toothbrushes, and shoes might also be useful.

We were taken to a guarded, "safe haven" area on a military post. From there, wearing a civilian coat over my uniform and traveling in different vehicles using circuitous routes, I went to work every day. My daughters walked to the post school each morning: Laura, thanks to her mother's intervention, nicely clad in suitable, though frequently repeated ensembles; Karen, our seven-year old, big smile as always despite lots of recent revenue from the tooth fairy, poking along with her yellow lunch pail. Both were, I believe, oblivious to the security personnel that trailed at a discrete distance.

Together as a family in the small apartment that was our "safe haven" home, we planned for the 'worst case'. If we came under immediate threat, the girls would go to an enclosed interior hallway. My wife would join them after securing the shutters in the adjoining room. I would jam the kitchen table against the door and lock the remaining rooms.

Inside the tiny dwelling, we spent all of our "free" time together: reading, playing games, listening to records, and talking. We remained there for 42 days until *caribinieri*, Italian national police, freed General Dozier from his captors.

On the first day, when the news of the incident reached my boss in Germany, he called to ask if I wanted to leave, to be reassigned elsewhere either temporarily or permanently. After I declined his well-meant offer, he asked if he should move my family – perhaps bring them to Germany for awhile.

We talked about it that night at our "safe haven." Around a tiny table in the kitchen, with the windows shuttered and barred, and an armed guard outside our door, we held a family conference. I explained the offer that had been presented to us. The youngest always spoke first. Karen said she was staying and continued playing with her dolls. Laura said she was staying and went into the other room to listen to her records. My wife said she was staying and resumed reading her novel.

I've never loved them more than I did at that moment.

Lonely at the Top

One of the first times I truly appreciated how differently commanders of military units are looked at from "other people" was on a softball field. The small Air Force unit that I commanded at Vicenza, Italy competed against teams from the nearest Army post the local softball league.

About midway through the season, many of the Army units were called for an extended period of training in Germany. That caused the softball season to be suspended until they returned, and when they came back it meant that we had to play every night to "catch up." It was one of the nicest times of my life, a true "major league" schedule. It was delightful.

We played 11 nights in a row. In nine of those games we were behind or tied very late in the game. Several went to extra innings. We won them all.

There was a different hero every night. One night it was Willie Dickerson with some daring base running and a slide that just beat the throw at home. Like all the other times, a massive celebration followed: a huge dog pile at home plate; shouting, back slapping, everyone pounding on Willie. The next night it was Mark Malinoski's turn with a last inning double down the right field line that drove in the two runs we needed to win. Again, complete pandemonium: Mark was engulfed at second base, swarmed under by a mob of guys who each night were finding ever more creative ways to commemorate a victory.

Then one night it was my turn. We were clinging to a one run lead in the bottom of the last inning, but the other team had the bases loaded with only one out. I was close to the bag, playing third base. Their batter absolutely crushed the ball, a cannon shot right down the line. It was a totally spontaneous play: a backhand stab that would have made Brooks Robinson proud, step on third, fire to first. Double play. Game over. We win. Tremendous uproar.

The dugout emptied and the guys on the field came racing towards me, ready to pounce. Then, all of sudden, about ten feet away they all stopped as if deactivated by switches that sent identical messages to all of them: "Hey, wait a minute, this guy's the COMMANDER." Magically, looking somewhat embarrassed, they all simultaneously slowed to a walk and somewhat sheepishly ambled up to me, deciding that shaking hands might be the proper decorum, some seeming to clear their throats and saying things like "Gee, nice play, sir" and "Attaboy, major." All the while I'm thinking "That's all right guys, beat on me, I'll love it." Apparently still a little unsure of the protocol, several of them stopped by the office the next day to again clear their throats and compliment me on the play.

At any rate, I never did get pounded on and thrown into the dirt like the other guys. Worse the luck. I feel like there is a void in my athletic experience. It's like winning the Kentucky Derby and not getting the roses, or taking the Final Four without being able to cut the net.

Maybe some day.

Headquarters Strategic Air Command, Offutt AFB Nebraska

I didn't write any letters requesting to get out of the assignment to SAC Headquarters. Perhaps I had out grown all of that. But, for sure, I didn't want to go. My feelings had nothing to do with my respect for the command: SAC in my view was one of the premier military organizations in the entire world. What concerned me was the reputation the headquarters had even in areas like personnel (human resources) for doing business lock step, using a checklist-like approach that defied attempts at innovation.

The checklist mentality was derived from SAC's nuclear mission. It was absolutely justified, at least in the operational area. There is no room for free lancing when dealing with nuclear munitions or the nation's strategic deterrent forces. The rigor the system imposes on bomber and missile crews is a source of enormous strength and at the same time its surest safeguard. Our nation is well served by it.

Even though Offutt AFB, home of Headquarters, Strategic Air Command, was only a stone's throw south of Omaha, Nebraska, and thus only 60 miles from where I grew up, I just wasn't sure it was for me. I had come from command of a small unit that had confronted a terrorist threat. Adjustments and innovations were required every day as we invented things "on the fly" to respond to shifting circumstances. That environment "fit" me well. By comparison, SAC's method of doing business seemed unchanging and pro forma.

For the first couple of years, it was like that. Even making a change to the format of a routine document was a hassle. Over the years, the SAC personnel staff had sent quarterly "letters" to wing commanders highlighting recent changes in programs and policies. These epistles were lengthy and written in "personnelese;" some even directed commanders to obscure references in regulations. It was like asking the CEO of General Motors to read the instructions on a carburetor repair kit as part of his daily mail. It was not the sort of service you wanted to provide to some of the busiest people on the planet. I called several wing commanders and, sure enough, few said they read the quarterly letters: they were too long and the language too arcane; they just didn't have time to plow through them.

The next time around, I gathered the staff inputs and wrote short, one paragraph "vignettes" capsulizing each new program or policy. Then, in lieu of the narrative, I used a few "bullet" entries to summarize the key provisions. Most commanders did not want, or need, details beyond that. I included the full-blown policy announcements as attachments so the commanders could simply pass those on to their technical experts.

The approach seemed to make good sense. At least it did to me. It did not, however, to the SAC administrative community and the Deputy Chief of Staff, Personnel. Both were reluctant to make the change: it deviated from the approved official format. In fact, there was no such format in SAC's administrative regulations. Finally, with the intervention of some ex-wing commanders on the headquarters staff, accompanied by my continued supplications, common sense prevailed and we received approval to press on.

Things were not much better on operational issues outside the nuclear arena. In Vietnam, SAC had been involved in conventional war in a major way. B-52s were among the most feared and effective weapons in the conflict. But, since that time the command's emphasis on non-nuclear matters had receded.

I hadn't been at SAC very long when Muammar Qaddafi decided to attack Chad. A few days before, a friend in SAC's intelligence community and I had been talking about Libya. With a smile, my colleague told me that it was his considered professional opinion that "about every six months, Qaddafi goes crazy." He didn't know if it was the phase of the moon or if Muammar periodically neglected his dose of lithium, but whatever it was, the periods of irrationality were almost predictable.

Whatever the reason, the attack met with initial success and a response cell was formed at SAC headquarters. By later standards – indeed, by *any* standard – SAC's participation was minuscule. In a nearby country, we positioned a tanker or two along with some maintenance troops and some carts for the water-injected engines. The tankers' mission was to support a tiny F-15 package sent to the area as a show of force deterrent and to be available as needed. As it turned out, Chad's regulars and irregulars, mostly in Toyota pickups with machine guns mounted in the back, were sufficient to discourage Libya's incursion.

What was interesting to observe inside the headquarters was the ponderous nature of the whole business. Nothing about it was *agile*, to coin a phrase too commonly used in later years. Preparations were rough and once the SAC element arrived in-country, communications with the on-scene commander were difficult. A large response cell inside the headquarters was cobbled together. As a member of the response team, but still a "new guy" in SAC, I came away with the impression that the command hadn't had much practice in doing that kind of thing.

That was soon reinforced during "Bright Star," an exercise where SAC deployed a number of planes, crews, and support personnel for an extended stay in Egypt. There in the desert we practiced dropping conventional weapons and did some training with the Egyptian military. As part of the planning group, my modest role included two tasks. First, my crew helped with the deployment processing from various SAC bases. Second, we built a brochure for deployed personnel. The booklet drew from inputs around the staff and included, for example, information from the medics about buddy care, immunizations, preventative medicine, and health issues in the desert environment. Chaplain, JAG, supply, and other "chapters" were included and I inserted a couple of extra items – maps and a synopsis of Egyptian history and customs – that played well with the troops.

The exercise director asked us to put the book together the first day the group met. Two days later, he seemed nonplussed when I handed a printed document to him complete and coordinated through the staff. The overall run-up to the exercise was lengthy and cumbersome. He was apparently surprised to have something done quickly. Conversely, I was surprised that more was not. In the terrorist environment, turning things quickly had by necessity become fairly routine. That was not the prevailing mindset in the headquarters. Non-nuclear issues were a long way from achieving parity in the SAC community.

That attitude changed quickly, thanks to the next two "CINCSACs" (Commanders-in-Chief, Strategic Air Command). Generals Larry Welch and Jack Chain had the foresight to realize that the shape of the world was changing. While the Cold War was certainly not over, other influences were altering the way the nation needed to train, configure, and employ its armed forces. The new landscape required different capabilities. SAC would provide one of the most significant: quick response, long range, massive conventional firepower.

Welch and Chain were two of the smartest people I've met. Their personalities were totally different. Welch was cold, austere, articulate, brilliant: perfectly formed sentences flowed into perfectly formed paragraphs on issues as arcane as the nation's nuclear war plan and officer assessment. Unlike Welch, Chain was not an intellectual. He was ebullient, a fiery leader and an inspiring speaker. Placed in a room full of people, in thirty minutes he would have met all of them and remembered their names. I once overheard a four-star at a different base disparage Chain as "charming" – the word was said with a sneer – but his gift for interacting with people, whether in sessions with Congress or with young people deciding whether to make the Air Force a career, served the command and the Air Force very well.

Both generals placed enormous importance on staffing the organization with good people. The quality of the officers filling key Deputy Chief of Staff positions throughout the headquarters improved by orders of magnitude. Sitting as an along the wall observer in senior staff meetings, it was obvious that every chair around the main conference table was filled with a more capable individual than the one who had occupied it previously. Welch and Chain were very good at what the civilian world would call "executive development." For several years before they came to the command, SAC officers had not done particularly well when competing for promotions to general. Beyond that, less than impressive numbers of the ones who were selected progressed on to the very top grades.

That situation changed. Chain constructed a plan for moving gifted officers through challenging positions that tested and, for those who succeeded, groomed them for higher stations. It was masterfully done. When General Welch moved on to become Chief of Staff of the Air Force, many observers believed that the general officer corps he built around him was the best the service had seen.

When they finished, even the base itself looked different. What General LeMay, SAC's legendary early leader, inherited as his headquarters was an old cavalry post called Fort Crook. Rechristened as Offutt AFB, LeMay worked long, hard, and successfully to rehabilitate and modernize the old fort. It was not an easy task. When the command first moved to Offutt, there was a large stock yard nearby. Even LeMay, a man not noted for his humor, wryly commented that the feed lot lent a distinct aroma to the place when the wind was in the right – or wrong – direction.

LeMay's upgrades now had some years on them and his successors, strained often by leaner budgets, placed less priority on maintaining the base's infrastructure. Even some of my civilian neighbors commented on how shoddy the place looked to them as they traveled past the front gate on Highway 75.

Within a year of Welch's arrival, the same friends were complimenting Offutt's new appearance: buildings repaired and freshly painted, historic areas restored. The entire base looked trim and neat.

The emphasis continued when Chain took over. Both generals sought to make the base a place befitting SAC's importance; so special that Air Force people would seek it out as an assignment and take extra pride in a "SAC tour." Helped by a remarkable group of local benefactors and Omaha businessmen, they succeeded in transforming Offutt into a marvelous blend of past, present, and future. The place sparkled.

The Welch-Chain tandem revitalized SAC. The tempo was upbeat, exciting. Every part of the staff got caught up in re-vectoring the command's mission toward major conventional capability. Welch was a devotee of Tom Peters' book *A Passion for Excellence*, so barriers to change and initiative vanished overnight. Outside of nuclear matters, a no holds climate of innovation took root command-wise. It was a fun place to be.

It was a surprise as well as a great privilege to be able to see much of this up close and personal. General Welch brought with him the concept of a small, special staff group that worked directly for him. I joined the two original members and worked for him for three or four months before he moved on to become Air Force Chief of Staff. General Chain kept the group intact, and when the original leader departed soon after to become a wing commander, I was tabbed to lead it.

I was flattered to be chosen. I sometimes wondered why: I was still fairly new to the command and did not have an operational background in it. Maybe General Chain just wanted an ex-farm boy too naïve to be anything but straight with him. The staff group was, in fact, a "sounding board" on issues where the boss wanted a non-parochial second opinion. We led projects that cut across staff lines or where the CINC for whatever reason chose not to assign it within the main staff group. It was intense, fascinating duty. I found myself dealing with a constellation of diverse issues and questions from the CINC: "depressed trajectory launch" possibilities by Soviet submarines; a "Spouse Sponsorship" program for the spouse of SAC members being transferred between SAC bases; an analysis of headquarters manning as a prelude to shifting slots from the headquarters to operational units.

Projects like those were enough to keep the three members of the group off the streets at night, but we also helped prepare the command's policy statements and wrote the CINC's speeches and briefings. It was intriguing to hear words the small group had put on paper being spoken to audiences as diverse as Congress, Foreign Affairs Councils, and Chamber of Commerce gatherings. In front of the "right" audiences, Chain was a forceful, emotional speaker, so we developed a basic "Red, White, and Blue" speech for Chamber of Commerce-like programs that we could ratchet up or down depending on the technical background of the audience members.

The abilities and backgrounds of the staff group trio complemented one another very well. Chip Franck was a SAC pilot with a Harvard PhD in Economics and extensive work in military history, nuclear policy, and international relations. Dave Nolting had a PhD in math. A SAC missileer, he became our best researcher and analyst. My background was more eclectic, so I was dangerous in several areas: commander-specific issues, personnel and other "support" matters, history, unconventional warfare and other cats and dogs. Together, the three of us formed an effective team.

For speeches to Chamber of Commerce groups and other "pep rally" type venues, we sometimes incorporated comments others had made about SAC into the CINC's remarks. We discovered that adversaries and allies alike had said some marvelous things.

- A statement attributed to Nikita Khrushchev: "I'm afraid of only two things: God and the Strategic Air Command."
- Lord Tedder, Marshal of the Royal Air Force, in a speech to the House of Lords: "For nearly a hundred years wars were prevented from spreading and world peace was kept by a very effective deterrent – the British fleet in being. Those days are over but there is no doubt that in recent critical years the peace has been kept by a new deterrent – the American strategic bomber force and its atomic weapons."
- A Rand Corporation report summarizing the outcome of discussions with captured Viet Cong: "Fear of B-52 attack seems to be widespread and not confined only to the areas that have experienced them. The B-52s were described as being the most devastating and frightening weapon used so far against the Viet Cong and were said to have great effect on Viet Cong morale."
- General Westmoreland: "When in contact, the enemy tries to hug our units to escape the supporting fires. And we know from talking to many prisoners and defectors that the

enemy troops fear B-52s, tactical air, artillery, and armor, in that order."

- Admiral Thomas Moorer, Chairman, Joint Chiefs of Staff: "This Command (SAC) enjoys the worldwide reputation of being the ultimate in professionalism and readiness and it has set the standard for all other military organizations in the world."

The longer I was in SAC the more I came to realize that Admiral Moorer's words and legions of similar ones correctly described the command and its extraordinary reputation. It was a privilege to be part of an organization so influential in keeping Americans alive and free.

When orders came for a follow-on assignment, it was crystal clear that writing a letter would have been yet another mistake. Now, far from complaining about being assigned to SAC, I was reluctant to leave it.

R & R

A MORAN STORY: THE

PAINLESS VETERINARIAN

The Foreign Legionnaire trekked for many miles across the desert to see a veterinarian in a town at the edge of the Sahara. Despite his out of the way location, the French veterinarian had an international reputation for curing hopeless cases that had baffled even the most renowned of his colleagues.

It was his fame as a healer of large mammals that had not responded to any other form of treatment – "lost causes" beyond hope of recovery – that brought the Legionnaire hurrying to see him. The problem concerned a much beloved camel. With great emotion, the Legionnaire explained that the creature was incredibly brave and had carried him through several battles, once even saving his life. The Legionnaire wept as he told the vet that the animal was lethargic, refused to drink, and was slowly withering away. His loss would be irreplaceable; he meant so much to all the people in the fort – in fact, over the years he had become the mascot of the entire Legionnaire unit.

The soldier became increasingly despondent as he described the animal. "You are our last hope," he told the veterinarian.

They talked for a few minutes more before the Legionnaire shook hands and got up to leave. "I have only one stipulation," he said as he headed for the door, "whatever therapy you employ must be painless. The Legion has a reputation to consider; we recruit from all over the world and the animal means so much. I must insist that the treatment be devoid of pain."

"Mon Dieu, hie hunderstan'," said the veterinarian, "Hie would 'av eet no ozzair way." (Moran in his most flamboyant French accent.)

As soon as he could break away, the veterinarian traveled to the Legionnaire fort and was taken immediately to see the camel.

The situation was exactly as had been described to him. The camel was completely rigid and unmoving. Despite coaxing and the efforts of attendants to make him drink, the animal refused to accept any liquid. Time was running out.

"For God's sake man, you must help him!" The Legionnaire was frantic. "You must save him, but I must have your word that the cure will be painless."

Quietly confident, the veterinarian set immediately to work. He gave orders for the camel to be transported to a nearby water trough. The animal stood beside the tank with a glazed expression, completely still and oblivious to all that was going on around him.

Moving quickly, the veterinarian instructed the attendants to hold the camel's head in the water, then went around and crouched between the animal's back legs. He reached into his medical kit and extracted two bricks. Taking a brick in each hand and swinging with every ounce of strength he could muster, he slammed the bricks together against the camel's testicles.

The camel's eyes opened wide with surprise and as he gasped for breath and opened his mouth to bellow with rage, he swallowed gallons of water. The animal went berserk, bucking, kicking with his two front legs, then his two back legs, then alternately with all four legs, rolling over, sliding along the ground, banging his head against a tree, before finally making several laps at tremendous speed around the perimeter of the fort.

The veterinarian observed quietly and nodded his satisfaction.

The Legionnaire was livid. Too furious to speak, he shouted incoherently "Y-y-y-you, you SONAFABITCH!"

The veterinarian was surprised. "Jus' a minute," he said, "what are you upset about? You 'ad a camel zat wouldn't drink and couldn't move. 'Ee jus' drank 'alf a tank of water and now 'ee ees running aroun' ze fort so fast zat you can't see 'eem for ze dust 'ee ees raising. Hie 'av cured 'eem."

"You sonofabitch," the Legionnaire snarled, seething with anger and hardly able to restrain himself, "you promised me the cure would be *painless!*"

"Eet was painless," replied the veterinarian, "ze only time eet ever 'urts ees when you get your fingairs caught between ze bricks."

EAGLES

The Readiness Center

Lieutenant Colonel Jim Ermis stood beside me in the Readiness Center as we watched the opening strikes of *Desert Storm*. It was quiet as the thirty or so people in the room stared transfixed at CNN's coverage of the maelstrom forming in the skies over Baghdad.

We had "stood up" the readiness operations at the Air Force Military Personnel Center on August 4, 1990, not quite two full days after Iraq invaded Kuwait. Almost instantly, the place became a 24-hour a day beehive of unremitting activity. The building's main conference room had been converted in a much altered form into our readiness ops center. The facility's original function was now fully disguised by the maps, clocks, and status boards affixed to the walls and by the banks of telephones, planning tables, message books, manning documents, directives, computers, and other accoutrements of a space age Air Force arrayed across the breadth of the room.

Now, on the evening of January 17, 1991, at Randolph AFB, Texas, the waiting was over. That relief, I think, was the most prevalent feeling although there were several other emotions as well. Certainly there was a sense of suppressed excitement in the room as the TV image presented the drama to us in real time. The sentiment was intermixed with tempered uncertainty about what the future might bring and concern about good friends traveling in harm's way. But most of all at the moment, there was relief: now, after six months of buildup and tension, the waiting was over. Underlying all of this was confidence, and pride, and conviction. Saddam had sown the wind; he was about to reap a whirlwind.

I was mid-way through a second tour at the Air Force Military Personnel Center at Randolph AFB, on the northeast edge of San Antonio. Sixteen years previously, I had been a young captain in the Plans, Programs, and Analysis Directorate (later, the name was changed to "Personnel Operations," a more descriptive title.) Now, as a colonel, I was back as its Director. As a captain, my desk sat by a window. Now, as a colonel, my office was a few steps away in an interior room. I told anyone who would listen that during the intervening decade and a half, my career progress had been 15 feet and I'd lost access to a window!

If anything, the "Taj Mahal" looked even more exotic with the passage of time and the appearance of the already beautiful base was further served by the advent of a new clinic, new Base Exchange, and other projects that preserved the architectural style of the original "Randolph Field" while modernizing its facilities.

Years before, Nita and I talked idly – more conversation than dream, more rumination than possibility – about what it would be like to live in one of the marvelous old houses that sat shaded from the sun on broad, tree-lined streets laid on in concentric circles in the interior of the base. Now, we were privileged to find out.

29 Outer Octagon: what a neat place to live. It was clearly a 1930s home – small rooms, non-existent closet space, but with a great sun porch and family area. We delighted in it and in a shared sense of the history of the home and officers and families that lived there before us. 1930s it may have been, but it was built to last; I had to use masonry bits to drill into the cement walls just to hang pictures in the living room! Of all the 14 places we have lived and the dozens of places we have visited or stayed at in transit, Building 555 ("triple nickel") – 29 Outer Octagon – on Randolph AFB remains one of our favorites.

Jim Ermis was one of eight division chiefs who worked for me in Plans, Programs, and Analyses. As chief of the Readiness Division, Jim ran the day to day operations of the Readiness Center. I doubt that anyone has done it better. A medically grounded F-4 pilot, he knew the operational side of warfighting as well as the "support side" human resources business. Plus, he was inexhaustible and one of the most determined individuals I've ever met. I'm glad he was on our side.

Jim and I stood there watching the coverage for awhile. Another set was turned to NBC and soon, as the cameras showed F-15s launching, Tom Brokaw made some observation about "young Americans in those cockpits." And, of course, that brought it all home. Whatever those kids needed we'd do for them. Whatever their commanders asked for, we'd get for them. Everyday, throughout *Desert Storm*, that's what we did. It was one of the most intensely busy but fully satisfying periods of my life.

To support the commanders and accommodate the around the clock operations, the peacetime readiness staff was augmented by 220 technical experts from every function in the Air Force Military Personnel Center: officer and enlisted assignments, promotion, casualty notification, awards and decorations, personal affairs, chaplain, medics, and many others. Wizards that managed 200 enlisted specialties handled "filler replacement" requests from deployed units. On the officer side, every specialty was represented. Fighter, bomber, tanker, reconnaissance, and airlift "resource managers" had especially important places at the table in day to day operations. Additionally, there was a sizable administrative function set up to prepare and transmit messages and to receive and follow-up on the more than 25,000 "action items" that flowed through the Center during the course of the conflict. Communications were intense and constant with our policy-making colleagues in the Pentagon, with major command headquarters around the world and with embedded specialists in the field.

Somewhere in the distant past some staff officer had probably received a medal for inventing the acronym "PERSCO" to cover "Personnel in Support of Contingency Operations." PERSCO's were tiny teams that moved with Air Force units to take care of the human resources business in deployed operations. Generally, whenever there were pockets of Air Force people, there was a PERSCO team. Occasionally, the "team" was only one person; typically, it was three to five. In the rare instance where greater numbers were required, the pre-packaged teams, along with their configured "kits," were combined into larger elements. Teams were dispatched on the first planes to Southwest Asia under the plans for *Desert Shield/Desert Storm* and adjusted for size and location as conditions changed. PERSCOs were the eyes, ears, and voice of the human resources manager in deployed operations. They were invaluable.

PERSCO operations formed one of the first lessons of the Gulf War. All the prior planning focused on PERSCOs performing three main tasks: strength accounting, casualty reporting, and force accountability. Strength accounting – keeping track of the forces at hand – was, of course, vital to the commander for warfighting purposes. In recent years, the area was increasingly in the spotlight for another reason as well. Congressional oversight -- micromanaging to the point where, for example, our strength accounting had to ensure that at any one time there were no more than 70 Air Force people on the ground in Honduras – placed a premium on timely and accurate reporting. Casualty reporting was an obvious and essential requirement. Force accountability meant maintaining the structure, providing the fillers, and sustaining the flow of replacements to the deployed units.

Everyone realized how important those three functions would be. Before deployment, what was not anticipated was the strong desire of commanders and troops to sustain full blown human resources operations in the field. It was quickly obvious that deployed troops wanted a "mini personnel office" where everything from performance reports to skill upgrades to follow-on assignments to eligibility for Good Conduct Medals would be managed on site.

No doubt the six-month ramp up to action contributed to the demands for additional services – lots of units sat in lots of desert locations for extended periods – but the point was well taken. We found that we could indeed structure PERSCOs to be "mini personnel offices," and we quickly did so. Mostly that was due to the superb people assigned to the teams who promptly expanded their roles and took on new duties. We sent copies of regs and forms on computer disks, wired the tiny teams to technical experts at headquarters, and made it work in a fairly seamless fashion.

The readiness center eventually oversaw the transfer of 65,000 Air Force people to Southwest Asia and other locations in support of *Desert Shield/Desert Storm*. Once the units were in place – sometimes even before – a major task was to respond to commanders' requests for additional personnel or filler replacements. Many of the initial filler queries spoke in a broader sense to the climate of the times in which modern military services operate. For example, early on we "sourced" heavy, repeated requests for firefighters, cooks, and rapid runway repair technicians. Finding them was not always an easy chore: so many of these functions had been contracted out or "civilianized" that the pool of military people available for deployment was often quite small. Similarly, the irony could not be escaped that often a deployed commander's first call for assistance was for public affairs troops to help handle the media.

Some specialties, such as intelligence technicians, were at a premium throughout the conflict. Others bubbled up spasmodically depending on real world experience. Senior NCOs in fuels specialties were shorted in the original planning. When units actually put feet on the ground and began operations, it became apparent that more were needed. That type of situation was to be expected. Nothing in the planning, practice, and wargaming had prepared the nation to transfer 660,000 people – the population of Oklahoma City, along with all the attendant skills and vehicles needed – half way around the world ready to fight in such a short period of time. All in all, it was nicely done.

Making it happen necessitated a multitude of "workarounds" and inventing things on the fly. The "real world" prompted an avalanche of "firsts." "Stop Loss" was invoked, prohibiting service members with established dates of retirement or separation from exiting the service. Statutory "Recall Authorities," mobilizing reservists and calling back members of the inactive reserve were exercised by the Secretary of the Air Force as well as the President. Retirees with special skills were recalled for the first time in decades. The Civil Reserve Air Fleet was activated and the civilian airliners and crews helped immeasurably in flying the Oklahoma City-sized equivalent to the Gulf.

Problems popped up and lessons were learned almost every day. For some actions, operating a full "mini personnel office" in a deployed environment posed unique challenges. For example, keeping commanders informed of major events affecting their troops was not always easy. Like other services, the Air Force reserves the right of first notification to the commander of a person being promoted. That means the promotion lists and information about them must be kept "close hold." That is tough to do on a main base personnel office; it is ever so much more difficult when the "personnel office" is a tent in the desert.

One of the first major surprises that *Desert Shield* brought in the human resources area was that the computer systems of the active duty, Air Force Reserve, and Air Guard components were not fully compatible. The files that contained essential personal data and information on skills and experience would not automatically transfer to build composite data bases as we melded people from all three sources into combined units. Some splendid computer technicians working non-stop eventually gave us that integrated system capability. Until that happened, an equally superb group of people – many of them secretaries volunteering their own time – "fat fingered" the required mountains of data into the system and did so on such a timely basis that the overall effect was transparent to decision makers.

Similarly, when statutory recall authorities were invoked, plans, procedures, and computer routines were premised on activating entire reserve units en masse. Instead, we found that sometimes we did not need an entire unit but rather only certain people or skills within it. Here too, initially the automated system had no capability for activating only portions of units. Again, we manually input the data until we could make the system work.

Each seemed a difficult problem at the time. All were quickly and thoroughly overcome. That it worked so well was a tribute to our colleagues at the Pentagon, in headquarters and personnel offices around the Air Force, and to the kids on the small teams in the desert.

When *Desert Storm* was over, I had special certificates created for all the people that had supported the readiness center operations. Overall, we presented well over three hundred of them. All were deserved; all were important. I was especially proud to give certificates to so many civilian secretaries who gave of their time around the clock to enter data that was essential to our operations. Every one of them had volunteered, saying they "just wanted to help" or "just wanted to be part of it."

When I have returned to San Antonio and to the Air Force Military Personnel Center over the years, I invariably glance into that room. It has, of course, long since been transformed back to its original function: it is once again a conference room. The pristine appearance and serenity of the place belie the intense activity and the importance of what took place there over those difficult months a decade and a half ago – although that is the picture I always carry in my mind.

I've always thought that a plaque on the wall or some similar commemorative marking the spot might have been appropriate. But, in the big scheme of things it is enough to know that what we did there was very important and that we did it very well.

"No One Ever Tried So Hard": The Search for Heidi Seeman

Although this story transcends purely military issues, it illustrates an aspect of military life that I especially admire. In the best military units there is a sense of "oneness," a warmly enfolding bond that encompasses not only those who wear the uniform but their families as well. Simply put, the people in these organizations take care of one another. There is a mutual sharing of highs and lows, triumphs and tragedies, organizational and individual, personal and professional.

Each of the Services share this ethic and conviction. I suppose that all have expressions that address this feature of military life. In the Air Force, its essence is captured by the phrase, "The Air Force Takes Care of its Own."

The saga chronicled here began with one special unit trying to take care of one of its own: a tiny girl abducted in a major metropolitan area. As events unfolded, almost magically the example it set and the leadership it provided inspired an entire American city.

/////

To the hundreds who labored there during that August more than a decade ago, the small fire station on the northeast outskirts of San Antonio will always remain a place with special memories. They recall it as the scene of intense activity and high drama and the setting for a most unusual story – a story of how from the deepest tragedy there emerged something rather extraordinary: the "coming together" of an entire major American city in an unprecedented outpouring of emotion and support. For several days in early August 1990, the little building on a semi-rural section of Judson Road was the busiest place in Texas, the headquarters for the largest search in the state's history. Conducted over a 1200 square mile area in and around the city, the search involved more than 6,500 volunteers on foot patrols, as well as horses, ultra-light aircraft, all-terrain vehicles, helicopters, and the Civil Air Patrol. Scores of Air Force people and countless numbers of individual citizens, scout troops, fire departments, service clubs, mounted posse units, and law enforcement agencies took part, all looking for one little girl.

Heidi Seeman was the eleven year-old daughter of Curtis and Theresa Seeman. Her father Curt, an Air Force Master Sergeant stationed at Randolph Air Force Base, worked for me in the Directorate of Plans, Programs, and Analysis at the Air Force Military Personnel Center. Heidi was an avid reader of Nancy Drew books, jumped rope with the Foot Notes, a club at Stahl Elementary School, and was an especially well liked member of the school's bus patrol. A search flier, one of the thousands posted in public places all around San Antonio, described her as being 4' 10" tall and weighing 70 pounds. She had light brown hair and green eyes. Indeed, years later it is the marvelous eyes and the delightful smile, recalled from the picture on the flier, that many of those involved in the search remember most of all. The flier described the clothes she was wearing and the small white and turquoise bag she was carrying. The contents of the bag befitted those of an eleven year-old who had spent the night at a nearby friend's house: a night gown with a bear on it, a toothbrush, and two cassette tapes, one by Bon Jovi.

On Saturday, August 4, 1990, at about 11:55 in the morning, Heidi was walking home after spending the night with her friend. The Seemans lived less than a mile away in the High Country II area of San Antonio, and the two girls decided to walk part way together. Heidi's friend went halfway with her, then said goodbye and began walking back to her home. Both had noticed a small red car with a white stripe drive past them several times as they strolled along Stahl Road. Soon after they split up, Heidi's friend looked back but did not see either Heidi or the red car.

The search began on a small scale almost immediately. When Heidi failed to return, neighbors from the close knit group in the Seeman's cul de sac quickly began looking around the housing area and along the road where Heidi and her friend had walked. Some jumped in cars and vans and drove through the neighborhood looking for the suspicious red car. This small first step, beginning with a few hopeful friends and neighbors, would soon be transformed into a massive, community-wide endeavor.

The effort began growing the following morning, when the search was joined by large numbers of volunteers from the Air Force Military Personnel Center. When a colleague of Curt's called to tell me of Heidi's disappearance, I ran a "telephone recall" of people in the directorate, asking that if possible, they contribute to the search. The recall and the request were probably academic. Some were already on their way to the search and many had learned of Heidi's disappearance through telephone contacts with co-workers. As the numbers continued to grow and expand far beyond the people in Curt's immediate organization, hundreds were drawn to the search throughout the day. It became clear that a work site and an organization of some sort would be necessary to make effective use of the surprising, almost overwhelming, numbers who were coming to help.

By mid-day on the first Sunday, a "command post" site was located: the Fox County Volunteer Fire Station not far away on Judson Road. Close to the Seeman home, the station became a central point for volunteers to arrive, congregate, and receive assignments. For the next several days, the white frame one-story building with the crushed rock drive way would be the hub for around the clock activities involving hundreds of people.

Leadership soon emerged from among the people assigned to Curtis Seeman's organization at Randolph AFB. Colonel George Greenwood, Lieutenant Colonel Tom McFarland, and Major Robert Eric Duncan had major roles from the outset. I tried to serve as the group's "fourth musketeer" during times I could break away from my duties as Director of the Personnel Readiness Center at the Air Force Military Personnel Center (Saddam Hussein had invaded Kuwait two days earlier). Soon after, as the community effort deepened, businessmen and city officials became actively engaged as well.

Given the background of the leadership group, it was not surprising that the command post came to resemble a military organization. A Personnel Section logged in volunteers, organized search teams, provided instruction sheets, and appointed search team leaders. Intelligence debriefed returning teams and passed on recommendations to the Targeting Section which identified areas to be searched, assigned priorities, and kept track of the areas covered (not an easy task in a search that eventually encompassed more than 1000 square miles). Logistics arranged the transportation of search teams to and from the field, and provided food and water for the volunteers. Logistics also handled the mountains of food, water, and soft drinks donated by grocers, convenience stores, pizza parlors, and fast food restaurants – as well as the sandwiches, cookies, and snacks brought in by caring individuals who just wanted to help in some way – in gestures of support that continually astonished search participants. The printing of fliers, so critical to the search effort, was also a Logistics responsibility. A Security Liaison worked with the FBI, the Air Force Office of Special Investigations, and the several police jurisdictions involved in the case. The Information Section conducted daily briefings and assisted the throngs of media representatives who visited the site and did a remarkable job of informing the public about search activities. Lastly, there was a small First Aid Section to tend to sunburns, insect bites, scrapes and scratches.

During the first day, a plan was developed which guided the staff's efforts throughout the search. The idea was to initially focus on areas close to the abduction site and then expand the search in an outward spiral, each day sending teams further out into new areas. As a continuing "double check," teams systematically returned to areas previously searched. Specific attention went to sites that surfaced in any tips or leads.

Additionally, areas of especially high concern, such as vacant lots and deserted roads, were designated for search every day

By Sunday night the basic command post structure was in place and search patterns based on the plan had begun. By the time the last teams returned late that night, all public areas near the abduction site had been searched as well as 2,700 acres along Judson Road, a major access route through the area.

Even at this early stage, search leaders began to notice something unusual and unexpected: sizable numbers of concerned citizens who did not know the Seemans and had no affiliation with the military were arriving at the search site. They were but the initial surge of the hundreds of residents of San Antonio who soon came to help. Adopting a work schedule which would later be offered by several businesses and labor unions, employees at the Air Force Military Personnel Center who wanted to help with the search were given an afternoon off to participate.

The effort that had begun on a quiet Saturday afternoon with a small stream of eager, but mostly unguided, friends and neighbors turned into a flood of volunteers from the Air Force base and throughout the city, each assigned specific tasks and search areas. On one representative day during the first week, more than 1200 volunteers showed up at the fire station to help look for Heidi. Twenty-six search teams patrolling on foot, 30 horseback riders, dog teams from the San Antonio Police Department and other jurisdictions, two volunteer fire departments, the Texas State Guard, 150 private off-road vehicles, a squadron of ultra-light aircraft, and two private planes scanned a 50 square mile area on the northeast side of the city. The FBI also joined the search, eventually signing eight agents to the case.

Two important initiatives quickly followed. Saturday, August 11, was designated "Find Heidi Day" in San Antonio. Citizens were asked to spend at least an hour scouring their neighborhoods for any clues. An estimated 300,000 did so, including the mayor and members of the San Antonio Spurs basketball team. Sunday, August 12 was named "Take Heidi to Church Day." City officials asked San Antonio residents to "in spirit, take Heidi to church and pray for her" during their worship services. Almost all local churches participated; sixty distributed small bookmarks with a biblical verse that spoke to Heidi's return. Meanwhile, "I'm Looking for Heidi" buttons – donated by local vendors – fliers, and yellow ribbons were handed to shoppers at malls throughout the city.

Many of these initiatives were inspired by Tom McFarland, an innovative, brilliant leader. When Tom's abilities were melded with George Greenwood's intensity and organizational talent, the resulting combination of skills was truly formidable. Each activity had a specific focus. The fliers, buttons, bookmarks, and yellow ribbons were meant to increase awareness and keep Heidi in the public's consciousness. "Find Heidi Day" was aimed at involving the community in a comprehensive way. "Take Heidi to Church" was an appeal to conscience: the hope that someone who knew or suspected the abductor might come forward. Finally, there was a monetary appeal as well. The list of reward donors reads like a litany of San Antonio businesses: grocery chains, service stations, fast food outlets, hotels, and many more. Contributions to a reward fund began almost immediately and eventually totaled tens of thousands of dollars.

Nine days into the search, the size of the effort outgrew the small fire station. Operations were moved to a donated space in a nearby mall as efforts continued unabated.

During the hot, grueling days of 6:00 AM to darkness searches there were occasional minutes of amusement and hours of human drama. Those among the searchers who found that humor helped cope with the bleakest moments had reason to smile when George Greenwood, an imposing colonel, set out to search after widely proclaiming the virtues of his go-anywhere, do-anything all-terrain vehicle -- and immediately got stuck not far from the command post. The smiles got wider when another colonel – me -- had to hop up and down on the back bumper to free the vehicle.

For the thousands directly involved, participating in the search meant living through a roller coaster of emotions. There were cruel rumors, "dead end" leads, and pain inflicted by prank callers.

Through all the distractions the army of volunteers remained hopeful and the search sustained its vitality. Then, on the 25th of August, 21 days after it began, despite the best efforts of legions of caring people the search ended in tragedy. At about 4:30 in the afternoon, in a rugged area of Hays County eight miles from Wimberley, Texas, Heidi's body was found by a rancher as he rode with his son on an all-terrain vehicle. Identification was confirmed and announced late the following day.

It was an especially difficult time for the volunteers working at the search command post that Sunday night. Many had given almost every waking hour – a total commitment of time, energy, and emotion – for the entire three weeks of the search. They had cried and prayed and shared highs and lows and hopes and fears with the Seeman family. Many of the Air Force people involved in the search knew the Seemans personally. Some had gone almost without sleep for several days as they helped with the search while also working greatly extended duty hours as the United States geared up for Operation *Desert Storm*. For them, these were moments of soul-tearing anguish.

Still, the community that had embraced Heidi was not ready to let go. Visitations at the local funeral home drew hundreds. An overflow crowd attended the memorial service at a Randolph AFB chapel. And still the outpouring of support and generosity continued: funeral and mortuary costs were donated; a local airline flew Heidi's grandparents to San Antonio and later returned the entire family to Minnesota, the site of Heidi's interment, at no cost. Countless hundreds of sympathy notes were received from the citizens of a city brought together by one little girl.

The search was over. The grief and the memories of family, friends, and volunteers would remain, but Heidi's story had ended. Or so it may have seemed during those dark hours. But time has brought perspective and clarity: out of tragedy emerged something extraordinary.

The response from the community was so overwhelming and the volunteers, representing a cross-section of people and skills in San Antonio, had formed such a close, effective team that many saw the need to keep the group and the structure intact. Planning began immediately to establish an organization that could be called into action to respond to similar cases. The result was the Heidi Search Center.

Dedicated in an emotional ceremony on September 8, 1990, the Center operates today out of a major shopping mall in San

Antonio. Chartered to provide a place where search efforts can be mobilized and preventive training and education can be offered, the Center has been a continuing success. In recent years, the organization has enhanced its education efforts with visits to schools and presentations to groups of parents, and has expanded its program to include helping locate runaway children, Alzheimer patients, and other missing, at risk adults.

/////

The "command post" fire station on Judson Road looks different now: it seems larger somehow; the driveway is paved and the building is mostly surrounded by homes. At the time of the search a crushed rock road led to the station and in two directions it was at the edge of the inhabited area. It is hard to picture the intense activity that took place there. Other reminders are more visible. There is a plaque at the Air Force Personnel Center commemorating the search and those that participated in it. There are still yellow ribbons, buttons, and bookmarks that so many have kept under glass desktops or elsewhere as mementos of a special time, and of Heidi. And there is, of course, the Search Center, still saving and changing lives — scores of them — as a result of Heidi.

Yet it was the stunning, overwhelming response of the people, the embrace of a city and a major military installation, the thousands who helped, that remain the search's finest legacy. The inscription on the plaque at the Air Force Personnel Center reads "No one ever tried so hard. No one ever cared so much." Those words apply to all of the thousands who took part. No one — military or civilian -- who helped look for Heidi will ever forget.

Operation Fiery Vigil

This is another small story that goes beyond issues of strategy and war-fighting. It is important, though, because it illustrates one of the aspects of military life that makes it unique. In some ways the account chronicled here is the Heidi Seeman story written on a larger tablet. Heidi's was a saga of the care and sustenance an organization provided to one family. The story that follows is about an entire military service working to "take care of its own."

In August 1991, while we were still in the latter stages of reconstituting forces from the Gulf War, danger suddenly threatened from an entirely different source. As if man's inhumanity to man in Southwest Asia were not enough, halfway around the world in the Western Pacific nature exploded on a horrific scale.

With limited warning, Mount Pinatubo erupted in the Philippines. Immediately, Air Force families on Clark Air Base were placed in peril by the mountain's unrelenting fury. With the massive detritus of the explosion – ash, rocks, choking dust – raining down on the base, evacuation began at once. Leaving cars, homes and most worldly possessions behind, carrying only quickly packed suitcases, families were hurried by convoy to Subic Bay. Still under threat, they remained there only momentarily before most were flown to sanctuary bases in the United States.

At the Air Force Military Personnel Center, we "flight followed" the evacuees while making arrangements with bases on the west coast that would receive the influx of returning families. The objective was to have *every* Clark family met by a host family from the receiving base. Hosts would help care for the returnees and shelter them until they moved on to their newly assigned home stations.

The process matched ranks and, where possible, even family sizes and children's ages of Clark evacuees and host families. Thank God for computers. Almost all credit must go to the commanders and project officers on the west coast bases and especially to the volunteer host families who went "above and beyond." They were blue suit guardian angels for people who had lost everything. The solicitous care and the haven they provided worked a healing magic. Many of the families thrown together by this random act of fate remain in touch to this day.

In the meantime, Air Force assignment makers rushed new assignments to Clark personnel to minimize the period of uncertainty and help them get on with planning their lives. Many received their orders soon after stepping off the plane. Existing statutes were invoked to quickly compensate them for their losses.

Altogether "Operation Fiery Vigil" was a plan quickly conceived, rapidly assembled, and masterfully done. Considerations of resources aside, few other organizations would have made the attempt; and for far too many, the idea would simply never have occurred to them.

///*//*

The same general concept applies to traveling the other way. For newly arriving families, especially the ones who have not previously had an "overseas tour," stepping from an aircraft onto foreign soil for the first time can be a daunting experience. To some, it must seem like *everything* is different: language, customs, food, architecture – all layered on top of the normal butterflies associated with a new job, new friends, and a new place to live. Sponsors are always appointed, and the guidance I gave to those representing my organization was that when the newly arriving family came off the airplane "The first thing they need to see waiting at the bottom of the steps is a smiling face in a blue uniform."

Commander, 1141st USAF Special Activities Squadron, Stuttgart, Germany

In the spring of 1992, I "got orders." At the very top of the page in the "Position, Organization, and Station of Assignment" block were printed the words "Commander, 1141st United States Air Force Special Activities Squadron, Stuttgart, Germany." Hallelujah! The message conveyed on that much-handled piece of paper was special indeed:

- In my entire career, it was the only job I asked for that I actually received;
- It was my second quasi-"dream" assignment;
- It was the parent unit of my first – and up to this point, only – real "dream" assignment: Commander, Detachment 9, 1141 USAF Special Activities Squadron at Vicenza, Italy, ten years before;
- It would be my last assignment in the Air Force prior to retirement.

Nita and I had first seen Patch Barracks in Stuttgart more than a decade earlier when we traveled from Italy, where I was a detachment commander, to attend Commanders' Conferences at 1141st Headquarters. Now, it was an extraordinary feeling to be working at the desk where Colonel Bob McCartan, who had recruited me into that job and Colonel Jackie Sikes, who had provided such strong support during the Dozier kidnapping episode, both used to sit. The floor in the commander's office even creaked just the same as it had the first time I reported in. It felt like being "home."

On old maps of Stuttgart, Patch Barracks is labeled as "Kurmaeker Kaserne." The Germans built it in the 1930s as the headquarters of a panzer unit that later spearheaded the invasion of France. Visible still on some of the buildings is the outline of garage-like doors that betray the structures' original functions as tank bays. Rommel was posted here for awhile. The world has turned over many times since then; and it is a positive sign of the new era that during our four and half years there, Rommel's son, Manfred, was the mayor of Stuttgart. He is a delightful gentleman, avidly pro-American, who speaks the Queen's English contaminated with American slang and corrupted by American humor. He is a warm, funny man. For many Americans, one of the highlights of their tours is a visit to his office, where he held weekly open houses for Americans newly assigned to the city.

Eighty percent of the built-up area of downtown Stuttgart was destroyed during the war, the target of repeated, massive bombing raids that struck Porsche, Mercedes-Benz, and other factories that saturate the area. After the war, the remains of those obliterated buildings were transported to a place on the edge of the city – appropriately called "Rubble Hill" – where they were piled into a tall mount, covered with dirt, landscaped with paths and trees, and made into a park. It takes several minutes to walk to the top – there were hundreds of thousands of tons of rubble and the place is really a small mountain – but the trek is worth it because the view from the peak affords a marvelous vista of the rebuilt city. At the very top is a small amphitheater. Protruding through the dirt and the wild flowers are shattered columns and pieces of masonry that once formed the edifices of buildings in pre-war Stuttgart. Swastikas have been exorcised from the circular recesses where they once resided at the top of the columns.

"Rubble Hill" was a frequent destination for my family's walks and bike rides. So was the forested area just behind Patch Barracks. As elsewhere in Germany, the woods are kept "clean" and there are excellent paths, many of them paved. It was one of my favorite destinations after a long day at work. In the middle of the wooded area, reachable only by hiking or bike trail, was a small restaurant that served sandwiches, ice cream, and cold drinks to fellow wanderers through the forest. Those walks, jogs, and bike rides in the woods replenished my soul: I looked forward to them with growing anticipation as the weeks and months went by.

I was not always on hand to enjoy them. The nature of the squadron's business and the far-flung locations from which it operated – north to south we took care of people from Stavanger, Norway to Nairobi, Kenya; west to east from London and Lisbon to Moscow – kept me in the air and on the road much of the time. That experience though – traveling to some of the world's most intriguing places – was for the most part just another form of enjoyment. Oslo, London, Berlin, Prague, Paris, Cairo, Bratislava, Naples, Riyadh, Sarajevo, and dozens of other venues with names both recognizable and unrecognizable where my unit did business were a long way from the cornfields of Nebraska. Not every destination was "fun," or easy, or benign, but all of them were fascinating places to be.

The 1141st was, and is, a one-of-a-kind organization. My job description read:

"**Duty Title:** Commander

"**Key Duties, Tasks, and Responsibilities:** Provides command, administrative and personnel service to 4,200 USAF officers and airmen assigned to major joint and international commands throughout Europe, Africa, and Southwest Asia. Responsive to senior USAF officials of Supreme Allied Powers Europe, North Atlantic Treaty Organization, Allied

Command Europe, Headquarters United States European Command, and Air Force Security Assistance Offices. Functions as the Major Air Command Director of Personnel for joint- and internationally-assigned Air Force members. Supports 28 general officers including 3 four-stars. Exercises Uniform Code of Military Justice jurisdiction over assigned personnel. Functions as a wing-equivalent commander with budget, finance, disciplinary, and other command responsibilities."

Those attuned to military mindsets will understand how that structure caused gas pains for our brethren – there are many – who prefer "one size fits all" types of military organizations. In different slices of its responsibilities, the unit has characteristics of a squadron, wing, and major air command operation. The reality of it – and this should be the real measure of merit – is that organization functions with enormous success in one of the military's most unusual and difficult support environments. The more than 4,000 Air Force people supported by the squadron and its ten detachments are at 250 locations. The contrasts are extreme. The largest groups, about 350 people at each place, are at Supreme Headquarters Allied Powers Europe (SHAPE) at Mons, Belgium, and Allied Forces Southern Europe (AFSOUTH) in Naples, Italy. The smallest are a considerable number of "onesy-twosy" situations with attaches, trainers, or isolated blue suiters in tiny "joint" (more than one U.S. military service represented) or "international" (U.S. forces intermixed with other allied forces in parent organizations such as NATO) units. The "1141st" provides a national-blue suit "home" for Air Force men and women assigned to these outfits. During the 50 years of its existence, the "touch" the squadron has developed for handling isolated units – "no organization has ever done it better" one of many citations reads – and working with unique international forms and requirements is marvelous to behold. Different indeed is its structure. Looks aside, it serves our people well.

The latter consideration has been what has preserved it over the years. Because it "looks different" as a one-of-a-kind organization, in every "cut drill" over the years it has inevitably been regarded as low hanging fruit to be plucked for closure or modification. So far, its obvious successes – "Best Customer Support Unit in the United States European Command" ad infinitum – and its legions of supporters, some of whom wear multiple stars, have been sufficient to sustain its existence, if not its name.

In a classic case of "one size fits all," in the mid-1990s a senior Air Force official came down from his office in the Pentagon with the revealed revelation that Air Force units needed to be renumbered so that, for example, all squadrons would have three numbers in their designations. This was a non-concern to the remaining half million members of the Air Force and the cost of reconfiguring computers and changing official documents was not inconsequential at a time the Service's budget was already under stress. Nonetheless, no more "1141st." The designation was first revised to the "641st" and subsequently has changed three times more.

The name change was unfortunate. The "1141st" had a great history, tradition, and reputation. It was one of the most frequently and highly honored support units in the Air Force. The designation evoked the same sense of pride from the youngsters assigned to it as names like the 555th Tactical Fighter Squadron and Strategic Air Command did for those assigned to operational units. What a shame.

Regardless, at the same time the name was changed, the unit won a considerable victory of sorts by making a convincing case for its continued existence. We worked hard to ensure that although the unit would be packaged differently, the traditions, pride, and professionalism of the 1141st would carry forward under the new label(s).

Through much of my assignment, the 1141st had nine detachments: Det 1 at Mons, Belgium (SHAPE Headquarters); Det 2 at Brunssum, Netherlands (Allied Forces Central Europe); Det 3 at Oslo (later Stavanger), Norway (Allied Forces Northern Europe); Det 4 at Naples, Italy (Allied Forces Southern Europe); Det 5 at Izmir, Turkey (Headquarters, Sixth Allied Tactical Air Force); Det 6 at Kapaun Air Station, Germany (Allied Air Forces Central Europe); Det 7 at

Geilenkirchen, Germany (NATO AWACS); Det 8 at RAF Molesworth, United Kingdom (Joint Analysis Center), and Det 9 at Vicenza, Italy (Headquarters, Fifth Allied Tactical Air Force). Detachment 8 had an interesting heredity: when the Shah was in power in Iran, there was a Detachment 8 in Teheran. When that unit got blown away (almost literally -- one of the senior NCOs was assassinated on a street corner), the designation lapsed for a few years until the Joint Analysis Center was built at RAF Molesworth and the Detachment 8 descriptor was assigned to the new unit formed to support it. In addition to the detachments, there were at times three operating locations: Brussels; Daws Hill, United Kingdom; and Rheindahlem Air Base, Germany.

Missions, "personalities," sizes, and situations were different from place to place. So, decidedly, were the physical contrasts. Even after I got used to the smaller, telescoped distances in Europe, I never ceased to be intrigued that, as one example of many, even in the 70 miles from Stuttgart, Germany, to Strasbourg, France, *everything* changed: architecture, cuisine, language, agriculture. Fascinating.

Trips to each of the detachments were always interesting. At Detachment 1 at SHAPE Headquarters in Belgium, the coffee bar at the headquarters building was a kaleidoscope of uniforms: 16 nations (at the time), many represented by all three military services, plus several Partnership for Peace countries. Nita was enthralled by it, all the colors and variety. I loved taking her there.

Norway has, I am convinced, some of the most attractive people on the planet. On one staff visit a group of us went to a restaurant in Oslo for a dinner hosted by the small crew at the local detachment. A young officer and I were trundling up to the salad bar when he saw a particularly striking young lady. "Colonel," he whispered to me, "that's the most beautiful woman I've ever seen." We filled our plates and were wending our way back to our table by a different route when he saw a different blue-eyed blonde in a far corner booth. "No," he whispered again, "*that* one is."

Studying Naples would be a sociologist's dream come true. *Nothing* works: stoplights, garbage pickup, and – often -- lights and water. *Nobody* pays attention to stop signs or stoplights (when they work), or condescends to wait in line. Petty crime is rampant. Yet, Neapolitans were the happiest, most carefree people I met in all of Europe. No one seemed to work particularly hard; at night most of them are out in the streets or in one of the small squares abundant throughout the city. There, they talk, sing, or play cards on benches under the trees or at one of the adjoining sidewalk cafes. In Naples, food and conversation are the staples of life.

The energy of the city comes out at night and is focused on personal relationships, not business or official ones although there is undoubtedly some carryover. It is a Mediterranean custom and lifestyle; there is much to commend it.

One evening, several of us were dining at a very good restaurant when without warning all the lights went out. The waiters did not miss a beat – this happens all the time – they simply brought out their ready supply of candles and continued serving the meal. Even Headquarters, Allied Forces Southern Europe, a place teeming with three- and four-star admirals and generals, is not immune from the foibles of life in Naples. On two occasions during my visits there, the building was without water. Each time the difficulty was of prolonged duration – in Naples, nothing less is expected – so 50 gallon drums of water were brought into the restrooms. That supply, dipped out in long ladles, was used for drinking, washing, and flushing commodes.

When the G-7 Summit was held in the city, the streets were cleaned for the first time in years and for a short while garbage collection occurred on a reasonably systematic basis. During Summit week, even the stoplights worked. Ironically, there were more accidents that week – with *il semaforos* in working order – than there were in the preceding and following weeks when eye contact, gesture, macho games of automotive "chicken" and blatant disregard for rules were what got drivers through an intersection. Neapolitans can't cope with law and order.

My own "adventures" at various hotels in Naples reflected the ambience of life in the city.
- On my first visit, the clothes bar in the closet collapsed, spilling my freshly pressed uniforms onto the floor.
- On my second trip, the seat fell off the commode. Fortunately, when the crash occurred, I only had a foot propped up on it as I brushed the dust off a shoe. Luckily for me, I was not more seriously engaged or I might have been badly hurt.
- On a later trip, early in the morning one of my troops came racing down the hallway in the hotel, in his haste knocking over one of those sand-filled receptacles where smokers snuff out their cigarettes. We had sent him ahead to another colleague's room to awaken that teammate so he could join us for breakfast. Unbeknownst to us, during the night our team member had switched rooms, the one he was assigned to being hot, noisy, and having no water. Then – and this is *so* Neapolitan – the front desk clerk had simply put a later arrival into the same room just vacated by our man. That was the room where my colleague knocked on the door, entered the room (the lock was broken also), and shook the body on the bed he presumed to be that of his friend – only to discover that the occupant was a massive, snarling, Mafioso-looking character who instantly made a threatening gesture, hopped out of bed and began advancing on my diminutive sidekick. That's when we caught sight of our man as he tore past us down the hallway, here and there spilling things on the carpet. We eventually caught up with him in the coffee shop where, after catching his breath, he explained what had happened. I thought my words of advice were particularly sage: "Terry,' I said somberly, "if you go back to your room and there is a horse's head under your sheets, don't wait to pack your suitcase."
- I suppose it could be argued that by the time of my final trip to Naples there were signs of improvement. My team stayed at a newly constructed hotel. Here, the seat did not

fall off the commode ... but that was because *there was no seat on the commode*. Toilet seats and other amenities had not been installed at the time the hotel opened and in typical Neapolitan fashion the decision was made to overlook the minor considerations and open the door to commerce.

There have in fact been serious studies of the Naples lifestyle and the ambience of the place. One researcher soberly concluded that Mount Vesuvius plays an influential role in a Neapolitan's attitude towards life. (Pompeii is really an extension of Naples; Vesuvius is visible from every part of the city.) To wit, the damn thing may blow at any time and take us and everything with it, so don't worry about tomorrow and don't sweat the small stuff – and, by the way, *everything* is small stuff. Whatever it was, I enjoyed the city – and when I could find a place on a hillside sheltered from the sights of uncollected garbage, pot-holed streets, and broken stoplights, the view overlooking the Bay of Naples was extraordinary.

I especially looked forward to trips to our detachment at Izmir, Turkey, because the contrasts were so sharply defined. At the top of a hill is a castle built by Alexander the Great around 330 B.C. From it, a winding road leads down the mountainside into the city. Along that narrow lane on the way down the mountain, everything changes. The landscape, the architecture, even the periods of history ease very gradually into different eras entirely. Near the top of the mountain there is a portion right out of the Middle Ages; a bit further down the hill that melds into an ancient Muslim section with souks, minarets, and open air bazaars; then, at the bottom of the hill near the waterfront resides a glistening, glimmering modern city with Hilton Hotels and neon lights. Even here, though, the street scenes preserve the contrasts. On the sidewalks fully robed Muslim women walk side by side with stunning Turkish girls in the shortest possible mini-skirts. On the broad avenues, the procession is often lead by overloaded donkey carts followed immediately by the latest model Mercedes. Izmir became one of my favorite places.

Molesworth, Great Britain, was also a favorite but for entirely different reasons. There is a steadfastness and tranquility about rural England, a sense of permanence and constancy. Biased by my background, I savored the pastoral landscapes and the small towns. More than that, the place is just *English*. The young officer who commanded the detachment at Molesworth lived in a village near the base. On occasion, Ed Bachl sent me clippings from the town's tiny, once-a-week newspaper. In one memorable issue the editor devoted much of a front page column to fuming over the fact that in that very town *a resident's garden hose had been stolen!* But, the writer reassured his readers, "The constable is in active pursuit."

In Sarajevo and other places, I thought about that column many times. How nice it would be if the extent of our problems – those that warranted front page headlines no less – were bounded at the upper limit by the disappearance of a garden hose.

There was much to enjoy and be proud of at the 1141st. The unit won repeated honors and a "Heritage Hall" dedication ceremony celebrating the unit's long history and many accomplishments was the subject of considerable media coverage. When the Dayton Peace Accords were signed, the 1141st was given the task of supporting Air Force people assigned in Sarajevo and in the British and French sectors of Bosnia-Herzegovina. That was a sizable added obligation for a unit that had only 75 people at the headquarters and another 55 or so scattered through nine tiny detachments. Still, with that small complement of people for the first several months of the deployment, we ran around the clock operations from a readiness center at the headquarters and manned forward operating locations at Zagreb, Croatia, and Sarajevo. In a long history of going "above and beyond," those accomplishments may have been the unit's proudest achievements of all.

Stuttgart became our home for four and a half years. I was asked to "extend" my tour twice. I agreed both times and would have volunteered had I not been asked. I loved the location and the job. With Bosnia visibly heating up, the 1141st was the right place for me to be.

Even now, Nita and I periodically get "homesick" for Stuttgart. Nestled right at the edge of the Black Forest, it is but a stone's throw from some of the most picturesque vistas in Bavaria: King Ludwig's fairy-tale castles, incredible small towns, "half-timbered" houses with flowers exploding from boxes on the balconies, majestic lakes, and snow caps in the Bavarian Alps. Although the "on call" demands of the job too often precluded it, when the job allowed, Nita and I would sometimes hop in the car on a Sunday morning and drive the three and a half hours to Zurich for lunch.

We keep hoping for an excuse to go back to the unit and to Stuttgart if only to visit for awhile. Perhaps one day we'll find one.

Riyadh

Riyadh was still officially on "scud alert," but the scuds had long since stopped flying when I arrived there. I was TDY to the Kingdom visiting a support operation, having just moved to my new job as commander of the 1141st.

The affluence of the place was almost overwhelming. Take my temporary lodgings, for example. Although my visit lasted only a few days and I was rather "small potatoes," I was given quarters larger than my colonel's residence back in Germany: kitchen, living room, formal dining room, two spacious bedrooms, plus den and library. I actually paced it off; it *really* was bigger than my permanent quarters. Brand new furniture, TVs, stereo system, and entertainment centers scattered throughout. Library fully stocked with new editions. They mistook me for someone important.

The downtown vista was dramatic. There is a magnificent appearing building that looks for all the world like an inverted step pyramid. The base is the smallest "step" and then each higher level gets larger as the structure extends skyward. Incredible. Except that it isn't used. After construction, the Saudis found a flaw in the design or a cracked foundation, so now they just turn the lights on at night to add beauty to the skyline. Another tall, modern building also remains vacant because it was found that part of the top floor overlooks a prince's compound.

An entire section of modern apartment complexes has an interesting history. Originally built to house desert tribesmen, the nomads for whom it was intended refused to live there. Block after block of new dwellings stood empty until they were provided to American troops deployed to Riyadh during the Gulf War.

On my group's first night in town we were taken for dinner to a compound on the outskirts of the city. On the way we noticed a late model Mercedes pulled off by the side of the road. It had been involved in a fender bender and it had some modest dings, but it appeared to be in good shape overall. Three nights later we drove past the same spot and saw that the car was still there. When we remarked about that to our driver, he said "The guy probably just left it and went to get another one. It happens all the time."

Sarajevo: Getting Started

It is fitting, I suppose, that just *getting* to Sarajevo was a far – "way far" one of my young sergeants said as we approached the city – from ordinary experience. My team hitched a ride on a Norwegian C-130, climbing aboard at a NATO air base in Germany. The word on the street was that if you needed to get into Sarajevo – or out of it – in a hurry, go with the Norwegians: they fly through anything.

Other than two port holes at the rear, there were no windows in the cabin of the aircraft. In this case, that was okay for there was not much to see. It was late in the evening when we arrived over Sarajevo. In the darkening skies few details were discernible, except that it looked like most of what was down there had been blown apart and scattered as if savaged by a storm of incalculable proportions.

Earlier in the war an Italian aircraft was shot down flying the same pattern, so as we prepared for landing, two crew members positioned themselves by the port holes to watch for tracers or signs of attack. The pilot made an excellent combat approach, essentially flying straight at the ground, then flaring out for landing at the last moment.

We taxied full-speed to the ruined terminal building, and then quickly turned so the rear of the plane faced the destroyed building and the protective berm that surrounded it. The ramp at the back of the aircraft swung down; I grabbed my gear and along with the rest of the passengers made a crouching run to the inviting safety of that sandbag wall.

As I jogged across the tarmac I noticed that the "Welcome to Sarajevo" sign on what was left of the airport terminal building had been mostly shot away. From what I could see of the rest of the city, already that seemed rather fitting. The airport complex was heavily damaged. The control tower was sandbagged, pockmarked with shell holes, and missing most of its windows.

We quickly sorted ourselves out and piled into our three-humvee caravan. The first sign outside the building cautioned that flak vests and helmets were to be worn at all times. The second, near the edge of the protected area on the only road leading from the airport, told travelers in bold letters "DO NOT STOP FOR THE NEXT THREE KILOMETERS." Guidelines required travel by convoy and a minimum of two people per vehicle. All had to be armed and at least one had to carry a "long rifle" (M-16). Soon, after a continued series of sniping incidents the rule was changed to mandate three passengers per vehicle with at least two long rifles. The two lane road traversed important real estate: no man's land, the scene of heavy fighting; the zone of separation between the forces, and Sniper Alley, a long, straight thoroughfare leading into the heart of Sarajevo. We traveled, very fast, into the city with vehicles in trail.

The area from the airport into the southern outskirts was one of the most heavily damaged parts of the city. Residential as well as industrial, before the war the suburb was predominately Bosnian Muslim. Fighting was heavy over a long period and the district was shelled by Serb forces from positions in the nearby mountains. Burned out and bullet riddled hulks of vehicles were pushed – just barely – off the road. Despite an observer's best attempt to sort it out and remember it devastated house by devastated house, the acres of shattered real estate eventually blended into a desperate sameness. Gutted facades with crumbling chimneys marched like an army of skeletons toward the far horizon. What once was a Volkswagon assembly plant sat distorted and mangled by the side of the road. From a distance the twisted girders resembled a hideously deformed roller coaster, long since abandoned and crumbling, devoid of the life and sounds that once energized it.

There was a crazy-quilt pattern to the damaged areas. Entire districts were almost obliterated, yet short distances away other suburbs – usually Serb – were relatively unscathed.

We eventually weaved our way through the sniper barricades and arrived at our temporary quarters. Within a few days, we contracted to rent two floors of a house of a Bosnian family. The place was within a block and a half of the American Embassy and Implementation Force (IFOR) Headquarters. It was in reasonable repair; a mortar round had hit the gate area and taken a chunk out of an exterior wall, but the inside was in good shape. We used the ground floor as office space and the second story as sleeping quarters. By early the next morning, we were in business, dispensing pay and taking care of other matters with Army and Navy colleagues, all of us melded together in an informal "joint" organization that worked remarkably well, as these things often do when they aren't encumbered by egos or hamstrung by Service policies and regulations.

When our three-service operation was up and running, we turned day-to-day supervision over to a sharp young Navy Lieutenant, Dave Hamby, who, along with one of my troops, Air Force Technical Sergeant John Ennema, became legends for taking care of all the troops, regardless of service affiliation, in Sarajevo. Overnight, the small office transformed into a magnet for GIs posted in and around the city and for Embassy personnel as well.

The kids quickly converted a parlor in the residence into an improvised "orderly room" and affixed an American flag to a wall. Other than the one flown from the American Embassy, it was one of the few in Sarajevo and because of the traffic drawn to the place by pay, mail, paperwork, coffee and conversation, it was probably the one most often seen by Americans stationed anywhere near the city.

The house that we rented belonged to a "mixed" Bosnian family: one spouse was Bosnian Muslim, the other, Serb. Inside a universe of hostility, they provided an atom-sized example of affection and cooperation from which others might draw. Within days the young Americans had ingratiated themselves with neighbors up and down the block and at a small café across the street. They were our best ambassadors and the friendships they built were our surest protection.

The Greatest Compliment

There have been countless times in my life when I have been especially proud of the uniform I wore and the country it represented. Some occasions, though, are so completely unforgettable that they carry a special memory all their own. Given all that has happened to our nation in the recent past, events can sometimes delude us into thinking that we are alone and unappreciated in the world. When that feeling strikes me, I find it useful to recall a marvelous moment when I witnessed an individual's gratitude toward America and heard him express it with transcendent beauty.

My small unit was one of the first to arrive in Sarajevo after the signing of the Dayton Peace Accords. A day or two after our arrival, I began making the rounds visiting other units in and around the city.

One of the American communications outfits I went to see had set up in an old Ottoman fort high on a mountaintop overlooking the city. The road to the fort was along a mountain path, barely passable in our humvee. At one point the road squeezed between a sheer vertical drop on the left and a small village on the right. Absolutely pressed against the road, the tiny community was wedged into a miniscule space between the path and the wall of the mountain.

I was riding in the front side passenger seat of the humvee with my arm out of the window. In the arcane reasoning of the military, because we were part of an international force, the national flag emblem was affixed on the right shoulder of our uniforms (not on the left as was normally the case). That meant that the American flag was showing on the sleeve that was nearest the open window.

Especially at the outset, there were many mixed emotions about the mission in Bosnia. But whatever our individual feelings, it became immediately clear that the people who appreciated us most were the very old and the very young. Our presence allowed the old people to live their lives in dignity and the young to play in the sunshine, and both groups were grateful.

As our vehicle inched through the village, two elderly Muslim gentlemen were drinking tea at a small table set right next to the road. We were so close that as we inched by, one of them reached out and touched the flag on my arm and said something to me in very passable English.

I returned his smile and for the rest of the drive, wondered at his words. When I arrived at my quarters I asked about the significance of the expression the old gentleman had spoken. It turned out that he had used an ancient phrase – words with meaning so deep they were reserved for use in his culture only to express the most profound appreciation.

What the old man said when he touched the American flag was "We will love you for a thousand years."

Sarajevo: Trip Reports

Within a few days after the Accords were signed, there appeared small but useful indications that the "comfort level" was increasing. The streets were no longer deserted at night and a few lights were on. Water was available in most places two or three times a day.

But, the killing had gone on too long and passions were too intense for any of this to be "easy." Vehicles remained frequent targets. On our first night in the city, a British soldier was wounded when his vehicle was hit. A French anti-sniper team killed one shooter and arrested another near the destroyed Volkswagon assembly plant along Sniper Alley. There was initial hope that this action would suppress future incidents; but, when vehicles continued to receive fire on succeeding nights, anti-sniper operations were continued. A few days later, a rocket propelled grenade hit one of the headquarters areas and two people were slightly injured when a city bus was fired on. Still -- remarkably, thankfully -- casualties were very light after NATO forces took control.

On my third day in Sarajevo, a U.S. Army colonel invited me and a few others along on a patrol through the surrounding area.

We took three humvees past the outskirts of the city, and then climbed on foot into the hills that enfold Sarajevo's river valley. During the fighting the Serbs had most of the artillery and held much of the high ground. They destroyed entire sections of Sarajevo from fire bases overlooking the city. The mortar and artillery positions were surprisingly close; we moved only a short distance into the hills before finding the first gun emplacements. Trench complexes around parts of the city harkened up images of World War I.

The main roads out of the city, those where there was an IFOR presence, were mostly cleared; but there remained mined areas, marked and unmarked, all over the countryside. The patrol made its way to a gravel quarry that was the scene of intense fighting. There were mined areas on both sides of the narrow road; all the buildings, earth moving equipment, graders, and trucks had been booby trapped. We drove in on a small path, and then backed out carefully, single file, because there was no room to turn around.

Estimates vary regarding the number of mines planted by both sides. Most agree that the number was in the millions. Right next to the road, not a hundred feet from a major headquarters, a French team spent several days removing mines. Many of the devices the Serbs got from the Russians were made of plastic. They are difficult to detect and they are not biodegradable; so, unless they are found and removed, they will be a threat for years to come.

The Army colonel who guided the patrol expressed hope that the locations of some might eventually be exposed by the freezing and thawing cycles of Bosnia's winters. He did not appear optimistic. Some mines were insidiously stacked one on top of another, so a mine sweeping team that disarmed the first mine was placed immediately in jeopardy by a bigger problem lying just underneath.

The Bosnian Muslims, more impoverished than the Serbs and with less access to military equipment, invented "toe poppers" made only of two pieces of wood, a nail, and a small explosive charge – sometimes just a shotgun shell. Those wicked little devices disabled foes by blowing off toes or parts of feet. They were built in countless numbers; they had an unintended side effect: there were lots of three-legged dogs in Sarajevo.

A subsequent trip took us to a portion of the city near the airport that we hadn't visited before. The place looked like the aftermath of a nuclear attack: several square blocks of high rise apartment complexes were absolutely shattered. There was an 800 meter covered trench leading from the gutted apartment buildings under a road out to a small section of the airport that remained usable during the early days of the fighting. The family that owned the house we rented for office space smuggled their daughter out of the city in 1992 using that trench. The daughter carried a few belongings, caught a small plane, and eventually wound up in France where she stayed during the siege. The trench was still visible, still in use. Near the airport, where the fighting was particularly fierce, the trench lines were notable for their numbers, length, and depth.

Still, despite the obstacles, a month later the changes in the city were eye-catching. The firing had mostly ceased. The streets were being cleared, there was a significant amount of vehicle traffic; busses and streetcars were in full operation, people were out and about, the anti-sniper barricades had been removed from major intersections, and new shops and restaurants opened almost every day. The city was coming back to life.

Time, money, and patience would be needed for years to come to resuscitate it completely. Most windows were still covered with plastic wrap. Gas service to homes and apartments was problematical and sometimes dangerous. The pressure was uneven and many outlets had been left open or damaged; there were frequent explosions throughout the city.

There were implausible scenes, the residue of violence imposed on people accustomed to tranquility and landscapes heretofore benign and beautiful. Near the destroyed apartment complexes two elderly ladies hoed a vacant plot of ground. The space was once a playground for the children who had lived in the apartments. Not 50 feet away was a roped off area with warning signs – still seen all around the city – indicating the presence of mines. On the hills overlooking the city there was unexploded ordinance strewn amidst sandbagged gun emplacements and fighting holes.

It was interesting to observe the differences between the population groups. The Serbs generally appeared more sullen and withdrawn. An Air Force officer who had been in Sarajevo the longest said that in his travels through the surrounding Serb communities, he had not yet seen a spontaneous smile. By contrast, the Bosnian Muslims and Croats seemed more upbeat. Conversely, several people who worked most directly with all sides on military issues regarding forces, weapons, and equipment reported that the Serbs were more responsive and reliable in the numbers they provided and the promises they made.

Americans were posted at about a half dozen locations in and around the city including the airport, the ice stadium, a site several miles outside of town built as a venue for the 1984 Olympics, an old Ottoman castle high on a hillside, and a large former telecommunications office. The Allied Rapid Reaction Force headquarters was at a former Olympic hotel complex adjacent to a Serb suburb, and Implementation Force (IFOR) headquarters was situated in central Sarajevo next to the American Embassy.

NATO's presence was everywhere visible. IFOR vehicles traveled streets all over the city; trucks and armored personnel carriers were spaced every few blocks along Sniper Alley. Some of the headquarters facilities looked like World War II revisited: dozens of trucks, tanks and APCs parked around the complex; tents, communications vans, antennae, and camouflage netting all over the Headquarters area. Throughout Bosnia more than 30 nations were involved in the effort to one extent or another. Sarajevo was in the French sector so there were large numbers of French troops as well as British, Italians, Turks, Americans, Scandinavians, and others. It made for some interesting conversations.

On every visit, indeed on every trip around the city, Sarajevo left a kaleidoscope of impressions:
- On several street corners people sold plastic containers of gasoline. Since there were no operating filling stations within miles of Sarajevo, some people made a living hawking one, five, or ten liter cans of fuel.

- The Holiday Inn in Sarajevo: still open for business. Not all of the rooms had windows; some had heavy plastic seals that replaced the broken glass. On the higher floors, easier for Serb gunners to hit, some exterior rooms were entirely shot away; what was left of them was open and exposed to the elements. One eighth floor interior hallway had a gaping hole left by a shell from a heavy caliber weapon.
- On our second trip we were privileged by circumstance to witness an historic occasion: being in Sarajevo on "G+45" (Peace Accord signing date plus 45 days) and watching the barricades between zones of separation being removed. People from both sides queued up at checkpoints waiting to return for their first look at the houses they had left months ago. I wondered at their thoughts. They surely must have felt a jumble of emotions: excitement and anticipation at returning to their homes, tempered by dread of what they might find waiting there.
- At about the same time, another – albeit major -- sign of a city coming back to life: the market that was the scene of a horrendous missile attack that had killed more than 30 people (an event that helped spur the international community's decision to intervene), opened again for business.

Easter Sunday, 1996: a memorable day. Along with a few team members, I took a British Chinook helicopter armed with a 7.62 mini gun to a British headquarters where we ate Easter lunch at a British dining hall. The headquarters, in Gornji Vakuf, was a considerable distance northwest of Sarajevo. The crew flew a combat profile: nape of the earth, fast and low, hugging the sides of mountains, popping up quickly over ridge lines and then immediately down again close to the ground as soon as we had cleared the crest, releasing flares to "spoof" tracking radar for anti-aircraft artillery and SAMs.

After lunch we took care of business with Americans assigned to the headquarters, and went with some Brits to look around the city. Gornji Valkuf was the scene of some of the war's initial combat, and had also been fought over the previous summer (1995) when the opposing forces grasped for advantage prior to a possible ceasefire. The damage was catastrophic: homes, businesses, schools -- the entire inhabited area -- imploded, literally and figuratively, on the central Bosnian plain. Before the war, Croats lived on one side of the major road and Serbs on the other. Now that shared community was a wasteland. During the most recent fighting, a last group of combatants holed up in a building along one of the main streets. It was a Balkan Alamo: more than 100 people were killed defending it. There was hardly a place in the building, inside or outside, unmarked by shell holes. Gornji Vakuf was the scene of the hospital atrocity. It remained a wounded city. The emotions were stunted along with the landscape. It was one of the world's most unhappy places.

The day was not yet over; an interesting event occurred on the way back to Sarajevo while the crew was looking for an alternate low level route because of periodic fog problems on the regular path. A few miles outside of Tuzla, as we popped up over a ridge, a large hawk hit the left center of the rotor housing about three feet above the cockpit. The crew had indulged me by letting me ride in the cockpit with them, so the view was up close and personal. There was no danger to the helicopter, no warning lights or signs of distress, but we turned back to Tuzla to check it out as a precaution. The crew found an impact dent of no consequence and within ten minutes we were airborne again. The new route zigzagged around mountains and brought us right over Sarajevo, fast and low straight down Sniper Alley, looking up at the taller buildings on each side of the street. What a great ride! I told the Brits that it even beat the roller coaster at the Nebraska State Fair. I think years from now I'll be able to tell people exactly what I was doing on Easter Sunday 1996.

/////

On our journey from Germany to Sarajevo, our stay in Zagreb, Croatia was noteworthy in a different way. Our hotel was also occupied by the twelve CEOs who accompanied Secretary of Commerce Ron Brown to Bosnia. All were fatalities when Secretary Brown's plane crashed in Croatia. The entourage had left from Zagreb with plans to return before heading back to the

States. Their rooms were scattered up and down the same hallway where my team was billeted. The evening of the plane crash there were American Embassy and Department of Commerce officials back and forth all through the night identifying, tagging, and bagging personal belongings in each room.

The Commerce Department established a command post in a conference room right across the hallway from us. Members of my group were up most of the night also, helping sort out who would do the casualty reporting and notifications for the Air Force crew members on Secretary Brown's aircraft. We wound up sending one of our NCOs to Dubrovnik to provide on-scene support. A somber occasion: we were ready to move on to Sarajevo.

Putting it all Together

Whenever I moved to a new job, I made it a point to meet individually with everyone in the organization. That was good, but eventually I got smart enough to realize that introducing myself to the unit as a *group* paid dividends as well. There was no better forum for sharing objectives and philosophy and giving everyone an idea of "where the boss is coming from." The session helped get us on the same page right away. More importantly, everyone from secretaries and one-stripers to colonels heard up front the importance I placed on teamwork, "oneness," and "family."

For the last several years of my career, I put these thoughts together in a short briefing, drawing on three decades of experience, mistakes, and lessons learned. The usual approach was to project the main points as "bullets" on a screen and spend about 20 minutes talking about them at a staff meeting or commander's call.

Often, my first words were something to the effect that in a shorthand way the list showed my thoughts on what we should be all about, how we should treat one another, and what we should stand for as an organization.

        PLAY IT AS A TEAM
        MAKE IT HAPPEN
        MAKE IT BETTER
        BE THE BEST

LEAD
READ
TEACH
GROW
DO IT WITH CLASS
MAKE IT A GOOD TIME
TAKE TIME TO SMELL THE FLOWERS

One of my smartass colleagues said the briefing reminded him of President Clinton's taped impeachment testimony – he wondered what "it" is – but cynics aside, I wound up being asked to present the talk to civic organizations, professional military education seminars, and sister organizations at nearby bases.

Each item drew a one-or two-minute "homily" as the "bullet" was revealed on screen. For example, when I spoke about "Be the Best: Lead," I mentioned an approach to guiding an organization that makes special sense to me. It is called "The Leader as a Servant." The idea is that the most effective leaders are those who serve their people and their organization (and in the military and many other forms of public service, a cause larger than themselves). The notion was expressed in its most extreme form by British Field Marshal William Slim: "I tell you, as officers, that you will not eat, sleep, smoke, sit down, or lie down until your soldiers have had a chance to do those things. If you hold to this, they will follow you to the ends of the earth. If you do not, I will break you in front of your regiments."

General Patton told his officers: "You are always on parade." I think what he meant was that all of us send signals – by how we conduct ourselves, by the way we treat others, by the way we prepare for things, even by the paperwork we choose to sign – and it is important that we send the right signals to those inside and outside our organization.

The concept of "leader as a servant" captured the essence of the sort of commander and leader I tried to be.

At some point in every discussion – after acknowledging that "What I am about to say is a gross oversimplification" – I mentioned that over the years I had observed two extremes to the practice of leadership. At one pole is the leader who persistently tells his people how "bad" they are, who continually drives them and "beats" them to a certain level of performance. It is indeed possible to raise a level of output by employing that style and inevitably some in the audience would nod when I said that probably many of us had at one time or another been subjected to bosses who used it. In practice, the problems I see with it – in addition to burning people out – are that improvements in output are likely to be transitory; if pursued over the long haul the approach is destructive to an organization, and once the baseline threshold is achieved there is likely to be little progress beyond it. There is no incentive or reward for innovation and staff members are too intimidated to come forward with new ideas.

Conversely, at the other end of the spectrum from the boss who tells his workers how *bad* they are is the leader who strives to give them a vision of how *good* they can be. The latter is much nearer my style of leadership, and each of these audiences heard my hopes that together we could create the sort of relationship that would achieve it.

Twenty minutes or so was long enough. So, at that point I would sum up and briefly mention a couple of things for them to carry away and think about.

First, I asked them to have the sort of courage that would allow them to tell me when they thought that I or the organization was headed in the wrong direction. That would not always be easy – *moral* courage is always more difficult than physical courage – but in snapshots of good organizations, the picture was one of the staff developing partnerships with their bosses and being ambassadors for them.

I, in turn, had an obligation to listen.

My final words were almost always about pride: "Pride is not something that you can tell a person to have; it has to grow and be nourished – it bubbles up from within a quality organization. I hope that together we can handle things so well that all of us come to take special pride in each other and in our unit."

The "briefing" was a bit off the beaten path and was usually pretty well received. The Junior Enlisted Council at Stuttgart asked that it be repeated once a year. That way, newcomers could be introduced to the message (and this pleased me no end: "to *our* way of doing business") and, at the same time it would serve as a reminder to the old-timers. From then on, we made it a squadron custom to present it at the first commander's call of each New Year.

/////

At the time, I'm not sure I intellectualized all the intended consequences of that presentation. I think that it was part of a deeper, almost subconscious agenda. What I was trying to do as a commander was to build organizations that were so good that people would want to be part of them. In my naiveté I have come to believe that perhaps, just perhaps, sometimes I may have succeeded.

R & R

A MORAN STORY: THE SIGN

One evening in a port city, it was so hot inside a house of ill repute that the lady of the night and her client decided to transact their business on the roof of the porch above the front door to the building.

Wrapped in the throes of passion, they rolled off the roof and fell to the ground below. There they remained: unconscious, still locked in love's embrace.

Soon afterward, a sailor well in his cups came wobbling up the street. As he passed the house he blearily noted the two figures impaled on the front lawn. Recognizing the establishment, and ever helpful, he staggered up to the front door and rang the bell.

The madam answered.

"Excuse me lady," the sailor said, pointing to the lawn, "I jus' wanted to let you know that your sign blew down."

Front left at Air Force Officer Training School graduation, 13 September 1966.

(Left) Newly minted second lieutenant at Orlando AFB, Florida.

At Orlando, I met a beautiful Air Force nurse. Twenty-two days later, I proposed. Foolishly, she accepted.

Travel was one of the many things my family enjoyed about military life. (Top) Our daughters Karen (L) and Laura in Venice, 1979, and (Right) at Hollenzollern Castle, Bavaria (Laura is at left) in 1995 during our second tour in Europe.

At Air Command and Staff College with my good friend Tao-Chien "Harry" Chen, Republic of China Air Force.

Good times in Italy prior to the terrorist episode. Picking grapes near Vicenza with Laura, Nita, and Karen.

Balconies and uninhabited rooms on lower floors posed security problems in many Italian homes. Our apartment was on the first two floors in this building. We were moved from it to a guarded "safe haven" area on 30 minutes notice after Red Brigades threat warnings were received by Italian police.

Celebrating General Dozier's freedom. Nita and I with U.S. Army Brigadier General James L. Dozier (second from right) and his wife Judy (right) at Verona, Italy, a few days after Italian police freed the General from a "people's prison" in Padova, Italy, where he had been held captive by Red Brigades terrorists.

My boss, General John T. Chain, Commander in Chief, Strategic Air Command, helps Nita pin on the eagles at SAC Headquarters, Offutt AFB, Nebraska. Chain and his predecessor, General Larry Welch, restored the command's conventional war-fighting capabilities.

Quarters 29 on Outer Octagon, Randolph AFB, Texas. I was a young captain when Nita and I saw Randolph for the first time. We wondered how it would feel to live in one of the marvelous old senior officer houses. When I came back many years later as a colonel, we found out.

With Technical Sergeant John Ennema (center) and Chief Master Sergeant Jerry Carney (right), examining the "ventilation" in our first set of quarters in Sarajevo.

Left and below, the most famous signs in Sarajevo.

(Top) A short distance ahead along this road leading from the airport is a hard right turn down Sniper Alley into the heart of the city.

(Below) A gutted tank near the airport. When the hulk was moved a few days later, two corpses were found beneath it.

Gornji Vakuf, Bosnia-Herzegovina. The long, white building in the center of the picture is the hospital where patients were dragged from their beds and shot. When we visited the scene, one of my young sergeants remarked, "We are pilgrims in an unholy place."

The "Alamo Building" in Gornji Vakuf. More than 100 people are alleged to have died inside it during a final spasm of fighting in the summer and fall of 1995.

"Streetcars were a favorite target ... There is an entire cemetery of murdered streetcars along Sniper Alley."

A French Army team checks for mines near IFOR Headquarters, Sarajevo, Bosnia-Herzegovina.

Riding with the Brits. In a British Chinook helicopter near Gornji Vakuf, Bosnia-Herzegovina, Easter Sunday, 1996.

British crewman checking for damage at Tuzla, Bosnia-Herzegovina.

Fast and low down Sniper Alley. Some of the buildings looked almost as if they had been melted by the heat.

Zetra Stadium in Sarajevo, where the 1984 Olympic figure skating competition was held. The stadium roof is mostly shot away and there are bullet holes in the Olympic rings.

Ancient Ottoman Fort at the top of a hill outside of Sarajevo. Along the narrow, winding road that lead to it an elderly Muslim gentleman touched the American flag on my sleeve and said, "We will love you for a thousand years."

Receiving a plaque from Lt. Dave Hamby, U.S. Navy (R), who ran the informal "joint" Army-Navy-Air Force support unit we built in Sarajovo. At the Ottoman Fort overlooking the city.

With General James L. Jamerson, Deputy Commander in Chief, United States European Command. Retirement ceremony. Stuttgart, Germany.

General Jamerson with Nita at retirement ceremony.

One last duty ...

Transferring the unit flag to General Jamerson.

"Sir, I relinquish command."

INCOMING ROUNDS

The Worst Duty

The conflict in Vietnam was reaching full fury in the late fall of 1967. Casualties numbered in the hundreds of killed and wounded each week. At Orlando AFB, casualty notification duties were performed by the officer in charge of the Personal Affairs Section, my friend and colleague, Dave Washburn. When Dave took a short leave, those duties were temporarily assigned to me to cover in his absence.

For a few days, I thought I might escape being called. Then, a day or two before Dave's scheduled return, my phone rang in the middle of the night. The voice at the other end was a Personal Affairs technician. He said he was typing the letter of circumstances that would be presented to the next of kin on a casualty case that had just come in. The letter would be done in a few minutes and he asked that I come to the base to pick it up. He would give me the address of the next of kin and fill me in on all the particulars. In the meantime, he would have a driver and staff car standing by and would contact the chaplain who would accompany me.

I shaved quickly, put on a "Class A" uniform, and hurried to the base. The technician had just taken the letter out of the typewriter when I got there. We both read it and then read it again. It had to be perfect. Any misstatements of fact or grammatical miscues would only compound the anguish we were about to visit on some unknowing family. Assured of the document's accuracy, I took the letter and went to the waiting staff car.

Fortunately for me, the chaplain I had drawn was Lieutenant Colonel Graydon TerBush, a wonderful "padre" and a good friend. Several weeks before, when Nita and I were married in the base chapel, "Chaplain T" officiated at the ceremony.

The next of kin – the mother and father of the young man who had been killed – lived on the outskirts of a nearby small town. We located the modest one-story white frame house without much trouble and walked up the front steps.

Preparing to knock on that door, I thought to myself that I would rather be doing just about anything else in the world at that moment. In the middle of the night we were about to visit sadness on a family so deep and enduring that it would surely remain with them through all their days.

The father, dressed in his pajamas, answered my knock. His eyes registered surprise at seeing two Air Force officers in full dress uniforms standing on his front steps at three o'clock in the morning, but either his mind had not yet had time to explore all the possibilities or he was not ready to accept the subconscious conclusion that it had already drawn. I introduced myself and Chaplain TerBush and asked if it might be possible for us to come in. He immediately assented and called for his wife.

Chaplain TerBush and I took chairs facing the father and mother who sat together on a small sofa. I explained why we were there and handed the letter to them, searching for the appropriate words to say -- only to discover that there are none.

We talked for a few minutes. At first, if only for a moment, the parents grasped for some non-existent hope that their son might still be alive. The chaplain and I comforted them as best we could and tried gently to guide them through the contents of the letter. When they had no more questions, we rose to leave. Chaplain TerBush said he would call them later that morning and that they would be visited by Air Force officials who would assist them with arrangements.

A veteran of such visits, Chaplain TerBush asked the couple if they would like him to contact their local pastor. They said they would. At their request, he offered a few words of prayer. As we left, the father shook hands with me and the mother, sobbing now, hugged me as I stepped toward the front door.

I'm not sure how long we were inside the home of those two nice people whose souls were now in anguish -- probably not more than a half hour. They struggled, mostly with success, to control their emotions, trying to be strong for each other and to hold it together in front of the two strangers seated in their living room.

The duty that night was one of the most difficult I have ever performed. Not "difficult" in the technical sense, but tough, emotionally wrenching. The memory remains vivid still.

Over the years, I've sometimes thought about that evening and the young man whose life had been taken, wondering – as his parents must have, countless times – what his life might otherwise have been. What accomplishments might he have made? What sort of person would he have turned out to be?

The answers are unknowable, unfathomable.

Across the country, thousands of parents, spouses, families, and friends wept over these imponderables, their questions precipitated by a visit from officers in uniform, often preceded by a knock on the door in the middle of the night.

In my later ruminations, I came to wish that every decision maker in a position to commit a nation's sons and daughters to war ought to *first* be required to make a casualty notification visit like the one that took me to that small frame house in the sad, early hours of the morning.

Perspective

Vietnam defined my generation. Most assuredly, it defined my generation of military officers. So overwhelming were its consequences that 40 years later, "lessons" from the conflict continue to influence, if not shape, our approach to war.

As America's involvement in the war deepened during the decade of the '60s, the size of our armed forces was steadily ramped up. Three million young Americans served in Southeast Asia. Directly or indirectly, millions more on installations all around the globe supported our operations there. At Orlando, the organization I was assigned to assisted Headquarters Aerospace Rescue and Recovery Service and Headquarters Aerospace Audiovisual Service with human resources support for the several subordinate units of both agencies that were scattered across Vietnam and Thailand.

Later, at Military Airlift Command Headquarters, we worked with those organizations as well as Air Weather Service, airlift, and medical evacuation units "in theater" and at bases throughout the Pacific. On trips to Hawaii, Japan, Guam, and the Philippines, I spent time with Military Airlift Command outfits busy with war-related taskings.

I never served "in country." I have enormous respect for those who were there and for the countless numbers who contributed more directly than I did.

For three decades it has been my fate, and that of colleagues in all the armed services, to study the conflict in professional military schools and civilian institutions. We have examined and debated it, cursed it at times, and tried to learn about it and to learn from it. We have rejoiced with the families of service members who returned from 'Nam and have grieved with families who wept when their service members did not.

Thirty years after Saigon fell, the war's residual influence continues to "touch us where we live" as a society: it remains part of the public debate, still impacting political campaigns, veteran's programs, attitudes toward war in general, and a host of other national agenda issues, many of them contentious.

Vietnam will not "go away." Like Valley Forge, Pearl Harbor, and 9/11, it has become part of the nation's psyche.

For me and other career officers, the war and its aftermath were part of the fabric of our professional lives for almost our entire time on active duty. For the past half decade, I have had occasion to further reflect on it from the distance and dispassion of life outside the military. Others may disagree with the conclusions and the scholarship that follow in the next section, but for me it is time to write down what I have come to believe about Vietnam and to offer it -- for solace, or judgment, or critique – to others whose lives were touched by the conflict.

Vietnam: A Retrospective

The picture of the helicopter on the roof of our embassy in Saigon is one of the saddest images in all of America's history.

Incoming Rounds / 151

To some, the photo evokes memories of a war frustratingly fought, ineptly led, and tragically "lost." To others, it connotes but a last bitter episode in a long downward spiral of divisive fury that for nearly a decade tore at the soul of our nation. Whatever the view, the poignancy of that scene cannot be escaped. A commitment that began with bright intentions and high expectations is captured as it ended: an impossibly long line of desperate people clamoring to board a solitary helicopter – all that remained of America's presence in Vietnam. Even today, I cannot look at the photo without feelings of frustration and anger.

Vietnam crept up in my awareness and in the nation's conscious like a blip on a radar scope – initially small, dim, distant; out near the edge – that slowly, persistently grew in intensity until it dominated the entire screen. I recall reading about the first of President Kennedy's "advisors" being killed. Then, when I was in Morocco, the *Stars and Stripes* newspaper carried an article about a place called Ap Bac where, in what has now become somewhat of a classic encounter, the Viet Cong mauled a contingent of South Vietnamese Army regulars. Vietnam was a topic of conversation in a general way, but although America's presence was clearly growing the conflict was far from commanding the headlines.

It began to do so during the time I was attending a civilian institution as part of the Airmen Education and Commissioning Program. Particularly after the 1964 elections and the Viet Cong attack on Pleiku Air Base in February 1965, U.S. forces began to be sent to the region in ever larger numbers. Eventually, the conflict became the lead segment on almost every evening newscast. It remained there for eight years.

Vietnam ushered in an entire range of new words, phrases, and acronyms into the military's vocabulary: "in country," "SEA tour," "Tet," "Rolling Thunder," "Buffs," "body count," "ARVN," "NVA," "VC," "KIA," "MIA," "POW." The nation got a lesson in geography as new places, some with exotic sounding names, were introduced almost daily in the media: Tan San Nhut, Phan Rang, Khe Sanh, Ben Hoa, U Tapao, Nakhon Phanom.

Eventually, three million young American men and women served there (the peak figure at any one time was 540,000).

Especially from the late '60s on, those who completed tours there often came back disillusioned. For the most part they continued to do their jobs and do them well – and although they would have preferred to be somewhere else, most did not object to the *idea* of the war or, initially at least, to our involvement in it. What did trouble them greatly was the ambivalent way we went about it. John McCain may have spoken for all of them: "No one who goes to war believes once he is there that it is worth the terrible cost of war to fight it by half measures."[1]

Vietnam remains our most enigmatic conflict. Nearly four decades later the debate endures. The most perplexing thing about it is that everything about it is perplexing. For every very strongly argued point there is an equally sharp counterpoint. Every aspect at every level evokes controversy.

Was it "legal" for us to be there in the first place?

If so, *should* we have been there?

If so, how should the war have been fought?

Now, three decades after the last helicopter left the embassy, for what little it may be worth, here is what I have come to believe.

I used to think that the "legality" issue was the "cleanest" part of the Vietnam question. In a general sense I still do although the unsullied fabric of my initial convictions has developed some frayed spots around the edges. In September 1954, the parties to the South East Asia Treaty Organization (SEATO) pact signed a protocol extending the treaty's protection to Cambodia, Laos, and South Vietnam. That had always seemed to me to put the basic issue substantially at rest. However, the historian Stephen Ambrose argues that the Geneva Accords that temporarily partitioned Vietnam prohibited either entity from "making a military alliance with an outside party."[2] The key, I suppose, is whether protection extended by SEATO to South Vietnam was tantamount to South Vietnam entering into a military alliance.

Ambrose also notes that the Geneva Accords specified that elections were to be held within two years to unify the country. He and many others assert that South Vietnamese President Diem refused to hold the elections, believing Ho Chi Minh's contingent would win. Dissenters state that Ho's faction was already assassinating village chiefs and other officials to gain control of the countryside, a process that would soon accelerate.[3] Thus, "real" elections were already beyond reach. Finally, it is Ambrose's contention that the entire legal situation surrounding South Vietnam was "fuzzy"; that is, at the time South Vietnam was not a nation but a territory to be administered by France until the scheduled elections in 1956.[4] The United States, however, interpreted – Ambrose argues, *redefined* – the Geneva Accords as having already established two nations: North Vietnam and South Vietnam. The whole thing is like looking through a glass, darkly.

The run-up to major U.S. involvement is almost as murky. The seminal events were incidents in the Gulf of Tonkin that occurred in early August, 1964. On two consecutive days North Vietnamese motor torpedo boats were thought to have attacked U.S. Navy destroyers. Of the first encounter, the facts have not been much in dispute (except only for the *why* it happened in the first place). Three torpedo boats attacked the destroyer *Maddox* and were engaged by that ship as well as by naval air from the carrier *Ticonderoga*. Two North Vietnamese vessels were damaged and one was reported dead in the water.

It is the second incident that has generated the most enduring controversy. Commander (later, Admiral) James Stockdale was the lead pilot on air strikes that took place on both occasions. On the second night, he did not see any enemy combatants. Later, the skipper of the *Maddox* acknowledged that the apparent attack may not have happened: weather phenomena and an inexperienced radar operator might have resulted in a misreading of events by his ship and the accompanying destroyer *C. Turner Joy*.[5]

Admiral Stockdale believes that administration officials must surely have been aware of the ambiguity surrounding the second "attack" but chose not to disclose it. He acknowledges the possibility that events were spiraling in a direction that made war almost inevitable under any circumstance, but he regretted that in this specific instance we were "about to launch a war under false pretenses."[6]

Peeling back an additional layer reveals still more contentions regarding *why* U.S. ships were there in the first place. To those on one side, the circumstances are clear: they were there to demonstrate our "presence" and to assert our right of passage along the coast of Vietnam – and at any rate, they were most assuredly in international waters. Those in opposition allege that the vessels were engaged in direct or indirect support for South Vietnamese commando operations on nearby islands. Thus, attacks on the ships – if in fact they did occur – were not entirely unprovoked.[7]

Those who challenge the legality of our entry into the conflict are at their weakest, it seems to me, when they argue that a declaration of war was required. Declarations of war have been the exception rather than the rule in our national experience. Critics who further assert that the "Tonkin Resolution" was an insufficient basis should note the numerous times in our history when Presidents have committed forces without a congressional imprimatur of any kind. Whether it was proper to use the Resolution as the continuing legal foundation for what became a long duration major conflict can be debated, but there was not a lot of pressure to do otherwise, particularly during the first years of the conflict.

Should we have been there?

Legions of PhD dissertations pro and con notwithstanding – and with due regard for the countless numbers yet to come – it has always appeared to me that the *should* question was almost moot to begin with. In the climate of the time, our involvement in Vietnam (but not the approach we chose to carry it out) was practically a given. Often lost in the debate is that the whole issue of Vietnam came wrapped inside a larger Cold War setting. Confrontations were frequent, widespread, and recent: Berlin, the Bay of Pigs, Laos, Cuba. This was not a passive time.

At his inauguration, President Kennedy had vowed to "pay any price, bear any burden, meet any hardship, support any friend, oppose any foe, in order to assure the survival and success of liberty." Impatient with, in their view, the insufficient energy displayed by the previous administration, the Kennedy White House was predisposed toward action.

Spring-loaded as they were and accepting the general credence of the "domino theory" as they did, the concerns they sought to address were not without substance. In 1959, the North

Vietnamese communist party plenum had voted to resume the armed struggle in the South.[8] By 1960, the Viet Cong were engaged in a nation-wide revolt. The pattern of events made it likely that the Kennedy administration framed the argument for action not as a *should we* question but as a *we must* issue. The dilemma was in determining the proper action to take.

How should the war have been fought remains the most contentious of all the Vietnam questions.

Until the late days of the conflict, the approach we chose was massive firepower from large ground formations and aerial bombardment. In concept, the infantry units would find and fix the location of the enemy and firepower would annihilate them: "search and destroy."

Accompanying the continuous aggressive series of infantry actions was the limited application of airpower in a slowly ascending escalation intended to induce the North Vietnamese to negotiate: "Rolling Thunder." "They can't even bomb an outhouse without my approval," President Johnson was quoted as saying.[9] "High value" targets were placed off limits.

Hindsight inspires genius, but even at the time many, if not most, in the military believed that parts of our approach missed the mark. The success of large ground formations in finding and holding the enemy was marginal: even when cornered the Viet Cong, and later the North Vietnamese forces, often simply evaporated into the conducive landscape only to reform and fight another time. As late as 1967, a U.S. Army study concluded that 88% of all land battles were initiated by the Viet Cong. Clearly, we were fighting on the enemy's terms.[10] Our opponents were not the heavy maneuver units of the Warsaw Pact. Even critics inside the Army worried that our forces – and through them by extension, the army of our South Vietnamese ally – were configured and trained for the wrong type of conflict.

To those in the Air Force the targeting strategy seemed almost criminal. Repeated bombings of barracks and similar facilities achieved little except to kill our colleagues who flew the missions. The North's major war materials were supplied by Russia and China. Much of it was coming through Haiphong; that harbor and other installations there as well as important facilities around

Hanoi were the target set that should have been assaulted. Worse still, the frequent pauses in the bombing campaign, intended to signal "goodwill" on our part, were interpreted as weakness and irresolution by our opponents. In every case, the North Vietnamese used the bombing halts to further improve their air defense system. In the meantime, imports of war material into Vietnam almost doubled.[11]

The "Rolling Thunder" concept seemed implausible to me. I remember an extended discussion with an Army colleague who argued the virtues of gradual escalation: just keep adding pressure and eventually the other guys will concede. What bothered me about that rationale was that it was open-ended; there were no boundaries to it. Better, I thought in my farm boy naiveté, would be for us to define what constituted victory or success and then establish the conditions to achieve it.

To a reporter in Vietnam at the time, our efforts seemed like a "holding action." Our national strategy "was about not losing as opposed to winning."[12]

Force management policies as well as strategy detracted from our ability to effectively prosecute the war. A "SEA tour" was 12 months long and in many Army units officers were rotated through combat units in six month intervals as a way of insuring that maximum numbers got their "tickets punched." Experience was the casualty, as were many young Americans as a result. John Paul Vann's famous comment was wry but astute: "The United States has not been in Viet Nam for nine years, but for one year nine times."[13] Then too, the U.S. commanders had no power to remove corrupt or inept South Vietnamese commanders, many of whom were appointed as a result of family or political connections.

Still, lest we get carried away with the brilliance of our critique it must be pointed out that by 1970 our policies had succeeded – I would argue that success came in spite of them – in placing more than 90% of South Vietnam under Saigon's control. In many areas a traveler could journey the length of the country in relative safety. Indeed, some have concluded that the U.S. part of the war was won at that time and that we should have declared it so and timed our withdrawal accordingly.[14]

Other equally frustrated but less sanguine observers had a different take on it. In the early days of the war Senator Richard Russell, Chairman of the Armed Services Committee, was alleged to have said to President Johnson "Let's arrange for another coup and have the new guys ask us to get out ..."[15]

Those who contend that our approach was flawed have an obligation to evaluate other alternatives. Many have suggested that the best, perhaps only way to have won the war was to invade North Vietnam and occupy Hanoi.[16] The Johnson administration discarded that option out of fear that it would provoke China's intervention. Support is given that contention by some scholars who assert there is evidence indicating China was prepared to enter the conflict if U.S. forces crossed the 17th parallel.[17] Still others offer the reminder that France occupied Hanoi – indeed, all of North Vietnam – and could not stop guerilla warfare in the South. (Conjecture regarding the relative capabilities of the French Army circa 1954 and the American forces of a decade or more later provides yet another area for discussion and debate.) Regardless, it is questionable whether an invasion of North Vietnam at any time after the mid-60s was politically feasible given the climate inside our own country.

The better approach it seems to me, again with the useful benefit of hindsight, would have combined pacification with a truly effective air campaign. In 1979, at Air Command and Staff College, a CIA operative who had been posted in Vietnam mentioned that the most effective prosecution of the war that he had observed came from small teams of Marines who lived in the villages and hamlets and worked directly with local South Vietnamese forces.

What he was talking about, as I came to realize in later years, was called the Combined Action Program. Teams of 6-12 Marines lived in villages, providing security, working with indigenous forces, and sharing food and living conditions. (Army Special Forces employed a similar approach in the Central Highlands.) Marine Lieutenant General Victor Krulak noted that 80% of South Vietnam's population lived in 10% of the countryside. Krulak's notion was to sever the Viet Cong from those population centers along the Mekong Delta and coastal plains and provide security for the villages. Getting to the Viet Cong in their jungle sanctuaries was difficult in the extreme. Cutting them off from the support of the civilian population would cause them to wither away or make them more vulnerable to attack.[18]

Where attempted, the Combined Action Program was marvelously effective. The problem was, it was employed too little (only 2,500 Marines were assigned to the effort at its peak) and too late.[19] The Combined Action Program was adapted from the Marines' experience in guerilla warfare in Central America and the Caribbean. What a tragedy that those lessons were mostly disregarded.

Except for the eleven days at the end of the war, almost every student of military aviation would argue that airpower was misused. The industrial base for the North Vietnamese was China and Russia; thus, airpower alone, especially as employed in South Vietnam, could not be decisive. By the end of 1967, more bombs had been dropped than in all of World War II. By 1969, more bombs had been dropped on North and South Vietnam than on all the targets in all of recorded history.[20] Air operations and the "search and destroy" campaigns of large American ground forces created five million refugees, most of whom fled to the major cities in the South, contributing to additional social problems.

From the earliest days of the war, Air Force planners urged the destruction of facilities around Hanoi and, most particularly, bombing and mining Haiphong harbor. Those actions, it was believed, would materially reduce the supplies flowing into North Vietnam and the ripple effect would contribute to efforts in the South. Sunday morning quarterbacking perhaps, but the comprehensive effect of a Combined Action Program along with a well conceived air campaign would have been interesting to behold. The former would have sought to disenfranchise the enemy and pacify the South. The latter would have focused on shutting down the North's war supplies at their point of entry, stripping them further as they moved south, and furnishing close air support to allied units engaged on the ground.

Rolling Thunder, for all its well intentioned signals of "good will," diluted the impact of airpower and squandered its effectiveness. The consequences of massive employment of air

More than just combat capability, it seems to me that Vietnam has changed, for the better, our *approach* to war. If *Desert Storm* and the War in Iraq are indicators, decisive force from the outset has replaced gradual escalation and sending "signals." The mindset is different: set the objectives, provide the resources, and let the professionals prosecute the conflict. The Commander-in-Chief has not been involved in choosing which outhouse to bomb.

Hopefully, we have matured as a society in the way we view men and women in uniform. Even those opposed to the War in Iraq separated their opposition to the conflict from the people we sent there to fight in it. If that assessment is correct, and permanent, it is significant indeed. Of all the things associated with Vietnam that troubled me, the hostility shown by the dissenting populace toward members of the armed forces was one of the most bothersome. Kids just returned from the war zone being spat upon: unconscionable.

It was difficult to fathom the depth of the hostility or understand why it was transferred as it was. The young people in military service were sent to war at our government's bidding. It was ironic to me that in a deeper sense they were fighting for many of the same things the protestors were concerned about – freedom of speech, freedom of assembly, representative government – only they were struggling to facilitate those processes in a distant place where they were under severe duress from the outside.

Although their objectives increasingly got lost in the escalating violence of their demonstrations – exacerbated at times, it must be acknowledged, by the heavy-handed responses of the authorities – the dissenters had every right to protest. Their quarrel, though, was too often misdirected. It should have been focused on the government that formulated the policies they objected to, not on the youngsters in uniform who had little choice but to carry them out.

High on my list of bothersome things was the notion expressed by the most vocal minority that a government imposed by the North would somehow be morally superior: that it would serve the Vietnamese people better than any administration constituted in the South. This was most often the view expressed by the high profile elite and thus frequently captured by the media. History, had they understood it, might have dissuaded them from that conviction. In 1954, after the Geneva Accords were signed, thousands fled from the north to the south because they knew full well what sort of government was about to be perpetrated upon them.

That tragic pattern did not change with the fall of Saigon. The horrific saga of thousands upon thousands of boat people provides eloquent testimony about choices between systems, views of the future, and quests for freedom. President Nixon stated that "The events following our departure from Vietnam disclose that a Communist peace kills more than an anti-communist war."[23] As others have observed, no one has ever tried to break into North Vietnam.[24]

As for myself, I have always wanted the opportunity to mention to the most vocal dissenters that – 30 years later – the world is still waiting for the first democratic elections to be held in Vietnam.

/////

"No other national endeavor requires as much unshakeable resolve as war. If the government and the nation lack that resolve, it is criminal to expect men in the field to carry it alone."[25]

Senator McCain's comment captures perhaps the most important of all the "lessons" from Vietnam. In Southeast Asia, the United States attempted to win an unpopular war – a war made unpopular in part by its own inconstancy and lack of conviction – with inadequate resources and misguided strategies. In the end, the price necessary to prevail was too high.

Those are bitter lessons. The early evidence from *Desert Storm* and the War in Iraq indicates we may have learned them. If that is correct, if indeed we have institutionalized that wisdom, its permanent place in our collective conscience will be the most positive legacy of all.

The haunting image of the helicopter on the rooftop is engraved in our national memory. We cannot erase, forgive, or forget it. What we can – must – do is use what the experience taught us to prevent anything like it from happening again.

Notes

1. John McCain, *Faith of my Fathers*, (New York: Random House, Inc., 1999) p. 334
2. Stephen E. Ambrose, *To America*, (New York: Simon and Schuster, 2002) p. 129
3. Ambrose p. 130
4. Ambrose p. 130
5. James Stockdale and Sybil Stockdale, *In Love and War*, (Naval Institute Press, 1990) p. 21
6. Stockdale p. 29
7. Jon Margolis, *The Last Innocent Year: America in 1964*, (William Morrow, 1999) cited in Brian Lamb, *Bookmarks: Stories from American History*, (PublicAffairs, 2001) p. 385
8. Max Boot, *The Savage Wars of Peace*, (Basic Books, 2002) p. 287
9. Boot p. 291
10. Boot p. 299
11. Boot p. 291
12. Peter R. Kann and Francis FitzGerald, *Reporting from Vietnam: American Journalism 1959-1969*, (Library of America, 1998) cited in Brian Lamb, *Bookmarks: Stories from American History*, (PublicAffairs, 2001) p. 412
13. Boot p. 299
14. B.G. Burkett and Glenna Whitley, *Stolen Valor*, (Verity Press Inc., 1998)
15. Margolis, cited in Brian Lamb, *Bookmarks: Stories from American History*, (PublicAffairs, 2001) p. 385
16. Ambrose p. 133
17. Boot p. 293
18. Boot p. 297
19. Boot p. 305-307
20. Ambrose p. 133
21. Kann and FitzGerald, cited in Brian Lamb, *Bookmarks: Stories from American History*, (PublicAffairs, 2001) p.414
22. Boot p. 313
23. Richard Nixon, *No More Vietnams*, <u>Strategic Review</u> Summer 1985: p. 70
24. Ambrose p. 147
25. McCain p. 335

International Relations ... At the Detachment Level

"Well, okay, Phillips," I thought to myself, "how are you going to get out of this one without causing an international incident?"

Darn those guys that ran the Command Track at Air Command and Staff College: they never mentioned that anything like this would be part of the job ...

Technical Sergeant Bobbi Stevens was the first woman assigned to Headquarters, Fifth Allied Tactical Air Force at Vicenza, Italy. Bobbi was a communications technician. She was excellent; she would soon be commended for almost single-handedly "saving" the communications part of a NATO exercise by helping clear the backlog of messages that had plagued it prior to her intervention.

But, there was this other thing about her. She was, er, ... a *woman*. No female of any branch of any service from any nation had ever been assigned to the headquarters. In the military forces of the other nations that furnished troops or liaison officers to "5ATAF" – Italy, Turkey, Germany, France – women were either non-existent or in miniscule numbers. For sure, none had ever ventured near Aeroporto Tomoso Dal Molin, the Italian Air Force Base that was home to 5ATAF headquarters.

Bobbi's arrival created considerable consternation. A woman in the military: most of her allied colleagues had never seen anything like it. In the machismo Italian culture, military service was outside the "accepted" role for women.

When the Italian *maresciallo*, the senior sergeant in overall charge of the headquarters communications center, posted the first duty schedule after Bobbi's arrival, Bobbi's duty title was displayed as *Mrs.* Stevens.

Bobbi was understandably upset. A total professional, she was proud of being a tech sergeant in the United States Air Force and rightfully expected to be addressed by that title. Not wanting to cause difficulties, she mentioned the situation only to a co-worker, who at any rate had already seen the roster and objected to it. Initially, nothing was changed. Her colleague, a USAF NCO, came to see me. During my time as detachment commander, I enjoyed a fine friendship with the base commander of Aeroporto Tomoso Dal Molin, Italian Air Force *Colonnello* Guido Cutry. On one occasion as we traded stories on commander-related issues, the conversation turned to the subject of how discipline was administered within each service. *Colonnello* Cutry commented that if caution or chastisement was the limited aim, the way the Italian Air Force often handled it was to ask a friend of the "offender" to speak with him about it. That way there was less embarrassment and minimal damage occurred to the relations between the supervisor and the subordinate. More importantly, it precluded a supervisor from having to get visibly and directly in the offender's face. That was regarded as bad form.

That approach seemed worth a try; it might be a way to handle the sensitivities and not overtly tick off any of the players. Senior Master Sergeant Jess Perry was the ranking American NCO in the headquarters and a friend of the *maresciallo* who ran the comm center. I asked Sergeant Perry to speak with him. In a low key way, over a cup of cappuccino, Jess said the right words: *Technical Sergeant* Bobbi Stevens is an NCO in the United States Air Force; that's the way we do things. We do not differentiate her rank from that of her male contemporaries. We expect her to do the same job they do. We are here because we are your ally. We are a very good ally. She is part of that effort. She deserves the courtesy of being called by her proper military title.

The roster was changed immediately and without fanfare. From there on it, it was "*TSgt* Stevens".

I was prepared to go to the Senior USAF Representative to 5ATAF (a one-star general) and ask him to speak with the Italian *commandante* of 5ATAF. He surely would have, and we would undoubtedly have gotten the duty roster changed – but not without ruffling some feathers all the way down to the *maresciallo* level. Other than Bobbi, Jess, and a few others in the comm center, no one else was aware of any of this. That was the way it should be.

Bobbi Stevens was the real reason things worked out so well. Her military professionalism and technical skills soon won over all her colleagues, including most assuredly, the *maresciallo*. I have thanked my lucky stars, and Air Force assignment makers, many times that she was the first Air Force woman to be sent to 5ATAF.

She set just the right example and paved the way for all the rest who followed. Had she been a dingbat, like the *second* woman that showed up several months later, initial success would have been more problematical. But that would be another story.

Women in the Military

At Air Command and Staff College in 1979, General Frederick Kroesen, Commander of U.S. Army Forces in Europe, spoke to our class. The "women in combat" issue was getting major press play at the time. It was a topic that magnetized constituencies at both extremes. Thus, it was no surprise when a member of the class asked General Kroesen for his views. General Kroesen's replied something to the effect that "Front line warfare is such an animal-like existence that I am not sure we could protect our female soldiers from their own colleagues, let alone from the enemy."

My thoughts took me back to General Kroesen's comments as I watched a "20/20" segment related to the War in Iraq. The subject was an Air Force woman pilot who flew the A-10 Warthog in close air support strikes against Iraqi armor. The story focused on her because she had brought back and safely landed a Warthog that had been badly damaged: a large part of the horizontal stabilizer had been shot away and the tail and fuselage were riddled with bullet holes. More impressive to her squadron cohorts was that the plane's hydraulic system was totally destroyed. The tiny captain had saved the plane using only manual controls. That in itself was a significant achievement, but the amazing thing was that in almost every previous case, the aircraft had been "broken" on landing. Not so this time. The young captain had fought it all the way home and brought it in for a perfect touchdown. No further damage was sustained. Even the squadron commander seemed in awe.

In a closing interview, the pilot spoke of her love for flying, of her special feeling for the A-10, her belief in the mission, and the importance of doing everything possible "to help the guys on the ground." There must have been countless numbers in the TV audience who, like me, felt like standing up to cheer.

I thought at the time and continue to believe today that General Kroesen's comments were valid for his frame of reference and the environment he described. (Women are still barred from front-line duty.) My observations – coming from inside a service that does most of its direct warfighting from different medium – have been shaped by a dissimilar perspective. I have come to believe that, at least for the Air Force, at least for now, the line is drawn at about the right place.

Presently, women officers are excluded from only one specialty: combat control. Enlisted women are excluded from only three: combat control, tactical air command and control, and pararescue. Portions of a few other specialties are restricted for entry, primarily in duties that work directly with special operations forces or with infantry battalions.

Not that some of the implications of all this – POW possibilities for example – don't bother me, both as a service member and as a father. There are few real protections available for our military personnel, male or female, while in captive status. Although their treatment will vary from one adversary to the next, inevitably some jailors will use these occasions as opportunities for misadventure. Considering the wide horizon of places where our military might be employed, it is almost a given that such episodes will occur.

I don't have an answer to these concerns. Nor does anyone else. I would not like my daughters to be subjected to that environment, but my daughters would say that they have a right to assess the risk and decide accordingly. I suspect that their views reflect where we're "at" in our society in terms of "climate" and interpretation of public law and policy.

Our military is a microcosm of the country as a whole, not only demographically but also in its translation of public attitudes. This is a major strength of our armed forces and, through them, of the nation. So, although I will continue to be troubled by the POW "aspect," I would not seek to change the policies affecting women in the service. I believe the best and perhaps only way to "protect" captured Americans – male or female – in future conflicts is to make it immediately clear to our adversaries that they will be held fully and individually accountable for the humane and proper treatment of American prisoners.

Thus, I suppose I have become as reconciled to this as I will ever be, in part because so many of the other concerns raised early in the debate have been dispelled. There is, for example, no significant difference between "time lost" for illness or injury or absences from duty between male and female service members. In fact, a study done in the mid-80s when I was at SAC determined that the amount of time lost by women was slightly *less* than for men.

My observations would indicate that study probably drew the right conclusion although occasional exceptions must be noted that severely impact the unit involved. In one SAC flying squadron, a woman navigator had two consecutive, very close together pregnancies. Because pregnancy causes removal from flying status, for two years she could not perform her aircrew duties. Nor could the unit get a replacement to fill the key position because the woman was assigned against a valid slot on the organizational manning document. In the Air Force, assignments are made based on vacancies in the "manpower system." Other squadron members had to take up the slack.

The effect of pregnancy and resulting time lost vary from unit to unit depending on the jobs and skill levels involved and the demands of the mission. There is *some* effect every time ... just as there is with longer than usual absences of any service members for any reasons. It is an issue that we need to accept, accommodate, and move on. It has not proven to be a show stopper.

Interestingly, the same study showed that the disciplinary rates for women were considerably lower than for men. That was not a surprising outcome. But, as commander of a military unit, I would caution against reading too much into it. Although the numbers of exceptions to this next statement are of epic proportions, *sometimes* – more frequently than is acknowledged – the best soldiers in combat are those that march to a different drummer in garrison duty.

Because we have decided as a society that women will play a substantive role in the armed forces, I have long advocated that we consider a leave of absence program for service members who wish to use it following childbirth. Indeed, statutory requirements might necessitate making the program available to both sexes and ascribing its use to purposes in addition to child-rearing. With long duration careers of 40 or even 50 years now being talked about, leaves of absence is an idea that also warrants consideration. Boundaries would have to be placed on length of absences, provisions made for special skills and, in many specialties proficiency re-training and the cost involved would have to be acknowledged. But, models can be found in successful counterpart programs in industry and in the armed forces of some allied nations (for both male and female service members).

America's women service members have been deployed in significant numbers and placed in harm's way in the Gulf War, Bosnia, Kosovo, and Iraq. If, as I believe, the measure of merit is capability to do the job and perform the mission, the proof has been demonstrated. Women now comprise about 15 percent of the population of our armed forces. Not all are as gifted as the young Warthog pilot and some aren't good at all, but overall the range of their abilities is on a par with their male colleagues.

At least that was my experience as a staff officer and commander.

The best of the women NCOs who worked for me were quite good indeed. They were masters of their technical specialties and capable supervisors as well: appropriately tough when the occasion demanded, but also exceptional listeners. It seemed to me that the good ones picked up on "signals" that some of the guys missed. In Stuttgart, I selected a woman First Sergeant for my squadron. Peggy Marquart was the right choice. She was the last "first shirt" I worked with in 36 years of active duty and she was one of the best.

During my Stuttgart time, four women officers worked for me as detachment commanders. Two were in the unit when I arrived. I curtailed the tour of one because of her general ineffectiveness. The other, Major Mary Wilson, was one of the top commanders in the organization. Mary commanded my old detachment at Vicenza, Italy, so I was probably spring-loaded to judge her performance with an especially critical eye. I needn't have worried. Mary's leadership made the unit one of the very best in the squadron.

Mary was a former enlisted person who had taught junior high school before joining the Air Force. I kidded her that her experience in handling eighth graders served her well in her dealings with colonels and generals. Given the egos of some of the ones we worked with, there was more than a small element of truth in that.

I selected two women officers to fill detachment commander positions during the time I was squadron commander. My only criterion was to choose the best officer available for what I considered to be the military's most important job. One of my choices was a bit disappointing: she turned out to be an adequate but not exceptional leader. The other, Major Lois Hansen, was superb. Lois took over our largest detachment after the previous commander had been reassigned on short notice. She immediately drew accolades from one-stripers to four-star generals for the quality of service her unit provided. Lois guided her detachment through an extensive reorganization in the critical spotlight of Europe's major international headquarters. Her energy level and capability to handle multiple tasks set high bench marks for her commander peers.

There are those who continue to voice concerns about women in the military and, most particularly, women in combat roles. I respect their views. As with General Kroesen's, their apprehensions may well be valid for the situations and frames of reference they describe.

My perceptions and the experiences that formed them have been different and, for the most part, positive. From my perspective the case for women in the military and, indeed, women in combat, has been made. The public's view appears increasingly accepting. At the same time, the major trends in the military – smaller forces and increased technological dependence – place a premium on attracting and keeping high caliber people.

That is the shape of the future. It would be foolish for us to exclude from it 50% of the brain power of our nation.

Location, Location, Location

For awhile, it looked like the situation could get nasty. Several weeks after our small "joint" support unit was up and running in Sarajevo, we were pressured to move our youngsters to a different site. Plans were being made to rehabilitate part of a mostly destroyed factory complex on the other side of the city. The idea was to house all the Sarajevo-area support functions under one roof and use several of the building's upper floors as a dormitory.

I received several phone calls, each more insistent, first asking, then telling, me to prepare to move the unit. A considerable amount of money had already been spent, I was told, and the callers insisted that the plan had been blessed at very high levels.

I was not eager to move. Our small unit was nicely situated in the middle of our "customers" and the security situation was excellent. My counterpart Army and Navy commanders with troops in our joint unit shared my reluctance. Eventually, we agreed to a meeting in Sarajevo to have a close-up look at the facility.

We were shown a massive building with two sections connected by a skywalk over a driveway leading to an interior parking and loading area. The support functions were planned for the wing on the left. The right section across the skywalk was mostly ravaged, still structurally intact but filled with junk and debris on every floor. At the extreme right end, a small factory employing 30-40 workers was still operating.

Right away, I didn't like it. The opportunity for misadventure by someone parking a vehicle filled with explosives under the skywalk seemed obvious. So did arson in the littered and untended half of the building. We were assured that "fire doors" would be built where the skywalk joined our section, but I was not comforted. Further, the workers at the other end of the complex had open access to the entire right side of the building. *Anyone* could get into it.

I voiced my concern. "There's a Turkish garrison just down the block," I was told in reply. I didn't think my kids were especially fluent in that language; besides, a straight out attack on the building was probably not the sort of threat we would face. I told our hosts that I preferred our present security arrangements where we were little more than a city block, in direct line of sight from IFOR Headquarters which in turn was next door to the American Embassy -- possibly the two most heavily guarded complexes in the city. Further, our present service arrangements were ideal. We were right in the middle of the troops we were there to support. Their time was minimized, and their safety enhanced, because we were so easy to get to. Anyway, I wasn't sure that clustering all the support facilities – and people – together was always a good idea, as testified to by the bombing of the Marine Barracks in Beirut.

That was where the meeting adjourned, but the calls resumed soon after we returned home. A few days later, General James L. Jamerson, Deputy Commander in Chief, U.S. European Command, came to my unit for a long-planned visit. He asked about the building situation in Sarajevo during our conversation. I explained my concerns to him, described the skywalk, the open access, and the flammable clutter in the adjacent wing, and closed saying "I think I could burn down the whole building with a roll of toilet paper and a cigarette lighter." General Jamerson said he was planning to send one of his security experts to Sarajevo to look at it. In the meantime, the overall situation became increasingly benign, further minimizing any justification for the move.

We stayed where we were. The facility was *never* used, by anybody. I regret that someone spent a carload of money on a vacant building, but I believe we made the right call.

"Don't Ask, Don't Tell"

Mark Twain was alleged to have said, "One positive thing about lawyers is that they are a good source of protein." There are lawyers in the military, too. Sometimes commanders have to deal with them.

Almost all of the ones I dealt with were excellent. The ones who caused trouble were those who tried to interpose their judgment on that of the commander. JAGs are there to advise, not to command.

Several months after Secretary of Defense Aspin promulgated the "don't ask, don't tell" policy, a young airman assigned to a nearby organization over which my unit had administrative authority went to see his supervisor and professed to be a homosexual. Under the rules, disclosure required discharge. Commanders were allowed no latitude. When the case was being processed, a JAG at command headquarters objected strongly, saying that the airman was using the provisions of the policy to get out of his service commitment and go home early.

My 'take' was different. There was no reason to doubt the airman's word. His coworkers and supervisors were impressed with his personal integrity; it was their collective judgment that he was almost painfully honest in his everyday conduct. There was nothing in his record, or in his daily interactions, that would hint of duplicity. His interview with me seemed to confirm the assessments of those who worked with him everyday. I suspect that he came into my office expecting he was going to be chastised, harangued, or worse. Not so; I mainly wanted to be sure he understood the consequences of his disclosure. We were simply trying to follow the rules. His demeanor was somewhat shy, but as his coworkers had said, he appeared sincere and assured in his convictions.

Thus, the JAG's objections were a surprise. I called to talk with him, explained the checks we had done and our rationale for proceeding with the discharge action. The lawyer continued to have problems with it. He thought the airman was playing fast and loose with the system as he had seen others do. He said he was going to "sit on the package."

Finally, I got both him and his boss (it is useful to remember that everyone has a boss) on the line. I again went through the sequence of events and noted that we were merely applying the rules and there was nothing to indicate deceit on the individual's part. Indeed, there were ample attestations to his honesty that would seem to corroborate the validity of his disclosure. Absent a video tape of him performing a sex act, that was the most we were going to get. We would have to apply our best judgment – the *commander's* best judgment.

When I finished my soliloquy there was silence on the line.

They still seemed uncertain, so finally I said: "What has to happen? Does this kid have to commit sodomy under the flag pole in front of the headquarters?"

Those words did it, I guess. Even the lawyers didn't have a comeback and the airman was discharged.

R & R

A MORAN STORY:

A GROWING FRIENDSHIP

When the new commander took over a famous regiment of the British Army, he called for the sergeant major to report to him.

The sergeant major did so immediately. As parodied by Eddie, the reporting process involved the foot crashing stomp the British use followed by an exaggerated open palm "windmill' salute: "SIR!"

"Sergeant Major," said the new commander, "as a check on the fitness of the men, for the next several weeks I want to inspect them as they stand naked in the ranks."

The sergeant major saluted and set out to make the preparations. After the first inspection, the commander called for the sergeant major (Eddie's foot stomping crash, open palm salute): "SIR!"

"Sergeant Major," the commander said, "I observed during the inspection that when I walked past him, Corporal Smythe-Pigeon was at *quarter staff.*"

After the second inspection, the sergeant major's presence was again demanded by the commander (foot crashing stomp, open palm salute): "SIR!"

"This week when I inspected Corporal Smythe-Pigeon I noticed that he was at *half staff.*"

The following week, when the commander completed his third inspection, he again summoned the sergeant major (foot stomping crash, exaggerated salute): "SIR!"

"Sergeant Major," intoned the commander, "this time as I moved though the ranks, Corporal Smythe-Pigeon was at *full staff*! What do you think accounts for that?"

"Well, sir," replied the sergeant major (Eddie's passable cockney accent), " 'oy'd say 'e seems to be developin' a *fondness* for you."

COMM CHECKS

Speech 101

The noncommissioned officers in America's armed forces are among the best trainers and teachers in the world. The reason is, they *communicate*. The language is not always pristine; in fact, quite often it is profane. But the line from sender to receiver is clear and direct. There is no mistaking the intended meaning.

Many of the very best NCOs paint pictures with their remarks. It is a gift. They capture the essence of a situation and describe it in such rich terms that it remains with the listener always.

When my small unit arrived in Sarajevo soon after the Dayton Peace Accords were signed, we quickly began setting up shop in the ruins of the devastated city. Those arrangements required extensive contacts – "coordination" in military parlance – with other allied and U.S. forces.

The process was not without its difficulties. After one less than notable session, one of my senior sergeants burst into my room shouting "Jesus Christ, Colonel, these assholes couldn't lead water downhill!"

Lessons about Uniforms and other Important Things

The first time I really had a chance to observe officer corps "psycho-socials" was as a captain at the Air Force Military Personnel Center, working on a new officer evaluation system. It didn't take long to realize that all kinds of emotions and anticipations came wrapped up in a military rating system. It later became equally obvious that "tickets," the service slang for evaluation reports, weren't the only example: things like titles, uniforms, and awards are also imbued with special auras that outsiders may never understand. These corporate views of the world result from traditions, experiences, and expectations within each service. They are vastly important to the institutions and to the professional officers who serve them.

The existence of these convictions, and their importance, is sometimes overlooked, particularly in matters that to some would seem to be of small consequence. But as witness the "brown shoe versus black shoe" tradition in the Navy and the explosion that inevitably results from even the hint of change or the short-lived attempt to restore the title of "commodore," those who would venture into these areas should do so with trepidation.

The Air Force has paid a price as an institution – in terms of lower morale and marginal acceptance – when service leaders have ignored their constituency on issues of intrinsic value to the rank and file.

Uniforms, for example.

The famous episode of the white ceremonial uniform was almost humorous in the way it played out. It would have been even more laughable had it not been for the high out-of-pocket expense officers paid for uniform sets that in almost every case were *never* worn.

The early '80s decision to introduce white and blue ceremonial uniforms came as a surprise to a service that prided itself on having a "functional" uniform ensemble: a basic blue uniform that could be worn with a "wheel hat," jacket and ribbons for dressier occasions and a mess dress uniform for formal affairs. That was it. Most officers seemed content with that; they appreciated the constancy and simplicity. The Marines are legendary for taking that approach with their uniforms and the consistency has served them well.

Nonetheless, as one version of the story would have it, the Air Force Chief of Staff was eager to match his Army and Navy colleagues with their array of ceremonial uniform combinations. Their wardrobes allowed them to adjust to the degree of formality of an occasion and to the time of day it was held. The Chief was perhaps getting ragged by his sister service contemporaries about showing up for every event in the same standard blue uniform. I believe it is charitable to say that most of the Air Force officer corps did not regard that as a problem.

The other version of the story is that the Chief's wife liked the looks of the Navy's white uniform and he was coerced into adopting one for the Air Force as well.

Whatever the reason, the idea flopped and caused considerable disgruntlement. The total cost of uniforms, tailoring, shoes and extras was quite high. I had the uniforms for several years until the Air Force discontinued them. I never wore either one. They were so unpopular that they were seldom designated for use at a ceremony.

Even when they were, there was sometimes an ulterior motive. Like, for example, the case of the crusty SAC senior officer who specified the white ceremonial uniform for his retirement festivities. He bitched about having to pay that price for a uniform that was of no use, but since he'd had to, he was by God going to wear it at least *once.*

Except at the tailor shop when it was fitted, I never had mine on. I once loaned the new white shoes to a neighborhood kid who was going to a '50s rock 'n roll dance. Other than that they were never worn either. I eventually took them to the Base Thrift Shop where they were scarfed up by a Navy guy.

The more serious uniform misadventure occurred a decade later when another Chief of Staff attempted to introduce significant changes to the Air Force's standard blue uniform. While no one would argue that *any* change in design will always be unacceptable – certainly the service should take advantage of new fabrics and "looks" that acceptably keep pace with the times – at least one of the proposed modifications was sufficiently radical that it alienated much of the Air Force population. (Changes to the fabric and less significant "tweaks", like removing the breast pocket from the uniform jacket, drew little flak.)

The Chief's notion was to make the Air Force blue suit look like the RAF uniform and other European versions that in his view had more of a classic "airman's appearance." The most substantial change was to remove the grade insignia from shoulder epaulets and, as in the RAF and U.S. Navy, display officer grades via braid arrangements on the sleeves of uniform jackets.

That part of the proposal in particular sparked an outcry from officers who felt it was too disruptive of the service's tradition.

From the time it separated from the Army in 1947, the Air Force had retained the Army's officer insignia and, like the Army, displayed it on the shoulder. Entire generations of Air Force officers had "grown up" attired in that mode.

To those critics, the Chief asserted that General Hap Arnold had intended to adopt sleeve insignia when the Air Force became a separate service. (General Arnold retired before the Air Force became an independent branch and died soon after.) Further, other air forces around the world displayed officer grades in that fashion, and like the RAF, a slimmer jacket and braids on the sleeves had an immutable "airman's look" about it. Indeed, he noted, even the airlines did it that way.

One of my bosses asked for comments about the uniform proposal in advance of a scheduled visit from the Chief to our organization. The idea was to collect inputs and provide him with feedback on an issue that was generating considerable buzz throughout the service.

My note said that it was irrelevant what General Arnold may have intended 50 years before. In point of fact, for all of its existence, the Air Force had used shoulder insignia. It was now part of our history and ingrained in our image of how we viewed ourselves. I also wrote that the fact that the RAF had a different look was also immaterial. "Without the United States Air Force, Great Britain would long ago have been the smallest province in the Soviet Empire. Maybe they should look like *us.*"

I doubt that my memo was passed on; even if it had been it would surely have made no difference. The RAF officer-braid-on-the-sleeve style lasted only a short time. The acceptance quotient was way too low and the style was a continuing source of heartburn. After a while it was made optional; officers could choose either the shoulder insignia or the RAF-type version. Soon, since almost no one chose the latter, the idea withered away and the style was discarded.

Part of the package of changes also did away with the "wheel hat" for the majority of Air Force people. (It is now authorized for majors and above when wearing the "service dress" uniform.) The Chief said he discarded it because on his travels it was difficult to stuff his wheel hat into the cockpit of his fighter aircraft.

Eliminating the wheel hat was less controversial; but in some ways I regretted it, also. Whenever I saw Air Force recruits from boot camp getting their first pictures taken in uniform, inevitably they choose to wear wheel hats for the photo. There just seemed to be an extra flair, some added pizzazz associated from wearing it in circumstances like that; clearly there was an element of special pride attached to it.

For the rest of us, wearing the "wheel hat" to certain ceremonies "dressed up" the uniform to a higher level of formality and did so without adding any other whistles and bells. (Ironically, in those cases it *did* make us more compatible in appearance with our international allies.) At any rate, since fighter pilots comprise less than one percent of the Air Force's total population, whether or not a hat fits comfortably inside a fighter cockpit should not be a matter of particular consequence.

The service uniform "hits people where they live." All kinds of feelings – pride and tradition foremost amongst them – attach themselves to it. This attempt to change it was wide of the mark. The Chief misjudged or misunderstood the convictions of Air Force people. Or, worse, he ignored them.

In Praise of Chiefs ... and Indians: Part II

For those who knew him, it would be impossible to write or talk about "wheel hats" without mentioning Chief Master Sergeant Frank Viser. The two subjects come in the same breath: they cannot be thought about separately. They are like ham and eggs or the ocean and the tides.

Chief Viser was one of the few people in the Air Force who wore the wheel hat as a standard part of his uniform. Most others saved it for special occasions and used the flight cap for daily wear: it was easier to handle (the Air Force Chief of Staff who abolished the wheel hat was right about that), and could be stuck in the uniform belt when not in use.

"The Chief," though, liked the appearance of the wheel hat; and when he was in uniform, he was never seen "covered" in anything else.

The morning he left the unit in Stuttgart for his final assignment in the States, we arranged to have the staff car transporting him to the airport swing by squadron headquarters. There, on the sidewalk outside the building, the entire squadron was lined up – all wearing *wheel hats*. Some of the kids had to dig deep into their wardrobes to find theirs; but we filled the sidewalk with the chief's wheel hat-wearing squadron mates, all of whom saluted as his car drove past.

The Chief's affinity for his wheel hat was an interesting detail about him although in the big scheme of things it was of secondary consequence. What really mattered – and what is always remembered about him – was his consummate professionalism, and the fact that almost everyone who ever met him regards him as one of the finest people they have ever known.

Soft-spoken, smart, known for his impeccable integrity, Chief Viser's counsel was sought by one-stripers and four-star generals alike. His wisdom was gently imparted: he is one of those rare individuals who teaches without seeming to teach.

Chief Viser was a legend in the 1141st USAF Special Activities Squadron. Half of his long career was spent in that unit, assigned at the headquarters in Stuttgart or to one of the squadron's outlying detachments. He loved that unit and the Air Force more than anyone I've ever met.

There is a cliché that NCOs are the glue that binds a military service together. If that is true, and I believe it is, none ever held it tighter – or closer to the heart – than Chief Viser.

Sexual Harassment: My Own Definition

As part of the annual conference for my detachment commanders, my unit brought in experts from the United States Air Forces in Europe (USAFE) Headquarters staff and international organizations to give presentations on the hot issues of the day. Briefings usually included intelligence updates, defense initiatives affecting Europe, human resources programs, disciplinary trends, and other special issues. In the latter category, I always requested a presentation on sexual harassment. Almost twenty percent of the population of my headquarters and subordinate units were women. Women officers commanded two of my detachments. It was a timely issue.

When the Social Actions expert from the USAFE staff was part way through the sexual harassment presentation, one of the detachment commanders asked him to specifically define sexual harassment. The briefer launched into a lengthy, technical explanation. He obviously knew his subject to a 't' but his extended and somewhat arcane remarks were costing him his audience.

I eventually interrupted. After apologizing to him for doing so, and then apologizing to the audience for some of the language I was about to use, I said I had developed my own definition of sexual harassment. It was this: "Sexual harassment is any action which, if perpetrated against your wife or daughter, would piss you off."

The Social Actions officer did not resume his definition. He stopped, smiled, and said: "I like yours better." So did I, if only because in a simplistic way it personalized the issue and provided a standard to apply.

GI Speak

Like many professions, the military has a specialized vocabulary all its own – code, slang, and shorthand words or phrases that communicate very well inside the service but sound like gibberish outside it.

Military jargon has a useful purpose. To those "fluent" in it, the terminology conveys specific images and meanings and does so in a concise manner. It's a great tool, and it usually works fine – unless the audience is forgotten.

At Strategic Air Command Headquarters, I received a call from a local businessman asking the status of Bill Nickerson, a sergeant who worked in my office. As duty permitted, Bill sometimes moonlighted at the caller's place of business. Bill was not available. At the last moment, a slot at SAC's noncommissioned officer academy had opened up with no advance notice. We were anxious for Bill to attend, so we had hustled him off to take advantage of the windfall opportunity. In the rush, Bill had not had time to notify the businessman of his non-availability.

It was the usual hectic day at the office. When the phone rang and the caller asked where Bill was, without thinking I quickly answered, "He's TDY at NCO PME."

There was stunned silence at the other end of the line. The moment I said it, I thought to myself, "There is absolutely no way this guy is going to understand *any part* of what I just said."

Then we both burst out laughing.

I carefully explained to the gracious caller that "TDY at NCO PME' stood for "temporary duty at noncommissioned officer professional military education."

Or ... in other words, "Bill is away at school."

R & R

A MORAN STORY:

THE IVORY FAN

This is a story Eddie loved to tell about himself. He told it frequently – slightly more embellished with each recitation. I was fortunate enough to be "present at the creation" and observe the event that precipitated it.

When we flew from Charleston AFB to Morocco, the Capital Airlines charter made a refueling stop at Santa Maria, a Portuguese airfield in the Azores. It was late at night when we rolled in but a coffee bar -- gift shop remained open in the small terminal building.

As we ordered, Moran immediately struck up a conversation with the proprietor. When we were being seated, Eddie had noticed a very ornate fan – one of those folding, decorative, genteel things that women sometimes carry on special occasions – on display at the counter.

Eddie commented on its attractiveness. The manager agreed that it was quite beautiful. As they chatted, Eddie continued to admire the fan and eventually asked the manager where it was from.

"Angola" (then a Portuguese possession), the manager answered, and then said almost in passing, "it is genuine ivory."

"Ivory?" Moran was incredulous.

"Yes, genuine ivory," responded the proprietor. "In fact," he said, pointing a snapshot on the wall behind the cash register, "this is a photograph of the elephant the ivory came from." After the elephant was found dead, he related, the tusks had been taken to Luanda where the carving was made.

The price seemed reasonable and, quite pleased, Eddie bought the fan as a gift for his wife.

As we flew the last leg of the trip from the Azores to Casablanca, Eddie showed the fan to everyone seated around him, delighted both by its appearance and by the fact that he had gotten such a good deal. It was, after all, carved ivory.

His running commentary eventually drew the attention of a flight attendant (aka in 1962 'stewardess'), who had flown the route many times. She smiled hugely and said "Let me see it." Eddie handed her the fan and she opened it as wide as possible. Way down at the bottom, where the folding pieces were held together, in the minutest possible print it said "Made in Hong Kong." Plastic. Totally.

For several weeks, Eddie showed his "genuine ivory fan" to everyone who visited our hooch. "Jeez, the guy even had a picture of the elephant ..."

SITUATION REPORTS

Lesson #1

When I became a commander, the first rule of management I developed was "No One Calls At Three In The Morning To Say You're Doing A Good Job."

On my first day in the chair, I was awakened at that hour to handle a contentious emergency leave situation. Fortunately, I stumbled through it, but from that time on my experience was that the most trying cases inevitably happened at inconvenient times or when the "experts" were not available. There was a reason the Japanese attacked Pearl Harbor early on a Sunday morning.

For me, that first time was a wake-up call. After that, I tried to always be sure that no matter what came up or who was missing, facts were at hand or some knowledgeable person was available to handle the situation all day, every day.

And So I Said to Carruthers, "Would You Rather Face Me or the Guns?"

"A good commander sometimes needs to be an actor," a senior leader once told me. He meant that communications are an essential part of the job and that occasionally commanders must be seen doing things that lend emphasis to issues of special significance. Images are important. So is impact.

I hope that I was a good commander, but I rarely saw myself as an "actor." There was one notable exception.

When I was on my way to Italy as a newly minted major to take over a detachment, I stopped by the unit's parent headquarters in Germany for a three day orientation. There, it was made clear that by most management indices my new detachment ranked at or near the bottom of the heap. After several months on the job, with the help of some fine NCOs, the unit was showing steady improvement.

Things seemed to be going well when in the NCO club on the Italian air base where the detachment was located, two three-stripers got into a drunken fight. Making the image even worse was that one was black and the other was white. The subsequent investigation indicated that the quarrel had no racial overtones; indeed, before the incident the two had been best friends. Rather, two drunken young people had let booze take control of their mouths.

The appearance was terrible. Not only had two American NCOs gotten into a public fight – that was bad enough – but they had done so inside a club operated by our host country. That made it even worse. Compounding all of that was that observers must surely have been left with the impression that race was a factor.

I was disappointed and incensed. I am not a talkative person and I do not speak loudly. In fact, my technique has often been to speak more softly and slowly when trying to defuse a situation. Sometimes in cases where emotions aren't completely out of hand, speaking quietly causes people to listen more closely. That was my usual approach -- and the only one people in the detachment had seen at that point.

Apparently, that was what the first of the two culprits was expecting as he stood at attention in front of my desk. But, the incident was so unacceptable and so far out of bounds that something special was in store for him. There had to be no doubt that a point was being made and that he should remember it, always. He was not going to get the usual approach.

I reamed him up his front side and then down his back. He learned quickly and loudly that he had embarrassed himself and disgraced our unit, our service, and our country in front of our friends; that what he had done was by God totally unacceptable and nobody in the organization, least of all me, was going to tolerate it; that he was about to get hammered big time with Article 15 punishment; that he was going to lose a stripe and some of his money, and that he was damn lucky that he wasn't getting court-martialed and kicked completely out of the Air Force.

Somewhere during the tirade, I picked up a stapler and threw it down on my desk. I was surprised at how far it bounced. In my mind's eye I found myself viewing this as from a distance, looking down on the scene. Did I really just do that? Wow, that thing really went a long ways.

Apparently, all this was so totally unexpected and out of character that when for further emphasis I slapped my open palm on the desk top, the sergeant began to visibly tremble. He was already sweating profusely and now when my palm hit the desk he began to wobble even more. My first sergeant, who was standing at the back of the room and whose eyes were getting progressively wider, stepped up to steady the culprit and help him to a chair.

"Just what I need," I remember thinking to myself, "this kid is going to have a heart attack." After the sergeant was safely a seated, I ratcheted things down considerably. The young man signed the Article 15 documents and walked rather unsteadily out of my office.

Still surprised and bemused, the first sergeant came in soon afterward. "Jeez, Major," he said, "I didn't know who was going to pass out first: me or the kid."

When the second participant in the fracas came in for punishment, we may have set the record for the fastest Article 15 ever handled: I've never seen anyone so eager to sign a document and get out of an office.

Firing a Commander

Removing a commander is a gut-wrenching decision. At least it was for me. My squadron in Germany had nine subordinate detachments and two operating locations scattered all over the landscape from Stavanger, Norway, to Izmir, Turkey. During the four and a half years I was commander, given short- and long-tour rotation policies and one or two humanitarian reassignments, probably 25 officers rotated through the commander billets. I fired two of them.

One was an officer that I replaced due to a combination of medical and personal problems and general ineffectiveness. The second was Franklin Chelvester (not the real name), commander of our largest detachment located at a major international headquarters. Frank was a highly regarded lieutenant colonel, "politically connected" due to his previous posting in Washington D.C. where he helped assign senior officers. He was also African-American.

Those who think that routine business as usual handling suffices in instances such as this do not live in the real world. Being "color blind" was, I believe, my reputation as well as that of my squadron; I urged my subordinate commanders to view everyone as being the "same color of polka-dot." Still, while I would apply the same procedures I would "normally" employ, quite obviously there would be some special mine fields to walk through.

Frank Chelvester was accused by two female NCOs on his staff, one of whom was African-American, of having made sexual advances toward them. The first alleged that Chelvester had come by her apartment at night, six pack of beer in hand. Nonplussed by the sight of her commander at her front door, she had granted his request to come in. Her statement asserted that while seated together on her living room couch he had made advances toward her that involved physical contact. Lieutenant Colonel Chelvester acknowledged stopping by her apartment, but said he did so only to confirm that she was okay after a contentious and difficult day at work. He denied everything else.

The second incident took place after a detachment Christmas party. When the festivities broke up, the black female NCO stated that Chelvester, perhaps partly in his cups, had walked her to her car and kissed her. According to her, it was not just a routine holiday buss, but an impassioned, tongue in the mouth, full monte. She had not reported it until the other allegation surfaced. Frank Chelvester contended that he had only kissed her on the check, as he had others, that holiday night.

There were no other witnesses to either episode.

The allegations contained inferences of both sexual harassment and abuse of authority. Thus, the issues touched the turf of the Social Actions program as well as the Air Force Office of Special Investigations (OSI). Each agency conducted investigations and interviewed people in the detachment and from around the installation.

Frank Chelvester's closest confidant on the base was an Air Force brigadier general. Through church, the wives' club, and frequent gatherings in each other's homes, Chelvester and his wife had become intimate friends with the general and his spouse. The general was apoplectic. He asserted that the reputation of one of the females was less than pristine (true) and that the charges had been trumped up as a result of personal vendettas. He hinted that he should see the results of the on-going investigations. I declined to supply them. The investigations were still in progress. More important, the information was proprietary within command channels, and I was the commander in the chain. It was further apparent that the general's close personal friendship with Chelvester had removed any semblance of objectivity.

Both inquiries took extended periods. The nearest Air Force base was a considerable distance from the international compound. The lawyers, Social Actions technicians, and OSI investigators had to travel back and forth to transact their business. While the investigations were underway I temporarily removed Chelvester from command and assigned him to duty at the headquarters of another international agency about sixty miles away.

The interregnum was difficult for everyone.

During it, I was reminded of an event that occurred during my first command job many years before. As a young detachment commander, I received a call from a commander at another base. He phoned to caution about an ethnic minority staff sergeant that was due to report in to my detachment. "Be careful of this guy," his ex-commander warned, "he's the type that will stop by the Social Actions office just to check their hours of operation even before he signs in." My colleague's comments were tongue in check, but there was some truth to them. There were indeed those on every side of the issue who were eager to push the envelope.

Sure enough, soon after his arrival the new staff sergeant sent the unit's Social Actions representative to complain about the disciplinary punishment that had been administered to one of his African-American friends. I provided a "no names" list that recounted every disciplinary episode that had occurred during my tenure as commander. The sheet contained a description of the incident that had provoked the disciplinary action and showed the specific punishment that had been administered. The list made it apparent that similar offenses drew identical punishments. Everyone was the "same color of polka-dot."

That seemed to defuse things. Later, after we helped the complainer with some tuition assistance difficulties and work place problems, he was quiet for the rest of his tour.

While the overall "climate" was better than it was when that event occurred, it would be naïve to think that sensitivities had subsided entirely. Considering his job, background, and acquaintances, Frank Chelvester's case carried heavy baggage with it. To Frank's credit, he did not, outwardly at least, play what would become known euphemistically in the O.J. era as the "race card." He was not at all uncomfortable though, in asking his friends in high places to weigh in on his behalf. As a result, I began to get letters on three- and four-star stationery with interesting autographs on them.

When the investigations were finally finished, neither reached clear cut conclusions. Both leaned toward suggesting there was likely some fire under the smoke, but absent any witnesses, it essentially remained, a "she said versus he said" contretemps.

I was prepared to take that situation and do with it what I could when I received notice that Lieutenant Colonel Chelvester had bounced checks and had major debts with payments overdue at his local post exchange. Overdue notices get sent to all commanders as a way of helping assure the welfare of the troops, especially in an overseas environment. More importantly, for people in senior positions or who hold high security clearances, indebtedness can compromise the individual in any number of ways. Considerable emphasis is placed on this issue; commanders burn lots of "commander's call" time drawing attention to it.

The list of payments overdue was three and a half pages long for the entire part of Europe served by that particular Post Exchange. Almost all of the names were of young two- or three-stripers. That was unfortunate, but not unusual. On the entire list, there was only one officer. He was a lieutenant colonel—and he commanded one of my detachments.

I called Chelvester, telling him to pay his debts, or explain why he could not along with a plan for reimbursement. Then I called his brigadier general confidant and explained the information I had received. I wanted him to hear it in an unfiltered form in case later action was warranted.

At about this time, I received several additional letters from senior officers who had written at Frank's request. It was noticeable that Frank had not mentioned the indebtedness issue when he solicited their support. The letters all mentioned his exemplary record and his sterling performance. I needed no reminders; I knew those comments were correct.

The next month I received another notice of payments overdue. This time, the amount was even larger.

The issue of how to adjudicate all this still remained. The three lawyers involved in it at one time or another and the various interested staff agencies all had different takes on it ranging from courts-martial to slap on the wrist. My decision was to place a Letter of Reprimand in Chelvester's permanent official records and to remove him from command.

That approach made sense to me but upset most others. At one extreme was Frank's coterie of heavy hitters who would have preferred the slap on the wrist approach, or nothing at all. At the other was the four star commander of the U.S. Air Forces in Europe. Because of sexual harassment incidents that were making headlines in the States at the time, he wanted to know why Chelvester was not court-martialed. Perhaps he was looking for an example; or he didn't want us to be one of the headlines.

At any rate, one of his colonel staff officers called at his request to relay his concerns. I explained that although I thought there was substance to the sexual harassment aspect, if it came to a court-martial proceeding the board members could interpret the "she said versus he said" as too ambiguous to be conclusive. Regarding the indebtedness issue, Chelverster had borrowed substantial amounts of money to pay off the debts identified on the second list. Thus, in a formal proceeding, board members might minimize the implications of the indebtedness issue as well. Further, lawyers said it was not certain that all of the testimony collected by the investigators could be used at a trial. That left some chance, modest perhaps, but real, that a court-martial could be lost. That would be bad form.

Conversely, the Letter of Reprimand would get us to main purposes we should be looking for: removing him from command and precluding prospects for future promotion. At the same time it would acknowledge the officer's past exemplary record by sparing him the embarrassment of court-martial proceedings (and, if the charges were sustained, a federal conviction). I thought it struck the right chord: it served the needs of the institution while best balancing the interests of the individuals. I don't know that the general accepted my logic, but I didn't get any more phone calls.

With the passage of time, I have become more comfortable with the decision. Some of that feeling may be rationalization, as over the years my deputy and I have run into several officers who, unsolicited, commented on Chelvester's "skirt chasing" reputation at the international headquarters. The detachment's very astute veteran first sergeant assessed Chelvester as being a binge drinker and lent additional credence to the assertions of the two women NCOs. For me, the Letter of Reprimand was justified by the poor judgment Chelvester showed. Even aside from the question of whether "harassment" occurred or was intended, showing up alone, unannounced, at odd hours at a junior subordinate's off post residence was a dubious action ... as was kissing the other NCO ... as was severe indebtedness sustained while he was in a position that required him to set an example. As Patton told his officers: "You are always on parade."

Nevertheless, the run-up to the decision was tough sloughing indeed. Every commander understands that heartburn and anguish sometimes come with the job description, but that realization didn't make any part of this any easier.

The Last Round Draft Choice

I "inherited" the two officers that I fired during my command tenure. One was on board and the second, Frank Chelvester, had already been selected for assignment when I signed in. In Chelvester's case, my predecessor had phoned me at my previous base to inform me that he had chosen Frank for the position and to make sure I was comfortable with the decision. It was a gracious, professional courtesy. I had no objection. Chelvester's credentials were excellent, and as a commander-designate I was pleased to know that an officer of his apparent caliber would be the commander of the flagship detachment of my new unit.

Those were the only two cases where I directly removed officers in command positions. There was one other instance, though, where I facilitated a commander's early departure. This time there was nothing inherited about it. This one was totally on me.

When an organization is staffed with good people, all things are possible. Magic happens. Thus, my philosophy of hiring is like the one the Dallas Cowboys used to employ when they drafted players for the team: "Pick the best athletes available and find a place to play them." That is the approach I always used ... except once.

That one occasion occurred when the commander of a large detachment in Southern Europe suddenly departed on a humanitarian reassignment. The detachment was at an important location; the Balkans were just heating up, and there were other important peripherals in play as well. For one, it was a unit that needed to be jump-started. For another, an extensive renovation of facilities was underway, and we needed someone to invigorate the action. During his short tenure, the departing commander had done a good job of launching initiatives that injected new life into the organization.

For all those reasons, it was important to fill the billet quickly, rather than having the detachment run by a rotating series of temporary commanders while tolerating the machinations of the normal lengthy assignment selection process.

I accepted an officer who was available immediately. Dwight Edwards' (not the real name) record looked okay but not great. Ditto the feedback from telephone checks. Since Edwards would be assigned on an unaccompanied tour status (short tour length), my expectation was that he would be adequate to carry the load for a relatively brief period of time. Then, when he completed his short tour, we would have everything lined up to bring in a real blue chipper.

It was the poorest decision I ever made.

Dwight was awful. In a situation that demanded a high energy person, Edwards' approach was beyond lethargic. He never seemed to grasp the commander duties. As weeks went by and it became apparent that we had lost the positive momentum generated by the previous commander, I sent my best detachment commander half way across Europe to spend three weeks with Dwight, thinking that over the shoulder mentoring might serve to show him the ropes and light a fire under him. That had little effect. On two occasions, I stripped the headquarters to send teams to assist him and his detachment. That didn't do much either.

When the lieutenant colonel selection board rolled around, Edwards was passed over. The performance reports I had written on him no doubt had something to do with that, but it seemed apparent to all that he had already been promoted past the point of his highest competence. Under a program available at the time, he was eligible to apply for early retirement. Dwight was a single parent who had plans to return to the States to build a more stable environment for his children. At the same time, it was clear that his future prospects in the Air Force were limited. I encouraged him to take the retirement option and get on with his life. He understood and agreed. I set out, successfully this time, to bring in a dynamic young major to replace him.

I read a lot of military history. I always thought that it was instructive to note that the general philosophy of many major units in the German Army during World War II was to "go short" in an officer billet rather than accept an individual of less than top caliber. That had always been my approach to filling key positions as well: be willing to wait for the very best. In this case, I had violated my own rule. I never made that mistake again.

A Death in the Family

There are things in the military called regulations. Most of them exist for very good reasons. Almost always it is best to follow them. *Almost* always ...

First Lieutenant Andrew Olberding was mortally injured in a car wreck nears Mons, Belgium. Andrew was traveling from our detachment at SHAPE Headquarters to conduct promotion testing for a group of Air Force NCOs assigned to NATO Headquarters in Brussels, about 60 miles away. In rural Belgium, country lanes like the one on which he was driving are narrow and tree-lined. Andrew's car skidded off the icy road and ran broadside into a tree, impacting at the driver's side door. Help was immediately available on scene, and he was transported to a hospital in Brussels.

Andrew had been assigned to the detachment at SHAPE while awaiting a slot at pilot training. His ambition was to fly F-15s. He was a neat kid: smart, loyal, dedicated to the Air Force. I thought his prospects were exceptional and that his sojourn in our organization would serve him well. He learned a bit about the personnel business, filled in for a time as acting detachment commander, and worked on projects with allied officers in the international arena. Those experiences and the responsibilities that accompanied them far surpassed most of his junior officer contemporaries. Appending that background to the pilot wings that would surely come made his future appear bright indeed.

The accident occurred near the start of a normal duty day, thus it was still early in the morning in Europe when I received the call from the detachment first sergeant. As almost always happens, initial information was sketchy. I asked the first sergeant to find out the severity of Andrew's injuries; we needed to know that because of family notification considerations and other reporting requirements.

The first sergeant called back several minutes later. The news was devastating. Trauma from a head injury had caused swelling of the brain. Unless that could be reversed, Andrew's injuries would be fatal. The doctor held out almost no hope. He would not speculate on how long Andrew might live. For sure it would not be long: perhaps a day or so at most.

The detachment commander was away on leave at the time – why does that always happen? – and it was clear that we needed a presence on scene to help take care of things. Chief Master Sergeant Jerry Carney wore many hats in my organization, one of which was Senior Enlisted Advisor. Chief Carney had come to us from Mons, where he had been first sergeant in Andrew's detachment. The Chief knew the area and the people very well. More importantly, he was the right guy to send. To say that Jerry Carney gets things done is like saying Randy Johnson throws an okay fast ball. If you've got problems, he's the guy you want to fix them. I put him immediately on the road to Belgium, while at the same time attempting to contact the detachment commander at her leave location. Late that afternoon we succeeded, and she left to return to Mons, arriving there the following day.

In the meantime, I called the youngsters in the headquarters, about 75 total, into a conference room. I told them what had happened, asked them to be ready to assist with arrangements, messages and reports, and requested that they not speculate or spread rumors.

But the hardest part still remained: the question of how to contact Andrew's parents. The standard protocol is to go through channels to the Air Force Casualty Reporting Center. That agency then contacts the Air Force base nearest the residence of the next of kin, where base officials form a team typically consisting of a notification officer (same grade or higher than the casualty) and a chaplain, and travel in an Air Force staff car to make a personal notification. It is a superb way to handle one of the most difficult and sensitive circumstances any family ever has to face.

I just didn't think it fit this situation. I reconfirmed through the doctor that we now faced a "no hope" situation and that Andrew's life span would be measured in hours. The Air Force base that would notify Andrew's parents was about a four-hour drive from the Olberding's home. It would take another hour or two to form the team and get it on the road. If the Olberding's had any inclination to travel to Belgium the time absorbed by the standard process would preclude any possibility of seeing him while he was still alive. In the time the notification would take, his parents could be journeying to a nearby airport for a flight to Belgium.

The commander of a "spook" organization on the floor above us had learned of the incident through a hallway conversation. When he came into my office to commiserate, I told him I was considering calling the family directly. He urged me to follow the normal procedure: let a notification team make the contact. Doing anything could easily come untracked with troublesome consequences. That was a true but not necessarily convincing argument.

I phoned the unit in Belgium asking if anyone in the detachment knew anything about the Olberding family. As it turned out, Andrew's parents had visited him in Belgium the previous summer. Those who had met Andrew's family said they seemed to be in good health and described them with words like "down to earth," "pleasant," "strongly religious," "even keel", "a typical Midwest farm couple.'

It was probably the latter phrase that did it for me – along with a question I asked myself: "If it was my child would I want the opportunity to see him alive one last time?"

I drew a particularly deep breath and picked up the phone.

In Kansas it was not long after sunrise. The Olberding family was already up. Mrs. Olberding answered the phone. I told her who I was and asked if Mr. Olberding was there and, if so, if it would be possible for both of them to get on the line. I knew in an instant I had made the right decision. There was a quality to her voice that told me she could handle this mountain that was about to fall on her family. When Mr. Olberding also came on, I had the same impression: quiet strength and heartland steadiness.

I recounted the situation to them and concluded by saying that we had made tentative bookings on a flight to Brussels for them if they wished to travel. Throughout our conversation, they had interjected only occasionally with questions or comments. Now, when I had finished, Mr. Olberding needed one final validation: "How bad is it really?'

"Sir, it is very bad."

Andrews's mother and father, and as it turned out, his sister arrived in Brussels early the following morning. Chief Carney met them at the airport. Mr. and Mrs. Olberding had valid passports from their visit the previous summer, but Andrew's sister had no passport at all. Jerry Carney smooth talked and browbeat the Belgian customs official into allowing her into the country with an explanation of circumstances and a promise to take her to the American Embassy to get a passport. Then he drove them directly to the hospital to see Andrew. A few hours after their arrival, he died.

As soon as I could break away, I went to meet them. While they were still in Brussels, I stopped at Mons to speak with the young people in the detachment and make sure arrangements were in order. It was a time of profound sadness, but I have seldom been so proud to wear that blue uniform.

The handling of Andrew's family was the embodiment of the motto "The Air Force Takes Care of its Own." We arranged their flight to Belgium and took care of their quarters. Chief Carney and members of the detachment drove the Olberdings everywhere they wanted to go and arranged for them to see everything they wanted to see. A memorial service was arranged at SHAPE Headquarters that drew contingents from throughout the international community. Lois Hansen, the detachment commander, gave the most splendid eulogy I have ever heard in the most difficult circumstance imaginable. The next morning, an Air Force Personal Affairs technician traveled a great distance to talk with the family and provide information on government benefits and funeral arrangements. Andrew's accrued pay was transferred to them. The following day, a sharp young officer friend of Andrew's escorted Andrew's remains on the flight back to the States and represented the detachment at the funeral.

Andrew's parents and sister seemed to appreciate the opportunity for closure. They wanted to see everything: the car, the accident site, the places where Andrew worked and lived, his favorite haunts, his friends. I was pleased that we were able to make those things happen for them.

His parents gave us something in return: an example of strength and graciousness. At the memorial service, when the final program had been completed, Andrew's mom and dad came forward and to that standing room only audience of 300 people or more, quietly and calmly told us about Andrew's life, how much he had loved the Air Force and the people in that room, and how much the past day or two had meant to them. I've seldom been so touched.

The phone call to the Olberdings turned out to be the right thing to do. But, there is no denying that the menu of possible outcomes could have been different: collapse, hysteria, confusion, heart attack. That's why the usual notification protocol has such merit. It sends the right signal of class and concern, and face to face certainly better accommodates unforeseen and unforeseeable reactions.

The decision to override those considerations is not one to be made casually. I chose to do so, recognizing that sometimes considerations of the heart as well as the mind should weigh in the deliberations. After 35 years in the service I was prepared to accept the consequences whatever they might be. I'll always be grateful – for me personally as well as for the Olberding family – that, this time, it turned out well.

Breaking Another Rule

In Germany, traffic violations are sometimes captured on film by cameras mounted atop traffic lights, affixed at key intersections or positioned along the autobahn. The camera snaps the license plate, and the nature of the infraction is automatically recorded. Eventually, a letter containing the photo and a description of the transgression is sent to the owner of the automobile, along with a citation and a return envelope for payment of the fine.

When the traffic offender is an American service member, the letter is sent to the commanding officer of the "GI's" unit. The commander or first sergeant then contacts the service member and assures the fine is paid. The military member – "sponsor" – (in whose name the automobile is registered) is held accountable for violations of "dependent" family members who drive the vehicle.

One morning near the end of my tour, I opened the by now familiar envelope from German authorities containing a photo and traffic citation pertaining to one of my unit members. The "sponsor," Rob Warren (not the real name), was a two-striper then away on extended temporary duty in Saudi Arabia.

The violation was recent, and the location was a site on the autobahn considerably distant from our unit's base in Stuttgart. The clarity of the photo, shot as the car approached the camera, was excellent. It showed Rob's wife Kelli (not the real name) accompanied by a male individual driving the car.

The episode captured in the photo may have been completely innocent: two friends out for a "get away" jaunt, sight-seeing through the German countryside. I tried not to impute anything more to it than that. Still, the Warrens were a young couple whose marriage was known to have its rocky moments. Rob was due back shortly from his temporary duty assignment. It did not seem appropriate to risk adding further strain to his life, or to the couples' reunion, by subjecting him to that photograph when he returned.

I removed the picture from the envelope, tore it up, and threw it away.

Appearances Can Be Deceiving

"Trouble waiting to happen" was my first thought when Alfred and Brandi Carson (not the real names) walked into Detachment 9's Orderly Room in Vicenca, Italy. Alfred was reporting in for his assignment with the Fifth Allied Tactical Air Force. Brandi was his newly acquired wife. They had been married just a few days before leaving the States.

Alfred was a withdrawn, scrawny looking "geek" (although the term was not popularized at the time), with a woeful appearing mustache and coke bottle thick glasses. His new wife, by contrast, was a harsh voiced, gum chewing, hip swinging blouse full. Alfred was her fifth husband.

I may have spent several years growing up on a farm, but I was astute enough to mentally acknowledge the possibility that for Brandi, the free trip to Italy was a major motivation for her most recent wedding.

Trouble soon developed. Alfred arrived in Italy about $13,000 in debt, some of it recently accumulated as a result of his perceived need to acquire a used sports car more suited to Brandi's tastes. That was a considerable amount of indebtedness for most people at the time, and it was a monumental amount on a staff sergeant's salary. Alfred should never have been "cleared" for overseas duty; I immediately called his former commanding officer and educated him regarding the rules.

Nevertheless, Alfred's supervisor, Master Sergeant John Messier, worked with Alfred to ease the Carson's financial difficulties. With John's assistance, Alfred constructed a budget and consolidated several of his debts. I wrote to creditors in the States, and Sergeant Messier and I were able to reschedule payments on many others.

Then, just as we thought we were getting a handle on the indebtedness problems, the other shoe dropped. Brandi Carson sought companionship from a paratrooper in a nearby unit.

For a short time, the situation festered. I arranged counseling; not surprisingly, it was unsuccessful. Then, a few days later my phone rang: it was the MP Commander at the U.S. Army base. He said his guys had just pulled Alfred Carson off the paratrooper in the Post Exchange parking lot, where Alfred "was beating the holy hell out of him." I was stunned. "Are you talking about *Alfred Carson?*" I asked. The MP officer assured me that he was. Sure enough, geeky Alfred Carson, droopy mustache, coke bottle glasses and all, had with righteous indignation accosted the paratrooper in front of the Post Exchange. When the MPs got to him he was astride the guy, beating on him and pounding his head against the parking lot pavement. Other than his pride, the paratrooper was not seriously injured.

I called the soldier's commander. "Look," I said, "we've got a situation here. I'll keep my guy Sergeant Carson away from your paratrooper if you'll keep your paratrooper away from Carson's wife." We did a telephonic handshake.

Soon after, I removed Brandi Carson's base privileges, and Brandi – by then officially separated from Alfred – returned to the States. Alfred completed a successful, although now unaccompanied, tour.

Even today, the thought Alfred in that parking lot still brings a smile.

The "Minuteman Award"

As a commander, I bought small mementos to present "on the spot" to the young airmen in the outfit who clearly had gone above and beyond in handling a job or in taking care of one of our military "customers." Whenever I observed that happening or received calls or notes from service members lauding the service they received, I went to the person's work area and presented the small token of appreciation. In Stuttgart, I used tiny nutcrackers that looked like miniature colonial soldiers. The youngsters in the squadron quickly began calling it the "Minuteman Award," not only because of the small figure's appearance, but also because they "got it in a minute" after doing something exceptional.

The "Minuteman Award" had an extraordinary side effect: the kids began competing for it. What had begun with the intention of being only a small gesture of appreciation and reinforcement for their good work (goodness knows we didn't pay them enough) became a much sought after motivator. The small figurines were quickly and widely displayed beside computers, in work areas, and in dorm rooms.

For two consecutive years the organization was recognized as the best customer service unit in all of the United States European Command. We had some great people in the squadron to begin with, but I believe those tiny "Minutemen" also contributed to the unit's success. They were among the best investments I've ever made.

R & R

A MORAN STORY:

THE DISCOUNT

A young soldier from deep, deep in the backwoods had just received his reenlistment bonus. He decided to spend it on his first-ever leave in the big city.

The soldier was stunned by the number of things there were to buy. His first day's purchases were substantial; he could hardly carry them to the cashier. When he arrived at the cash register, the sales clerk smiled and told him that because of the large amount he had bought, he would get a discount.

"Discount" was a new word for the soldier. He asked the sales person what it meant. "Well," she said, "it's an amount we 'take off' in return for a large purchase." The soldier thought that was really something and left with his arms full of packages.

When he got back to his hotel room, he counted his remaining money. He found he had a thousand dollars left and he resolved to spend it all the next day before returning to his base.

The next morning he walked into a large store to begin the day's shopping. Eager to exploit his new found knowledge and anxious to be sure he got his money's worth – but unable to call to mind the word "discount" – he walked up to a sales lady.

"Ma'am," he said, "how much would you 'take off' for a thousand dollars?"

"Soldier," she replied, "would my earrings be in your way?"

BULL SESSIONS

Oscillations

There is a rhythm to life; I'm convinced of it. Alternating cycles of good and bad oscillate through an individual's personal life and professional career. For my wife Nita and me, it always seemed that the bad things happened in patterns of three. As a young lieutenant with a net disposable income of about a dollar ninety eight a month, Nita and I moved across country to a new assignment and with most of our carefully hoarded savings placed a deposit on a small apartment. Within the next two days, the transmission went out on our car, the compressor died in our used refrigerator, and the picture tube blew up on our most prized possession, a color TV set.

Later in my career, getting ready to accompany some high ranking officers on a briefing trip, Nita stepped on my laboriously spit shined shoes as she kissed me goodbye at the door, then my necktie dipped into the topping of a coconut cream pie at the airport terminal. During the trip, the buckle fell off my uniform belt as I was getting ready to brief a four star general. That had never happened before and has never happened since. It was one of those slide arrangements that military belt buckles have, and the little metal roller that holds the belt in place somehow just slipped out of the slot. Fortunately, for some reason the secretary in the anteroom outside the general's office happened to have a pair of pliers in her desk. We managed to bend the roller piece and put it back in place. (That episode only served to compound my admiration for secretaries.) But, I kept one hand close to the buckle all through the briefing in case the roller came loose again.

I think the general thought I had a stomachache.

Timing

Timing is everything. Said another way, timing can *disrupt* everything. Just before I left the commander's job in Italy, a senior officer at Headquarters United States Air Forces in Europe called me. Terrorist groups were still rampant at the time: the Red Brigades in Italy, the Baader-Meinhof Gang in Germany, and several other misguided but lethal organizations spread terror across the continent, convinced somehow that periodically kidnapping or blowing up their influential countrymen would help achieve their political aims. My own theory was that for some groups the political aspect receded over time and the *process* of kidnapping and killing became the objective as well as the gratification.

At any rate, the colonel from the Directorate of Assignments opened by saying that I had an experience "that was not widely shared" – leading a unit through a terrorist episode. Therefore, he remarked, "we'll be keeping a short leash on you." The "climate" of the times was such that further instances were expected throughout Europe. "If that happens, we may bring you back after a year or two ... or sooner," to run an organization under threat or to assist commanders involved in terrorist situations.

Okay by me, I guess. I was grateful for his consideration that my present overseas tour was complete and that it would be good to take my young family back to the States for awhile. Still, the phone call changed everything. When we settled in at our new base we chose, for example, not to buy a house, thinking that we might have to leave after a short time and on short notice. Instead, we decided on an okay but not great rental convenient to the base and close to an elementary school.

Then, for the people of Europe, something very good began to happen. Astute police work, better intelligence, and popular disaffection combined to disassemble the major terrorist organizations. Even before we left Italy, the *carabinieri* made solid progress in tearing apart the Red Brigades, aided in no small part by captured gang members who felt no compunction at all about ratting out their colleagues.

All this was good to behold. It happened gradually, but visibly and inexorably. In the meantime, we were still in our okay but not great rental, still not knowing whether a call might come or if we were still "on the bubble."

Thus, the saga played out: we moved to Offutt thinking we would be there only for a short time; instead, during my entire career it turned out to be the longest I ever spent in one place. And here we were in our okay but not great rental house.

Eventually, the progress in Europe was so obvious and the time lapse so extended that we moved ourselves to a place that the entire family lusted after: a beautiful home in the woods with a stream flowing at the foot of the timbered hillside. Deer and raccoons were frequent visitors and an opossum enjoyed a tree by our back porch. Timing is everything indeed. A few months after that move to the neatest house we ever lived in, I got orders to my next assignment.

Military Brats

At certain random points in my life it has been abundantly clear that my children were raised in a military family.

The longest time we were stationed anywhere was at Offutt AFB, Nebraska. Offutt is a "big plane" air base. RC-135 reconnaissance planes and E-4B National Airborne Operations Center aircraft (converted Boeing 747 flying command posts) are permanently assigned there and, as was befitting Offutt's raison d'etre as Headquarters Strategic Air Command, SAC's other heavies – KC-135 tankers and B-52 and B-1 bombers – made frequent visits.

There is a unique sound associated with the engine noise of large airplanes. We grew accustomed to it: a deep-throated, reverberating growl that became part of the background noise during the years we lived there.

From Offutt, we moved to Randolph AFB, Texas. Randolph is the home of T-37 and T-38 aircraft. Small, very small, airplanes. The sounds were totally different. The engine noises had a high-pitched, tinny, almost whistling quality about them. Not for nothing is the T-37 nicknamed "Tweet."

One evening several weeks after the move we were sitting down to dinner in our quarters on Randolph when a low bass rumble in the distance immediately caught our attention. Ever louder as it moved over us, our windows began to rattle and it felt for all the world like the plaster would crack and the fixtures would shake loose from the walls.

Karen, our youngest daughter, ran outside. Sure enough, there in its beautiful ugliness, drooping wings blotting out the sky, a roaring, growling, 488,000 pound personification of lethal fury, was a B-52. "Now *that*," my young daughter quietly pronounced, "is an airplane."

Talk about a Job Description

The day after I left for a five-week TDY to the Pacific, the toilet in our home backed up, the car had a flat tire, and our youngest daughter was diagnosed with a heart murmur. Inevitably, a set of three. Fortunately, it all "worked out."

There was a reason that it did. My wife – the plumber – used a plunger to unstop the commode. My wife – the mechanic – changed the flat tire. My wife – the "medic" – handled the news of our daughter's condition with understanding and steady assurance.

Entire chapters of military family histories talk about dealing with emergencies and foibles of life that occur when the service member is a continent or two away. Almost always, things "work out." When they do, it is usually because of support provided by others in the military community and the resourcefulness of the spouse.

Most often, things "work out" because the spouse is a special person who, with an appropriate blend of humor, patience, and imagination makes sure that for every separation there is a homecoming; that the sorrow of changing schools and changing friends is tempered by the anticipation of new schools and new friends; that moving for yet another time is met with enthusiasm instead of the uncertainty of "here we go again"; that travel is appreciated as an opportunity for education and adventure and not as an inconvenience, and who sees to it that the car and the plumbing and the kids are cared for despite the difficulties and loneliness of separation.

That is a formidable job description. The duty title that goes with it is "military spouse." Very often, especially when the military member is away, several additional duties are also appended: chief of staff, CEO, scheduler, planner, tutor, counselor, cheerleader, chauffeur, resident med tech. The list goes on. Remarkably, many times all this gets done while the spouse has full time employment outside the home.

The longer I stayed in the military, the more I came to appreciate the enormous importance of the military spouse, not only to those of us who were privileged to share their lives but to the military service and to the country as well. America's tax payers truly get their money's worth when they invest in a military family. The military career is not for everyone, and the military lifestyle is not suited to every family. It demands special qualities, sacrifice, and commitment not only from the person wearing the uniform but from the spouse as well. How fortunate we are to have families who understand the importance of the military to the nation and "buy into" the extraordinary life that service to our country requires.

Nicknames

Maybe because of political correctness, nicknames aren't employed as frequently as they were when I first enlisted. Almost anything could be used to derive a nickname: physical characteristics, personality traits, occupation, ethnicity, homes of record, previous bases of assignment, transliterations of names ... almost anything would do.

Even when their use was more common, the weather detachment at Sidi Slimane was an anomaly: *everyone* had a nickname – that was a tradition in the small unit.

At Sidi Slimane my nickname became "Flip." In past locations, it had most often been "Phil," but the unit already had a Philip Durrett so it was just a shorthand jump to "Flip." That's what it remained for my entire tour in Morocco.

Generic nicknames, applied to incumbents in key positions, still exist. Regardless of age, commanders are inevitably "The Old Man." It will be interesting to see if the increasing numbers of women in the military might someday transform the title given to female commanders, but somehow "The Old Lady" doesn't sound as "right."

Likewise, First Sergeants almost always become "First Shirt," or just "Shirt," or "Top" (for "Top Sergeant").

Before political correctness set in, airmen from Hawaii were usually "Pineapple" and Native Americans were invariably "Chief."

Some last names always carried a specific nickname: Rhodes were always "Dusty;" Villas were usually "Pancho;" Crosbys were nearly always "Bing."

Nicknames could also be applied by place or areas of residence: "Tex," "Reb," "Gator." Some were a further stretch geographically: to some of the kids from the east coast anyone from west of the Mississippi was "Cowboy." (I began to doubt the geographic proficiency of some of my friends when a kid from New York City told me – at Boot Camp, in *San Antonio, Texas* – that he couldn't wait for our first afternoon free so he could go to Tijuana.) Anyway, I never minded that title. My dad was a tenant farmer. To me, "Cowboy," connoted a *ranch*, so I took it as a compliment.

"Keepers"

Like many people with military backgrounds, I accumulated a collection of plaques and other memorabilia. Most eventually found their way to a storage room or were discarded, but the "keepers," proudly affixed over the years to the walls of dens, basements, and offices, are special. Eventually, even the "keepers" will be boxed up or given away. But for now the intensity of the feelings and the memories they elicit keep them tacked to their customary places, each one a mini-celebration of an accomplishment that was significant to me or my family -- an instant recollection of a good time or an achievement recognized by friends.

There is a unique clock on the wall of my office. It was given to me by the enlisted men and women of an organization as I was getting ready to move on to a new assignment. After 36 years in uniform, it remains one of the "keepers" that I value most. The clock displays the insignia of the enlisted ranks and officer grades that I held, each placed in ascending order representing the hours around the clock face. At the bottom of clock is an inscription that reads: "You Always Had Time For Us." I've seldom been so touched by any gift; there was considerable throat clearing when it was handed to me – and a very long time before I could find words that would even remotely convey how much that gesture meant.

In Praise of Chiefs ... and Indians: Part III

There are two "keeper" plaques that I probably will not take down, ever. The first is small, made of polished wood. The youngsters from the joint Army, Navy, Air Force support unit that we built in Sarajevo presented it to me at the old Ottoman Fort overlooking the city. The other one is large, encased in a heavy dark oak frame; it was given to me at my retirement ceremony. Duly bestowed by Chief Master Sergeant Jerry Carney and Chief Ken Casey representing Headquarters, United States Air Forces in Europe, it confers on me the title of Honorary Chief Master Sergeant with "all the rights and privileges attached thereto." Plus -- and this may be the highest honor of all – I got a "Chief's Coin" to carry in my pocket whenever I'm in the company of other chiefs.

The Aftermath

To a World War II history buff, trips to Berlin were like graduate seminars taught in residence. Except for the shattered spire of the Kaiser Wilhelm church, left standing as a visible reminder of the war, the western portion of the city has been rebuilt and rejuvenated. Today it is a vibrant, gleaming, neon lights flashing, horns honking, ultra-modern metropolis. Eventually, with the city now reunited and serving once again as the nation's capital, East Berlin will no doubt be similarly transformed. In 1992, however, it was still cloaked in socialist drab. Row upon row of crumbling, cookie cutter, "wedding cake" apartment houses reflected the Stalinist architectural style. On the massive old buildings near the Brandenburg Gate pock marks and shell holes were visible in the masonry, testimony still to the ferocity of the enormous rolling assault that swept up the Unter der Linden and other broad avenues toward the Reichstag and the Fuhrer bunker sixty years ago.

Soon after I took command of the unit in Stuttgart, Nita and I went to Berlin for the first time along with a group of American officers and spouses from the United States European Command. It was an orientation trip; we were there mainly to listen and learn and to ask questions of, and answer questions from, our counterparts from each of Germany's military services.

During the trip it was my interest in history that led to my first meeting with a Russian officer, a lieutenant colonel in charge of a war museum in a suburb of East Berlin. The museum grounds included the building where on May 8, 1945, the Russians accepted Nazi Germany's surrender. (The capitulation ceremony on the western front was held at Rheims, France the previous day.) The German representative, Field Marshal Wilhelm Keitel, had walked into the building on that Tuesday morning and conducted himself with a pompous arrogance that surprised and infuriated the assembled allied dignitaries, who talked about it for the rest of their lives.

The museum is nicely kept. Except for a statue of Lenin in the entry foyer and a placard commemorating the Red Army's victory, the building looks untouched, exactly as it was on that day almost six decades ago. So, too, I later discovered, were the facilities at Potsdam, where the "Big Three" met soon after the war ended. Even the table placements and the chair arrangements remain intact, as do the small offices in the Schloss Cecilienhof used by Stalin, Truman, and Churchill (later, Attlee) to conduct business away from the conference room.

The Russian officer and I shook hands and spoke briefly. The thought could not escape me that the world had turned over many times since 1979 when my class at Air Command and Staff College wargamed a nuclear exchange between our countries: a Soviet attack on the United States followed by our retaliatory response.

To the students at Air Command and Staff College and to those who viewed the Soviet military "across the wire" during the span of the Cold War, the Red Army presented formidable capabilities. "Quantity has a quality all its own," was a favorite cliché – and, indeed, the Soviets had enormous numbers of almost everything.

Years before, one of the projects I worked on for a time sought to assess the possibility of a "depressed trajectory" missile launch (a low, ocean skimming shot) by a Soviet submarine intended to "decapitate" our National Command Authority. From the military's perspective, there was considerable logic for that specific concern and to others similar to it. Military organizations "train like they fight" and there was no doubt about the Red Army's training regimen. Their major exercises inevitably focused on offensive operations and their doctrine emphasized attack from the outset. In a conflict, there seemed little doubt about what the Soviets would do: strike first with a massive assault, sustain it, and prosecute it with unremitting fury.

Now, here were the two of us conversing, certainly not as friends but at least as something less than enemies, on the steps of a building that had been purchased in blood at a time when our countries shared a common objective.

The Russians still retained a sizable garrison in Berlin in 1992 although plans were well underway for the withdrawal of their forces. When a German officer showed my group the Russian military facilities in the city, we were surprised by their condition. Windows were broken, building exteriors were deteriorating, light bulbs were missing, plumbing was questionable, streets and sidewalks were cracked, and weeds overran the unmowed green spaces. The installations looked decayed and untended. The Germans had more than a passing interest in all of this because they were preparing to move into the facilities when the Russians left.

The Russian bases would need extensive rehabilitation. In the enlisted barracks, running water was sometimes available only a few hours a day. At times, Russian draftees had hot water for only a short time, one day per week. The Russians had no money and now, with withdrawal imminent, no inclination to repair broken items or make the places more habitable.

To the Russian youngsters stationed there, those few who were somehow able to glimpse the bright lights and shopping centers in West Berlin, the visual impact must have been jarring. The Soviet Union was a bona fide superpower militarily yet decidedly Third World in so many other ways. I recalled a memorable early 1990s CIA presentation during which the briefer, recently returned from Russia, told my audience that many of the toilet seats in Moscow establishments were made of wood – and that during the winter months many of the seats were stolen and burned for heat. At Air Command and Staff College, a senior intelligence official talked about the problems he faced in handling Russian defectors: some "short circuited," unable at first to cope with the extraordinary number of choices for *everything*: razor blades, chewing gum, after shave lotion, breakfast cereal, clothing, cars, houses ... *everything*. When MIG-25 pilot Viktor Belenko defected, he was eventually taken to a shopping center near Langley AFB, Virginia. He thought the place was a setup: it was not possible for such a variety of goods to be routinely available. In Berlin, the Russian troops having to sell their "great coats" in order to subsist must have felt confusion, envy, and anger, among many other conflicting emotions.

All of these things probably helped account for the somber demeanor of the Russian officer at the museum and the others that I met later. I do not recall a spontaneous smile. The impoverished state of their military was made obvious by the amount of Russian military equipment and clothing openly for sale on street corners. "Great coats," officers' caps, belt buckles, uniform blouses, badges, insignia – all the paraphernalia of a military establishment – were being hawked near the Brandenburg Gate and at other sites around the city.

The withdrawal of the Russian forces proceeded with fits and starts. The Russians had no money to pay for the move, so the German government picked up almost the entire tab. Once back "home" in Russia, many of the Russian troops and families repatriated from Germany were confronted by even worse conditions. At the outset, even the most senior officers were placed in tiny apartments and, if reports are to be believed, some officer and enlisted families were crammed into already occupied apartments or housed in tents.

These circumstances carried baggage beyond considerations of personal misfortune. Some analysts expressed concern that the presence of this large, trained, potentially dispirited cadre on Russian soil – particularly if combined with other elements in the disgruntled military – could pose problems for the nation's incipient democracy. Impoverished or not, the existence of several thousand nuclear warheads inside former Soviet territory was an objective reality not easily dismissed. Eventually, Germany, with a little assistance from others, provided money to assist with the transition. If there was an explosion waiting to happen, the conditions never reached critical mass.

Still, I came to believe that the United States should have acted at the outset to tie ourselves more closely to the Russian military and the Russian nation when both were at this vulnerable stage. Militarily, the advantages in terms of dealing with the nuclear problem seem apparent and if, as it may turn out, Russia's experiment with democracy does not reach full maturity, our lack of political engagement will be equally as regrettable.

In contrast to the deteriorating facilities, when the Russians eventually departed Berlin they also left behind excellent museums, well maintained relics from World War II, and a memorial containing the remains of thousands of Red Army soldiers killed during the battle for the city. Past a wooded walkway, through an esplanade framed by two gigantic statues of Russian soldiers, one shielding a small child, then down some steps are a series of large rectangular slabs flat to the ground, spaced evenly along a sunken plateau. Each represents a republic of the former Soviet Union. Buried en masse beneath each slab are the scores upon scores of soldiers from all parts of the Soviet Union slain during the battle. It is a humbling sight. One of the conditions for the withdrawal of Russian troops from the city was that the German government will maintain this memorial and other Russian venues related to the war.

I wondered if the nature of that memorial – it is in such stark contrast to the American military cemeteries – spoke to something fundamental about the orientation of each society. The Russians honored their slain soldiers by burying them in mass graves fronted by somber statuary enormous in size. Conversely, the American cemeteries seemed somehow lighter, more hopeful: *individual* glistening white marble crosses -- thousands of them; one for each soldier, all in landscaped fields of breathtaking beauty. I don't know if it is as profound as all that; I only know that each one – Russian and American – touched me deeply.

When they moved entirely out of East Germany, the Russians left behind an ecological nightmare. Polluted streams, coughing smokestacks, grimy cities; even the Trabant, East Germany's "national car," was -- like the Russian Lada -- a noisy, oil spewing, exhaust belching throwback. The Wall was down and the borders were no longer marked, but it was obvious in an instant when a traveler passed into the former German Democratic Republic (East Germany). Gone were the bright lights, clean landscape, and vibrancy of the west, replaced in a heartbeat by the drab dispirited shabbiness of the workers paradise. It was a mess.

The Mayor of Berlin, members of the Berlin Senate, and representatives from the Bundestag who met with us all expressed surprise at the extent of the damage and how much it would cost to rehabilitate the east. Still, as one political leader said, reuniting the country "is the sort of problem we like to have." The Federal Republic eventually imposed a sizable surtax to help pay for reunification.

Difficulties in putting the country back together again were not confined to money matters alone. Integrating the fire departments and – especially – the police departments and educational systems was an extraordinary chore. The protocols, procedures, and orientations that came wrapped inside each organization were radically different between east and west.

No task, though, was more daunting than combining the armed forces of the Federal Republic of Germany and the German Democratic Republic. In the end, the Federal Republic absorbed some of East Germany's MIG-29 fighter planes but not much else in terms of equipment. As for people, no officer above the grade of colonel from the East German military was taken into the newly combined armed forces. Even then, only *one* colonel was accepted: a medical officer with unique qualifications. The backgrounds of the remainder of East Germany's senior officer corps – socialist indoctrination, Soviet-style training and tactics – and the "cultures" of the two systems dissuaded the Federal Republic from offering billets to any others.

The Russian lieutenant colonel and I have traveled a long road since my classmates and I wargamed the nuclear exchange in 1979. And, although there are still open spaces of opportunities remaining on the map, our countries have also moved a considerable distance, albeit along a bumpy path, since the Cold War began more than a half century ago. As for how it *ended*, historians will no doubt debate the specific reasons for years to come. I gladly leave the discussion to them.

For a time, there was talk inside the Department of Defense about instituting a "Cold War Victory Medal." I understand the sentiment involved in that suggestion, but I don't believe a medal is necessary. It should be sufficient to recognize that generations of young Americans flying the "Looking Glass," manning missile silos, crewing ships, carrying rifles, and deployed in every manner of tasks all around the globe, stood to their duties – whatever they consisted of, however mundane or exciting or dangerous they might have been – and because of their skill and steadfastness, we prevailed. That is legacy enough.

I have modest sympathy for those who suggest that the breakup of the Soviet Union and the end of the Cold War have actually made the world a more *dangerous* place. They are, I believe, correct in part of their assessment: the world is now a *different* place, and more complex – and therefore our military establishment must transform itself to be able to operate successfully in it.

Proponents of the "more dangerous" school offer the rationale that there no longer exists a restraining central core to channel and hold back adventuresome former-client states. The absence of this centripetal force, they argue, makes it easier for events to spin out of control: the entire situation has become ambiguous.

That may be true, but I still remember being at Sidi Slimane Air Base, listening to the sound of my own heartbeat, wondering if that fifth klaxon was going to sound. As for me, I will accept the ambiguity.

/////

Berlin became one of our favorite short getaway places. On our first family visit we stayed at Tempelhof Airfield just before the American military facilities inside it were closed. It was a privilege to be part of that history, even if only in a small way. The eastern arch of the Berlin Airlift Memorial sits in front of the huge terminal building, reflecting the airfield's importance during those anxious months in 1948-49 when the city was blockaded and the around-the-clock flights by allied air forces kept it alive and free. The Pergamon Museum, home of the Ishtar Gate from Babylon and other of the world's treasures from Greece, Rome, Sumer, Babylon, and Assyria soon became a popular site for us.

On one December excursion, our daughter Laura bought a Russian "great coat" from a vender near the Brandenburg Gate. It hung almost to the ground, and indeed kept all 105 pounds of her toasty warm; but it was so heavy that she could only wear it short distances for a few minutes at a time

On that same trip we happened by the Olympic Stadium where Jesse Owens had embarrassed Adolph Hitler during the 1936 games. Hitler's box was still there. We sat in it. The Fuhrer must have had a nice view of Jesse winning four gold medals. From Hitler's chair it was easy for us to observe that there were no caretakers around; indeed, we and some friends were almost the only people in the enormous stadium. That being the case, I walked down to the field, climbed over a small retaining wall and in winter jacket and street shoes ran a lap on the Olympic track. I was quite sure in my own mind that my time was a little faster than Jesse's, but my family has assured me – repeatedly – that it was not.

R & R

A MORAN STORY:

THE PET MONKEYS

The soldier's young bride was very shy and had led a sheltered life. Their marriage was a happy one, but because of his wife's shyness they had few friends. They were, however, completely content with each other's company.

Eventually, the soldier received orders to go overseas. Worried that his wife would be lonely in his absence, he purchased two pet monkeys, a male and a female, to provide his wife with company while he was away.

It was the perfect gift; she was immediately charmed by the monkeys' antics. They provided her with delightful companionship, everyday.

Sadly, after a few months, both monkeys died. The young wife was stunned. She missed them terribly. Then, thinking that perhaps just the sight of them would bring pleasant reminders and make the house seem less empty, she decided to take them to a taxidermist.

Because of her extreme shyness she didn't go out much at all. Finally, summoning up all her courage, she walked into a taxidermy shop and handed over the monkeys.

The taxidermist asked what she wanted done with them.

Already flustered by being away from home, she struggled to find the right thing to say; "stuffed" was too harsh a word to contemplate.

Sensing her difficulties, after a few seconds the taxidermist interjected. "Ma'am," he asked, "do you want them *mounted?*"

The shy young lady blushed and whispered, "No thanks, holding hands will be fine."

AFTER ACTION REPORT

Differences

After a year, two months, and ten days I resigned from the organizational oil spill that constituted my first civilian job after leaving the military.

There was much not to like about it ... and much that was different from anything in my past experience. Totally absent was the "all for one and one for all," "service before self," "excellence in all things," ethic that had formed my professional life up to that time. In its place inside a "what's in it for me?" climate were divisive cliques, self-aggrandizement, and gesture politics transformed into an art form. The dissimilarities were profound, immediately noticeable, and evident every day.

Even the *act* of leaving was totally different this time. How strange it felt the night I resigned to walk alone down the skywalk to the parking garage. When I left Germany after my last assignment in the military, other than skeleton manning for mission essential duties, the entire squadron showed up at the Stuttgart airport to say goodbye. Even as a captain teaching ROTC, most of the sophomore class I taught surprised me with a visit to my home the night before I left for duties elsewhere.

The graciousness of those farewells, and others, will remain with Nita and me through all our days. But even beyond that, the memories recall the kinship, the sense of *oneness* that drew my colleagues to come and share those moments with us. All of those recollections of triumphs and adversities shared together, the recognition deep in our souls that what we did was very important and part of something much bigger than ourselves, were wrapped up in those never to be forgotten gestures.

When I took the job with the civilian firm, I knew the experiences that would come with it would be different than those that had been part of my life in the past. It was ironic that *leaving* provided the clearest example of all.

Staying in Touch

The material I read prior to leaving the Air Force said that the typical military retiree goes through three jobs before finding the right match. I reacted to the possibility of three jobs the same way the young GIs responded to a briefing before D-Day informing them that casualties in the assault platoons were projected at 50% or more. As told by the historian Stephen Ambrose, one young soldier recalled looking at the guys on either side of him and thinking, "You poor bastards." Ambrose recalled that they believed themselves to be "too good/too handsome/too lucky" to get hit. Three jobs? Surely that could never happen to *me*.

But of course it did. The eagerness to get settled, my wife's severe illness, and the fact that during my entire adult life I had always been busy doing *something* predisposed me to accept a position as Business Manager for a Midwest firm.

Fourteen months and ten days was long enough. I was more than ready to leave.

/////

The military is a young people's organization. That is an often overlooked fact. One of the things I missed most during my time at the civilian company was the opportunity to work with and around young people. Other than for a few part time college students who worked as messengers, the demographics of the firm did not include many young adults. After 36 years in the military that was an age group that I had come to immensely enjoy working with.

When I left the Business Manager position, I decided to seek out as a next job one that would allow interaction with young people. As it turned out, the opportunity presented itself almost immediately. The ad appeared in the paper the following Sunday. A nearby university was looking for an administrator to run one of its departments.

I updated my resume, carried it to the university's employment office, and within a few days received a call back. I went to the initial interview thinking that, following the usual form, it would likely be the first in a long series.

As I was leaving the building following the interview, the panel representative from the chancellor's office caught me at the doorway. She explained that the job would entail considerably more than implied by the job description in the paper. In fact, the university was looking for someone to plan and implement a redesign of the entire department. I was offered the job the next day.

The next several months turned out to be among the busiest and most rewarding of my professional career. The frosting on the cake was that I got to work with a marvelous kaleidoscope of great young people from all over the country and, indeed, from all around the world. Helping with everything from student loans to health insurance, living accommodations and parking permits, and arranging for visas and social security numbers for our international students turned out to be satisfying and enjoyable. I found myself being sought out for advice on the most unusual subjects and participating in the most intriguing conversations. Perhaps it was the gray hair, or the fact that I took time to chat in what can be a very impersonal environment, whatever – my surrogate father role resulted in a host of continuing friendships.

/////

There is one final thing for which I will always be especially proud. Hearing of my background, at different times two young graduate students came to talk with me about military service. When they received their advanced degrees, at their request I assisted each of them in being accepted into Air Force Officer Training School. Both have now graduated and received their commissions as Air Force officers. Mike Christensen and Greg Theriot will serve our country very well.

The Best Part

Some of the best recollections of military service aren't really memories of a specific moment at all. They are instead, *feelings* that are evoked by the total cluster of all the experiences that happen to an individual while wearing the uniform.

Not long after I retired, the obituary of the actor Jimmy Stewart (a retired general in the Air Force Reserve) appeared in the local paper. I recalled an appearance Stewart had made on the Johnny Carson show years before. Carson and Stewart were talking about wartime experiences – Stewart had led a squadron of B-24s on raids over Germany – and Carson asked him if he had prayed before going on a mission. Stewart's answer was that he prayed to not make a mistake that would harm his crew or his squadron. He explained in a marvelous way that he had become so close to that group of people and had shared so much with them, that they – each person individually and the unit collectively – somehow became more important to him than his own well-being. So, while he wanted to make it back as much as they next guy, his prayer was to do his job well and not let anyone down.

My experiences were far less dramatic, but I understood what Stewart was talking about. The good units I had been in over the years had an "all for one and one for all" outlook: a Band of Brothers (and now, Sisters) who cared for and supported one another, exalted in the highs, anguished in the lows, and worked together towards a shared objective.

To the people in those organizations, "service before self" and "excellence in all things" were more than slogans: they were, in fact, beliefs to live by. Their ranks were represented by Colonels Ed Jones and Dale Hess who, along with scores of others, worked hard and unselfishly to make my job easier and the organization more successful. Ed was my deputy director at the Air Force Military Personnel Center during *Desert Storm*. Dale was my deputy commander in Stuttgart during the run-up to Sarajevo. They, and the countless others symbolized by them here, had those qualities every commander looks for: they made the organization's problems their problems, they tackled issues without being asked, and they didn't flinch from making difficult decisions. They made the rest of us better. It is a privilege to have served with them.

Eddie Moran: One Last Story

In December 1995, Nita and my daughter Karen picked me up at my headquarters near Stuttgart after I returned from a visit to a distant unit.

Their greeting was subdued. When I was settled in the car, Nita handed me a letter. "We've been crying," she said.

Uncertain of the contents, but knowing somehow what I might find, I opened the envelope. Inside, the half sheet of paper said:

"Dear Flip:

Just a note to tell you that I have lung cancer. I expect a PCS move in the near future. I'll keep 'shortstop' open for you.

All the best.

Eddie Moran"

I didn't cry; I smiled. Somehow, Eddie had known the perfect words to say. My dearest friend knew exactly the right way to let me know.

Even with his final story, Eddie was still taking care of one of his troops.

Adding Things Up

Retirement Order AL-000087 certifies that I served 36 years 5 months and 2 days on active duty. The orders relieve me from "organization and station of assignment" and direct me to "proceed to home of selection." I eventually did the latter, although the routing was a bit circuitous.

Of that total time, eight years, two months, and four days were spent in "Foreign Service," to use the terminology from my DD 214, a document familiar to all veterans.

As nearly as I can compute, I went on 125 TDY trips that aggregated to about 650 days. I saw fascinating real estate and met interesting people on those journeys. I will always be grateful for those opportunities, but I am conscious of the fact that they came at the expense of considerable time away from home. Still, in comparison, many of my colleagues spent far more time on the road.

The Air Force sent me to nine technical schools and professional military education courses totaling 533 days. When I see those numbers, I am reminded of Harry Truman's comment regarding William Fulbright: Truman said that Fulbright was a man "who had been educated far beyond his intelligence." Surely that was a lot of learning to pour into a farm kid who intended to stay only four years and check out life outside of Lancaster County.

During the course of my career, combining enlisted and officer time, I made a total of 14 "PCS moves."

Counting PCS moves and times when they accompanied me on extended training TDYs (such as to Squadron Officer School), my family moved a total of 14 times.

The lifestyle – the excitement and anticipation of new places, new jobs, new friends – fit us well. We loved it. For me, it was over much too soon.

A Fitting Dream

I have worn the uniform four times during the years since I retired. Once was at Air Force Officer Training School to swear in and "pin on" the second lieutenant bars of a superb young man who had worked for me as a sergeant at two locations. The second was to promote to master sergeant a marvelous NCO who shared my time at Stuttgart. The third was to attend an awards ceremony for a young friend from my "civilian" life being honored for his work in the local Army Reserve. The fourth and most recent was to preside at the retirement ceremony for the chief master sergeant who accompanied me to Sarajevo.

The uniform still fits. I still miss it.

In my dreams, it remains part of me. I always have it on.

During a 36-year career in which he rose from "slick sleeve" recruit to colonel, Tom Phillips guided an isolated detachment through a terrorist raid, served as Director of the Air Force Personnel Readiness Center throughout Operation *Desert Storm*, helped conduct one of the largest searches in our nation's history, and led some of the first American troops into Sarajevo. He was the top graduate from Air Force Officer Training School, Squadron Officer School, and Air Command and Staff College.

A Pilgrim in Unholy Places recounts cataclysmic as well as quiet events from the career of an exceptional officer who went to boot camp as an airman recruit with no intention of being a "lifer" and wound up nearly four decades later as commander of one of the most unique organizations in the Air Force. Known for his innovative leadership, Phillips held an unusual variety of command and staff positions. The stories in *Pilgrim* reflect the scope of his extraordinary career: several describe people or units in peril; some offer reflections or recount anecdotes from headline crises as well as from everyday life in the military; many are hilarious, others so searing they tear at that heart. Whether humorous or tragic, official or unofficial, the episodes teach, inspire, and recall a lifetime in uniform spanning one of the most turbulent periods in America's history.